TRAINING PLANS FOR
CYCLISTS

Gale Bernhardt

VELO press

BOULDER, COLORADO

1830 55th Street
Boulder, Colorado 80301-2700 USA
303/440-0601 · Fax 303/444-6788 · E-mail velopress@competitorgroup.com

Distributed in the United States and Canada by Publishers Group West

Library of Congress Cataloging-in-Publication Data
Bernhardt, Gale, 1958–
  Training plans for cyclists / Gale Bernhardt.
     p. cm.
  Includes bibliographical references and index.
  ISBN 978-1-934030-18-9 (pbk. : alk. paper)
  1. Cycling—Training. I. Title.
  GV1048.B47 2009
  796.6—dc22

                    2009015186

For information on purchasing VeloPress books, please call 800/234-8356 or visit www.velopress.com.

Cover design by Bonnie Hofto
Interior design by Jessica Xavier / Planet X Design
Front cover photo by Tim De Frisco
Back cover photo by Don Karle
Illustrations by Tom Ward (Chapter 4) and Joyce Turley / Dixon Cove Design (Chapters 22 and 23)

09   10   11 / 10   9   8   7   6   5   4   3   2   1

This book is dedicated to all of the cyclists who trusted me to help them achieve their fitness and racing dreams.

CONTENTS

Part IV
Mountain Bike Training Plans

Part V
Building Foundation Fitness

Part VI
Supporting Information

ACKNOWLEDGMENTS

A good deal of credit for helping to nurture this book to completion goes to my husband, Delbert. His acceptance of my unusual job, odd work hours, travel, and passion for endurance sports is essential to my success as a coach and author. He also enthusiastically volunteers to provide sag support for my riding adventures and races. I couldn't do all the things I do without his positive attitude and unwavering encouragement.

My family has always stood behind me as well. When self-doubt or fatigue begins to dampen my enthusiasm, my close family members are always the first to tell me they have confidence that I will meet my deadlines and be successful.

My closest riding buddies not only provide encouragement for my professional life, they also provide the necessary distractions that keep me capable of creative thought. Those distractions include mountain bike rides, road rides, 24-hour relays, and weeklong ride adventures (much like the rides and adventures found in this book).

Certainly my extended riding family cannot go unmentioned. Every Sunday morning since about 1995, people have shown up on my driveway for "Gale's Ride." Though it is not really *my* ride, over the years these companions have kept me riding year-round in all kinds of conditions.

For my personal cycling support since 1994 and my go-to resource for information about the latest in cycling equipment, Trent Schilousky, Roy Gatesman, and the other staff members at Peloton Cycles in Loveland, Colorado, have been incredible.

Sometime in the early 1990s I began wearing Pearl Izumi gear and haven't stopped. I've tried gear from many other manufacturers, but Pearl is very hard to beat. I am a proud ambassador of their clothing; it's easier to ride and run when you're wearing the best gear.

The team at VeloPress closes my list of acknowledgments. Renee Jardine helped me flesh out the original outline for this book and has provided support for my work for years. Liza Campbell was on the front line of the editing process and made several great suggestions for improvement. Iris Llewellyn managed the editorial production, and Brenda Hadenfeldt had the challenging task of making sure all the plans were correct. Dave Trendler and Jen Soulé make sure cyclists like you know that this book is available. Ted Costantino has been a great advocate of my work, and his behind-the-scenes input has improved each book.

Writing a book is a long and not-so-easy process that requires a huge team backing the author. I appreciate every element of support that all of you have given to me.

INTRODUCTION

For years, cyclists familiar with my book *Training Plans for Multisport Athletes* have asked me, "When are you going to write a book for us?" *Training Plans for Cyclists* is an answer to that request.

Although my published work may be better known in the multisport world than in the cycling world, cycling is where I first achieved success as an endurance sports coach. I love cycling.

I have worked with a variety of cyclists, from local riders preparing for long-distance events to professional road racers and mountain bike riders. In my coaching business, I intentionally leave room for cyclists. One of the highlights of my career was working with Nicole Freedman, who secured her spot on the 2000 USA Cycling Olympic Team by winning the U.S. Pro National Championship Race that same year. My first trip to the Olympic Games was in 2000 to Sydney, Australia, as a personal cycling coach.

Coaching and teaching sport skills have long been my passion. I feel great when I can help endurance athletes reach success. I enjoy the challenge of figuring out the numerous steps that give an answer, or answers, to often complex problems. The end result is a successful athlete.

TRAINING PLANS

Because I can work with only a limited number of athletes at any given time in a one-on-one coaching situation and still deliver the quality of coaching that makes me happy, I wanted to find a way to help more people, including those who may not need or want a personal coach. In 1995, I began assembling ready-to-use training plans to help self-coached athletes reach their goals.

Plenty of books can give you principles of training and guidelines for assembling your own training plan, but if you have no experience in this kind of planning, it can be confusing and frustrating. For many athletes, it is overwhelming. This book features 16 detailed training plans that are designed to help you achieve a personal goal based on an athlete profile and a training plan goal or set of goals.

The plans are designed so that you can use this book for multiple types of events and goals. If you are a beginning cyclist, you can start with plans to improve your fitness. If you are an experienced cyclist, these training plans will give you more structure and more challenge in your workouts. If you are looking for training plan design methods to help you assemble your own plan, be sure to look at several chapters: This book has no cookie-cutter, computer-generated plans in which only training time or intensity level changes.

THE PLAN OF THE BOOK

Before you dive into a particular training plan, I suggest that you review the entire book. You'll find event-specific training plans as well as foundation fitness plans. At a minimum, you should review Part I (Chapters 1–4) before you begin following a plan.

Part I: Getting Started

Chapter 1 begins by looking at a reasonable question: "Can one training plan really work for many different athletes?" The chapter then looks at the parts of training that take place off the bike and in your head. Before you start physically preparing for your event, you should have a positive mental approach to training and racing. Chapter 1 also discusses goal setting and mental training tools.

Chapter 2 outlines training and periodization concepts and explains intensity indicators, such as the rate of perceived exertion (RPE), heart rate, and power output. Although some indicators can be measured with monitors and meters (see Chapter 4), this chapter will show you how to guide your training without gadgets by using RPE. In fact, I suggest that you—and every athlete—learn to use RPE as a training and racing tool, even if you use the fun gadgets, too.

> Before you start physically preparing for your event, you should have a positive mental approach to training and racing.

Properly fueling your body is essential to both your overall health and your success as an athlete. Fueling affects you from the inside out. Nutrition basics are covered in Chapter 3, beginning with macronutrients and micronutrients. From there, the chapter moves to more sport-specific material to help you decide what and how much to eat and drink during training and racing. The chapter closes with information on supplements and ergogenic aids.

Another significant factor in your cycling success is, obviously, equipment. Chapter 4 begins by outlining the differences among the most popular bike styles. After you decide which style of bike you need, you should find a bike that fits you. Appropriate bike fit is critical. Never sacrifice bike fit for a great bargain on a bike that is too large or too small.

Once you find a bike that is the right size, several adjustments can be made to get the bike fitted specifically to your anatomy. Using the information in Chapter 4, you can either do the fit yourself or be a better educated consumer when asking a shop to do it.

Several myths about women's anatomy and bike fit still seem to live on in cycling culture. Chapter 4 includes data correcting this outdated information.

Choosing the right clothing is also very important in making cycling more comfortable. Learn about recommended styles of shorts, gloves, and jerseys as well as cold-weather gear in Chapter 4. The chapter ends with information about how to select other equipment such as heart rate monitors and power meters.

After you complete the chapters in Part I, how you use the rest of the book depends on your individual goals as a cyclist. More than likely, what brings you to this book is the need to prepare for an event. You've decided to enter, and now you need to begin training. You want a plan.

Throughout the book, I use the words "race" and "event" interchangeably, so don't let "race" intimidate you. Whatever your goal, you are still looking to deliver the best performance possible for you. For some people, this means aiming for a spot on the podium at a sponsored event. For others, it means reaching a self-designed goal.

Part II: Event Training Plans

Part II contains plans for 30-mile, 50-mile, 100-kilometer (commonly called a "metric century"), and 100-mile (commonly called a "century") events. If you are just beginning your endurance cycling journey, the 30-mile plan in Chapter 5 is a great place to start. You can use it to prepare for a specific event or to jump-start your fitness. I think you will be encouraged by how easy it is to go from no fitness to a 30-mile ride in just 6 weeks.

Chapter 6 moves the goal distance to 50 miles or a metric century. This plan is designed with indoor cycling class enthusiasts in mind. It is perfect for the cyclist who attends indoor cycling classes and is looking for a way to capitalize on that fitness and ride for longer distances outside. This 8-week plan works nicely toward a late-spring or summer goal.

Riding 50 miles or a metric century is often the stepping-stone to a century ride. It is a significant milestone to ride a bicycle for 100 miles. The first time you ride a century, more than likely your goal is simply to complete the event. Chapter 7 is designed for a cyclist who wants to complete a century ride at the end of 12 weeks, with an aim of averaging 12 to 15 miles per hour (mph) for the ride. The athlete profiled in Chapter 7 is riding only 2 or 3 days per week before beginning the training plan. As in Chapter 6, this plan is designed with indoor cycling class participants in mind.

Let's say you have completed a century and are looking for a bigger challenge, or you are riding 3 or 4 days per week and want to improve your fitness. Check out Chapter 8, designed for the cyclist aiming for a faster century, perhaps aiming to average 16 to 18 mph for the entire 100 miles. Chapter 8 is also a 12-week plan, but the cyclist beginning this plan is starting out with a greater level of fitness than the cyclist starting the Chapter 7 plan.

Part III: Touring Training Plans

Part III contains training plans for multiday bike tours. Multiday tours are a great way to combine fitness with sightseeing. Pursuing a goal to ride a destination bike tour can be rewarding physically as well as mentally. The opportunity to escape from everyday demands and focus only on riding your bike, fueling, resting, and enjoying the sights for a few days can be rejuvenating. A nice side benefit is the added boost in fitness you will notice after recovering from the tour.

Chapter 9 begins with a 10-week training plan to help riders enjoy a 3-day riding tour covering about 25 to 30 miles per day. This plan is designed for riders who have base fitness from other activities and perhaps enjoy indoor spinning classes but do not consider themselves to be cyclists.

The plan in Chapter 10 is perfect to help you prepare for sightseeing tours and multiday charity events. This 12-week plan is designed for an event of 40 to 50 miles per day and includes event guideline instructions for the last week. It is for the athlete who is already riding 3 or 4 days per week for 30 to 60 minutes. At the end of 12 weeks, the athlete following this plan will ride the 3-day tour and average 12 to 15 mph each day.

> Is it possible to be ready for a weeklong ride if you are currently riding 3 days per week for about an hour at a time? The answer is "Yes!"

For those of you wanting to ride a 3-day tour with distances of 40 to 50 miles per day and who want to bump up your average speed to 16 to 18 mph, the 12-week plan in Chapter 11 is ideal. You are already riding for an hour a couple of days per week, and your long weekend ride is two hours. Because you begin with a higher level of fitness, this plan includes more volume and intensity than the plan in Chapter 10.

When investigating a bicycle adventure, perhaps you find a weeklong tour during which you plan to ride for 6 or 7 days. You look at the great photos in the brochure and wonder if it is possible to be ready for a weeklong ride if you are currently riding 3 days per week for about an hour at a time. The answer is "Yes!"

Chapter 12 shows how you can be ready for that weeklong bike tour in just 11 weeks and gives you guidelines on how to ride the 6-day tour during Week 12 to get the most out of it. You plan to ride the tour at an average of 12 to 15 mph. Following the plan in Chapter 12 will give you confidence that your goal is achievable.

If you wish to ride a weeklong tour at a faster pace, averaging 16 to 18 mph every day, the plan in Chapter 13 is for you. This chapter is for the serious recreational cyclist or perhaps a cyclist using a weeklong bike tour to boost fitness for racing purposes. You are currently riding 3 to 4 days per week, with weekday rides of an hour each. Your weekend rides are longer, with one ride around the 3-hour mark. One option is to use Chapter 20 to prepare for this event-specific plan. I'll talk more about Chapter 20 later in the introduction.

The five plans outlined in Part III bring us to the end of the pavement, and now the path turns to dirt.

Part IV: Mountain Bike Training Plans

Part IV is for the off-road cyclist. This part includes plans for weekend warriors or sport racing, 100-mile bike races (often called "mud hunnies"), and 24-hour off-road team events.

For those of you who like to get a little dirty, Chapter 14 is designed with you in mind. Your training time is pinched during the week, but when you hit the trails, you want to be fit. If the random-riding method of training has brought disappointing results, take a look at this 12-week plan, designed to help you build strength and endurance on your 2-hour mountain bike rides. If you come into this plan with limited fitness, follow its instructions on how to use the foundation fitness plan in Chapter 19 to help you roll right into it.

Chapter 15 is designed for the cyclist who wants to be stronger and faster on 3-hour mountain bike rides. Just between you and me, you want to thrash your riding partners and leave them in the dust. It doesn't matter whether you are doing weekend mountain bike races for which an entry fee is demanded or you show up to the group rides that turn into races: Chapter 15 is your best offense. This plan is 12 weeks long and requires solid fitness before you begin. You ride 5 or 6 days per week, and some of the rides include intensity. If you need some help building your foundation fitness, you can use the plan in Chapter 20 before beginning this one.

Instead of a 3-hour off-road event, perhaps you want to try a dirty 100-mile event? The 100-mile mountain bike events are becoming more popular each year. Chapter 16 is a 16-week plan to help a time-pinched rider prepare for a mud hunnie. Though your training time is restricted and you need at least two days off from training each week, you still want to ride as fast as possible. Your training time needs to be efficient. If you are not consistently doing 5 to 6 hours of training per week before beginning the Chapter 16 plan, you can use the foundation fitness plan in Chapter 19 to help you prepare.

The plan in Chapter 17 steps up the training volume and intensity to prepare for an off-road 100-mile event. This 14-week plan is for you if you are already riding about 9 hours per week before beginning the plan and are looking for a personal best time for the event. Your two weekend rides are 2 to 3 hours long. You are doing at least two weekday rides, and each is at least an hour long. If you take a look at Week 1 of the Chapter 17 training plan and find you need some foundation fitness before you begin, use Chapter 20 to aid your preparation.

Staying in the dirt but shifting to a team event, Chapter 18 is a 6-week crash training plan designed for a 24-hour mountain bike event. With the right group of people and the right training, a 24-hour mountain bike event can be loads of fun. In addition to the 6-week crash training plan, Chapter 18 gives you other recommendations to prepare for the event.

Part V: Building Foundation Fitness

In Part V, Chapters 19 and 20 feature plans to help you build or maintain foundation fitness. Several of the preceding training plans have suggested using one of these fitness plans, if needed, before you begin training. Chapter 19 is a 12-week plan designed for a cyclist who can devote between 3 and 6 hours per week to training. Chapter 20 is an 18-week plan for a cyclist who can train somewhere between 4 and 11 hours per week.

Part VI: Supporting Information

Part VI is the supplemental information to all chapters and contains the workout codes, strength training instructions, and stretching guidelines. To help keep the training plans manageable and to give you as many plans as possible, I use workout codes detailed in Chapter 21 to condense information. Chapters 22 and 23 offer fully illustrated strength training and flexibility programs, along with tips on how to implement these programs safely and effectively.

Additional Resources

In Appendixes A, B, and C, you can find more resources to help you be successful, such as a health questionnaire, an event-day checklist, and information on how to cope with illness or injury specific to cycling.

Armed with the tools and information in this book, you should be well on your way to improved performance. I hope the plans help you prepare successfully for a variety of events. Most of all, I hope you reach your riding goals and have a great time doing it!

PART I

GETTING
STARTED

The Elements of Training

To kick things off, let's address some of the most common concerns athletes have about training. Can a single training plan work for every athlete? To what extent is athletic potential genetic? What are realistic goals? How much of performance is mental? This chapter breaks down several factors that make athletes successful both physically and mentally. Knowing which factors you can and can't control, as well as how to assess a training program and set effective goals, will help you optimize your training and performance.

CAN ONE PLAN FIT ALL?

In all the years I've been coaching individual athletes, I've never written two training plans exactly the same—even if two athletes had the same race schedule. Sundry elements enter into creating a training plan, including the athlete's work schedule, family obligations, and ability to recover from training and racing. Other variables that may affect an individual's performance include level of experience, desire, nutrition, and genetics. As this chapter shows, different individuals following the same training plan can improve at different rates and levels.

The plans in this book are based on scientific principles and are designed to help cyclists meet specific goals. While any general training program has its limitations, I've found that athletes can be successful using training plans as a guide. This book will help you determine which plans will work best for you. At the beginning of each plan, you will find an athlete profile; if it is right for you, the plan should anticipate your goal, your current fitness, and the amount of time you have to train prior to your goal or event and on a weekly basis. All of the plans include tips on how to modify them to fit your needs. You can use each plan as a template or a home base as your own patterns of progression emerge.

First, however, you should understand what factors affect your athletic skills. So before you choose a training plan, read on for the answer to this question: "How much of my performance can I influence and how much is fate?"

THE ROLE OF GENETICS

Sometimes athletes blame or credit their parents for their performance, and it's true that genetics play a part. Several scientific studies have been conducted to determine to what extent genetics are responsible for athletic performance. Claude Bouchard, PhD, and a team of researchers at Laval University in Québec looked at identical twins and put a group of 20, or 10 pairs, on a 20-week training program. The twins trained four to five times per week, in sessions lasting 45 minutes, at an average intensity of roughly 80 percent of maximal heart rate. The result? Identical twins did in fact respond nearly identically to the training program. One pair gained 10 and 11 percent, respectively, on their VO_2max (a measure of their aerobic capacity), while a second pair gained 22 and 25 percent. Most of the variation in performance gains was between, not within, sets of twins.

> You can control approximately 70 percent of your performance.

Although this study on twins revealed that 82 percent of the variation in VO_2max was due to genetics, it also revealed that only 33 percent of the differences found in ventilatory threshold, or the point at which breathing and carbon dioxide output increase at a nonlinear rate, were attributable to genetics. This is important because ventilatory threshold and the closely related lactate threshold, or the point at which increasing exercise intensity causes lactate levels to accumulate, are frequently found to be the best predictors of actual performance. This is good news because it means that lactate threshold tends to be more "trainable" than VO_2max.

After conducting additional studies, the researchers at Laval concluded that genetic factors account for roughly 20 percent of the variation in the performances of endurance athletes. Nongenetic factors, however— including nutrition, lifestyle, past exercise patterns, age, socioeconomic status, and mental skills—were found to influence 40 percent of the variation. Gender differences accounted for 10 percent. The final 30 percent of variation was due to how a particular set of genes reacts to a particular training program. That is, some people respond to one training program but not to another.

What's the bottom line? First, what works for you won't necessarily work as well for another cyclist. Second, and more important, you can control approximately 70 percent of your performance.

TRAINING RESPONSE RATES

Speaking of cyclists and their responses to training, you may wonder about the differences in response between athletes who are on the same program. The researchers at Laval conducted another study to determine how much fitness gains would vary among people following the same training program. Twenty-four similar subjects (initially sedentary) followed the same training program for 20 weeks. After 20 weeks, the group's average gain in VO_2max was 33 percent, and one person gained 88 percent! Unfortunately, another individual sweating on the same plan increased VO_2max by just 5 percent.

In the same study, scientists measured power output on a bicycle ergometer, on which subjects pedaled for 90 minutes. The group's mean power output was measured before the training program began and again at the completion of the 20 weeks. The average power improvement was 51 percent. One happy person saw a 97 percent improvement in power, while another improved only 16 percent.

Why do some people seem to make big gains while others make minimal ones? The studies at Laval led researchers to categorize people as "responders" or "non-responders." Responders make big improvements in aerobic capacity and power as a result of their training, while non-responders barely show a gain, even after 20 weeks

> Knowing how you respond to training helps you determine when or how to make changes to a training plan.

of hard work. The scientists further estimated that, of the responders, around 5 percent of athletes are "high responders" who can see improvements of over 60 percent, while an equal percentage of athletes are "low responders" and may expect only a 5 percent improvement.

The studies also revealed a gradation in response rates—a scale of responsiveness. Some people saw gains after just 4 to 6 weeks of training, while others reached plateaus and made minimal gains in weeks 7 to 20. Others were late bloomers who were at a standstill for 6 to 10 weeks but then improved their aerobic capacities by 20 to 25 percent after 10 additional weeks of training.

So you can see why your response to training cannot be compared directly with the responses of other athletes. And as you use the training plans in this book to your degree of success, gauging your response to the training helps you determine whether or not it's a good idea to make calculated changes to the plan.

GOAL SETTING

Each plan in this book begins with a goal in mind. You may have other goals you want to achieve as well. Good goal-setting techniques make it more likely that you will achieve the success you desire.

Before you start a training plan, take time to identify the overarching goal of your training. Setting a major goal allows you to work backward and design a plan to reach it. If you set a goal that is weeks or months away, it is best to have subgoals to help you recognize progress and, of course, give you reason to celebrate.

Five Guidelines for Defining Your Goals

State Your Goals in Positive Terms

Your goals should explain what you want to achieve, not what you hope to avoid. For example, "I don't want to be dropped on Sunday group rides" defines what you *don't* want to happen. Instead, make your goal "Stay with the main group on the Sunday group ride." This means that even if you have to draft someone for a good portion of the ride, you will stay with the pack.

Make Your Goals Challenging

If you are already staying with the group on Sunday rides, "Stay with the main group on the Sunday group ride" won't challenge you as a major goal. Perhaps a goal could be "Go to the front and lead for part of a group ride twice each month." This goal is stated in positive terms and is challenging.

Make Your Goals Achievable

One of the most common mistakes is to make goals *too* challenging. If a goal is impossible to achieve, it is easy to get discouraged and quit. For example, an eager rider may make a goal to ride every day for the next six months. Missing one day, whether during the second week or the fifth month of the plan, makes the goal unreachable. This goal is too restrictive.

A more achievable goal that still provides health benefits is "Ride bike and strength train five to seven times a week for the next six months." You could even add an illness disclaimer if you like: "Being ill will not count against me." This kind of goal statement encourages healthy, consistent behavior while giving you room for unforeseeable interruptions.

Set Goals Within Your Control

It is best to set goals based on yourself and your performance. Setting goals based on someone else can be disappointing. For example, let's say you set a goal stated as, "Ride faster than Scott on next Sunday's ride." What happens if you do ride faster than Scott, but in the post-ride chat session you find out Scott has been sick with the flu for the past three days

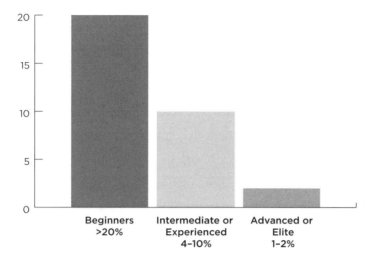

FIGURE 1.1 Average Annual Improvement for Cyclists

and is still trying to recover? Will you feel good about riding "faster than Scott"? Will you feel success or a shallow victory?

You can use other people as benchmarks for your fitness goals, but you have no control over their training or how they ride. If you want to use Susan for benchmarking performance, that's fine, but you should also have other ways to measure your success. For example, "Improve my 5-mile time trial speed from 16 mph." If you improve your speed, perhaps you will ride as fast or faster than both Scott and Susan. Measure success based on *you*.

Now that I've said goals need to be under your control, I have to qualify this statement by saying that some goals do involve other people. If your major goal is placing in a race, your spot on the podium—or not—depends on how you race relative to other people.

While you may want to win your category of Roots and Rocks Mountain Bike Race, you will need to think about what it will take to make that happen. Do you need to improve your speed by 1 percent or 50 percent? (The latter ambition would be another opportunity to consider whether your goals are achievable.)

Having a good understanding of your current and recent-past capabilities is essential to future performance planning. Although there are no guarantees, improving time trial times, power output numbers, and other benchmarks specific to you will help you get closer to obtaining your podium goals.

Every performance curve looks more impressive at the beginning. If you are just getting started in cycling, this is great news because it means you are likely to see big improvements in your first two years of training and racing. Your time and distance improvements could exceed 20 percent within a year (see Figure 1.1). On the other hand, improvements for athletes who have been consistently training and racing for over two years are typically in the range of 4 to 10 percent per year. Elite athletes who have been competitive for many years are looking at annual improvements as small as the 1 to 2 percent range, sometimes less. Once you reach the upper portion of the performance curve, it doesn't take a large percentage of improvement to break a world record—sometimes less than a hundredth of a second—but it takes years of work to achieve that record. Don't be discouraged if you don't see a 20 percent improvement in your first year, or a 4 to 10 percent improvement year after year—remember, every athlete is different. These differences are just another reason why you should set individual goals and keep track of your progress.

> Although the measurement is subjective, you can still measure your success.

Make Your Goals Specific and Measurable

This guideline is always a tough one. Before I begin coaching an athlete, one of the (many) questions I ask is "At the end of our first season together, how will we know if we were successful?" The typical response is "If I'm a better cyclist." But how will we know when this happens? What does a "better cyclist" look like? Let's look at a list of more specific goals that could help define this kind of improvement:

- Improve my average speed on my favorite route to be faster than 17 mph.
- Ride 50 miles in a single day.
- Improve my mountain bike climbing to ride Towers Road without walking.
- Feel strong on the group ride.
- Complete a 40-kilometer time trial.
- Ride 100 miles in a single day.
- Complete a three-day tour, averaging three hours of riding each day.
- Stay with the main group on hills on group rides.

Note that some of the goals are easily quantifiable. In other words, anyone could look at your performance and measure your average speed changing from 17 to 17.5 mph on your favorite route.

Other goals are more behavioral and subjective. While other people might notice that you are riding hills faster, only you will know whether or not you are feeling strong. Although the measurement is subjective, you can still measure your success. For example, on a scale of 1 to 7, 1 being best, how would you rate your hill climbing today? Ask yourself the same question every couple of weeks. Another example of a behavioral goal is "I will begin hills conservatively and plan to finish each one stronger than I started it." You can subjectively judge the difference between blasting up the bottom half of the hill and fading at the top and beginning with a smooth, relaxed cadence and finishing the hill strong.

Subgoals

The training plan chapters each display a detailed plan to complete a specific goal, such as "Ride 50 miles, averaging 14.3 mph, at the end of 12 weeks." Because it will be three months before you complete the goal, I suggest you look at the training plan and make one to three subgoals each week.

Your subgoals can come from the training plan, or they can pertain to nutrition, recovery, or another area you need to work on. For example, your goals for Week 1 might be:

1. Complete the Saturday two-hour ride.
2. Drink enough water each day so urine is light straw colored.
3. Get between seven and eight hours of rest each night.

If you were to add up the accomplishments of three subgoals each week for 13 weeks, you would have 39 reasons for why you made it to your ultimate goal. So give it a try: At the beginning of each week of training, jot down three subgoals you want to accomplish. As you complete each one, check it off and celebrate.

Celebrations

In our fast-paced lives, we often move on to new tasks as soon as the old are completed, without enjoying the accomplishments we've achieved. Go, go, go, do, do, do, faster, faster, faster. It seems we're all trying to fit a few more items into that nonexistent "extra" hour each day. When we pursue any goals, it's important that we take the time to pause, look at what we've done, and feel good about our progress. If we recognize and celebrate the goals we have achieved, our sense of purpose is renewed and we are encouraged to press forward toward a new goal.

Kids are the leading authorities on celebrating successes. They jump up and down and chatter excitedly about their accomplishments. They do victory dances. They celebrate when they've achieved even the smallest objective, such as being the first ones in a group to simply get on their bikes and on the road.

Celebrating each small success helps propel you toward a goal. Whether you share your accomplishments with others or choose to keep them private, take a moment to recognize success—and perhaps do a victory dance.

MENTAL TRAINING

Most athletes spend a great deal of time improving physical fitness and nutritional practices. Fewer spend time improving mental strength. Yet if all physical factors are equal, the athlete with the strongest mental game has the edge. This is especially true at the higher levels of competition, as elite athletes vary little in their physical abilities. In fact, it's not unusual for an athlete with strong mental skills to perform better than an athlete who is stronger physically but less prepared mentally. While you may or may not be aiming for a podium position, you don't want your head to get in the way of your success.

If you have never worked on your mental skills, you can start by taking notice of what that little voice in your head says to you. (Yes, I know you talk to yourself, because I do it, too.) The second step is to apply a filter to what you are hearing. Ask yourself whether the message is appropriate or exaggerated. If negative self-talk limits your performance as a cyclist, you can choose from many available books, seminars, CDs, and DVDs to help you work on mental toughness. Pick one to start your journey. Even if you have worked on mental fitness in the past, delving into a new book or reviewing your favorite mental exercises can be very rewarding. Just like any other skill, mental fitness requires maintenance and can improve with the proper training.

When You Play to Win, You . . .

- Show up and do your best
- Focus on yourself and your performance
- Take responsibility for what you can control; are accountable
- Embrace discomfort for growth
- Stretch your skills

When You Play Not to Lose, You . . .

- Show up only if you can do well at a race or be one of the leaders on a group ride
- Focus on others and their performance
- Blame your performance on the weather, equipment, other people; act like a victim
- Remain in your comfort zone
- Avoid new situations

Play to Win

I encourage the athletes I coach to "play to win." This means you push hard and use all that you have. If you attempt only to maintain security and comfort, you take a defensive strategy, or "play not to lose." Although the differences between these two strategies can seem subtle, they are important.

Playing to win means doing your best on a given day under given circumstances. No matter in what place you finish, you are the winner. The focus is on you and what you can control about your performance.

Training to ride faster is uncomfortable. At times, your legs will be burning and you'll feel like you can't ride one more second; then you'll ride 10. This is playing to win. Tolerating this type of discomfort, physically and mentally, is part of becoming a better cyclist. As your level of fitness increases, your tolerance levels for discomfort will improve.

Dealing with Pain

Physical discomfort and pain are not the same thing. Physical discomfort is typically muscular. If you feel discomfort during exercise, it tends to let up when you reduce your intensity. A second type of physical discomfort shows up a day or two after a hilly ride or a tough weight room workout. This is called delayed-onset muscle soreness. These discomforts are common to athletic training.

Pain, on the other hand, may lead to time off the bike or the attention of a physician. Here are some types of pain to watch for:

- **Pain that surfaces after a ride,** such as a bit of knee soreness, but goes away either the same day or within 24 hours is probably nothing to worry about. Some athletes use no treatment for such pain at all, while others prefer to ice a painful area when it is first noticeable.
- **Pain that occurs during the ride** but doesn't force you to stop can be treated the same way as after-ride pain. You may want to consider staying off the bike for a day or two to reduce further injury.
- **Pain that occurs throughout the ride** and interferes with your ability to complete the ride or pain that persists when off the bike needs attention. You are injured. Stay off the bike for a few days, use RICE (see sidebar, "RICE"), and consider using an anti-inflammatory, but also seek professional medical attention.

Too often, athletes try to train through an injury, which only makes it worse. To protect your longevity as a cyclist, you should be able to distinguish among physical discomfort, minor pain, and injury and should take care of yourself accordingly.

Mental discomfort can come from doing something you've never done before, something that is scary, or something that puts your self-image at risk. What happens if you don't meet the goal? What happens if you can't keep up with the group? What will people say? You are the one who determines your definition of success or failure. Stretching your limits and taking some risks will move you toward new levels of skill and confidence.

Using Visualization and Scripting Tools

For cyclists who just want to get going now and don't want to read another book on mental skills, a few basic exercises can help get you started. I often ask athletes to script the "perfect" race or event. Some write a description of how a perfect race day would go. For others, visualizing or scripting a movie in which they play a starring role works better. They may visualize the movie from a camera's perspective and watch themselves in action, or they may visualize the movie from their own perspective. Experiment with different techniques to find what works best for you.

If you are writing, try to find a quiet time and place, with no interruptions. If you are visualizing, begin by relaxing on the couch. Close your eyes, take a few deep breaths, and let the movie begin. You can start the script or movie with pre-race details, including preparing meals, transporting yourself to the start area, and readying your bike for the event. Be as detailed as possible, describing or seeing your equipment. Also make note of how you feel. You should strive to feel excited to race yet calm and confident.

The script I have written here can be used as a starting place for your personal script. Add more details and modify the story to personalize it. You can create a story to fit any race or tailor it for a particular event. Either way, the more detail you can add about the event, the better.

Visualize your final race preparation and the start line. Imagine how the start of your race will look and feel. What is the weather like? How does the air feel? What do the competitors around you look like?

What do you do that makes your start successful? What positive comments does the narrator make about your start?

As you are riding the first quarter of the event, how do you look riding the hills? How do you feel? Are spectators cheering for you? What can you see, smell, and hear?

Are you fueling and hydrating? What are you doing to keep track of your fueling and hydration pace? What you do now helps you finish strong.

You are nearing the halfway point and passing people. Do you say something encouraging to the people you pass?

As you continue into the second half of the event, riding the hills requires slightly more effort. But you handle them well; you are strong.

You focus on relaxing your face and shoulders and settling into a comfortable breathing pattern as you plan a strong finish. You are now pushing the pace while other riders fade.

Do you see the finish line? How do you feel? What do you look like? Can you see and describe a great finish for your event?

If you are visualizing and realize you forgot an important step, just rewind the movie and add that detail. You can rewind as many times as necessary to complete a successful movie and a perfect race. If you're writing a script, adding more detail is as easy as inserting more text.

Controlling FEAR

In training and racing, it is often false expectations appearing real (FEAR) that cause anxiety. Athletes worry about things that might happen, and FEAR churns up some stomach acid. Your script can help.

After you complete the script for your perfect race, work on a script for race-day challenges. Consider what things worry you the most about race day and write them down. Brainstorm solutions for each problem and positive outcomes for each unfortunate situation. The more options you can include, the better. For issues out of your control, such as the weather, how can you best be prepared? How will you deal with these issues and what will your little voice say?

You certainly don't want FEAR to cripple your race performance, but some level of worry is good for you in certain situations. It may keep you safe when you avoid riding a stretch of trail far beyond your ability. Concern that you won't complete an event may motivate you to train consistently. As Mark Twain once said, "Courage is resistance to fear, mastery of fear—not absence of fear."

Maintaining Cerebral Fitness

Solving training and racing problems is an intellectual exercise. As with physical skills, the more mentally fit you are, the easier it is for you to respond to problems. If you are a beginner at working on the mental side of the game, you will have to think your way out of even the simplest problems. You look for what is within your control and take action. As you advance in skill level, many actions become responses based on intuition and instinct, rather than calculated reactions based on a cumbersome intellectual process.

Of course, increasingly difficult problems will come along after you have mastered any particular skill level. This is a good thing. Problems are typically opportunities to gain new knowledge or experience, and they typically make you a better, smarter cyclist.

Now that you know more about these general training components, the next step is to understand the effects of exercise intensity and training volume. The next chapter explains these concepts, which help you define your own training zones for the plans in this book.

Training Intensity and Volume

Are you aiming to complete your first century? Ride a weeklong tour? Ride faster during an event? Whether you are aiming to go faster or farther, the paths to both goals are similar in process and strategy—as well as in the types of missteps that can leave you disappointed. In endurance training, one of the most common mistakes is to train at a fast pace all the time. You may think that if you want to be fast, you have to ride fast throughout your training, and this idea is true to some extent. However, you can't ride fast *all* the time and make progress. Cyclists who try to do so end up going one mediocre speed: not too fast, not too slow. They are never fresh enough to maintain a truly fast pace, yet they feel enough spunk to ride at a decent pace. This chapter will help you avoid that rut, by showing you how to use training and racing intensity and volume to your advantage, as well as giving you tests to estimate your training zones.

Perhaps you have been on a group ride during which the speeds were sizzling from the start. For a few moments you were right there, hanging with the pack. Then you were left in the dust. Your heart was pounding, your legs were burning, and you gave it your all, but the group intensity, or speed, was too fast for you to sustain. Yet others kept the pace. What were they doing that you were not?

Building or improving fitness is analogous to building a house. The foundation must be constructed properly or the house will not hold up—at least not for very long. Once you have a solid foundation, you can build the rest of the house, add finishing details on your own schedule, and make improvements as needed. The best results come from an orderly process in the initial stages of construction and good maintenance over time.

So it goes with fitness. A solid base is needed before long durations or long bouts of speed are added. If you attempt to ride for a long duration without having trained for it by gradually increasing your ride durations, your risk of injury is high. If you add long bouts of speed to your rides before achieving a good base of fitness, you can expect short-lived success and, again, a high risk of injury. Also, once you have reached a certain level of fitness, you need to maintain it. If you do, each season you can make further improvements. It takes years of steady improvement to become a world-class athlete or to achieve your full genetic potential.

PERIODIZATION

You may or may not strive to be world-class. Either way, a periodization plan will help you map out your journey to faster or longer riding. Briefly, a periodization plan is a plan that is created by manipulating exercise volumes and intensities over the course of weeks, months, and years.

The training plans in Chapters 5 through 20 are periodization plans. Some plans are designed for you to develop your depth of fitness to "survive" or complete a race. Other plans are geared toward increasing speed on an already established base.

A periodization plan for a world-class athlete spans the course of several years. The plan is designed so that the athlete will be at peak fitness and speed for a key event like the Olympic Games or the Tour de France. No athlete, even at this level, can maintain peak fitness year-round. A true peak performance is carefully planned and typically cannot occur more than two or three times per year.

> Your best results will come from building a solid base of fitness and maintaining it over time.

Although you may not achieve the time or distance marks of top professionals, your training process will not be fundamentally different from theirs. Rather, as you look into a training plan for an individual event, you'll find that any differences are simply further refinements of the training principles. For example, the details of the plan for a cyclist going on his or her first century ride look different from those of the plan for a cyclist training to ride faster. The plan for a weekend warrior looking to build basic endurance is different from the plan for a cyclist wanting to improve his or her ride time for a 100-mile mountain bike race. But all of these plans start with the same basic training principles and follow a scientifically proven process.

You've likely heard it said that "the devil is in the details." Here is a quick overview of the details and factors you must balance to be successful with periodized training:

- **Individual responses** to training vary, as discussed in Chapter 1. Given the same goal and training plan, different individuals may improve at different rates and may have varying gains in overall fitness levels.

- The **duration** of your longest workout may or may not be the length of your goal or targeted race. Generally, the shorter the event and the more time you have to train before it, the greater the likelihood that you will complete the event distance sometime during your training.

- **Frequency** of workouts scheduled will vary depending on each individual's current fitness, his or her race goals, the sport, and the training time available. Frequency applies to the number of workouts per week or per day. Some athletes will work out once a day, while others will do so two or more times a day. Keep in mind that although workout frequency is important, so is frequency of rest.

- **Volume** can be defined as the combination of frequency and duration. In any training plan, annual training volume is one piece of the puzzle. Monthly, weekly, and daily training volumes are equally important to break down in your plan. Don't try to establish your personal training volume based on what the professionals do. In order for you to see physiological improvement, your training volume needs to be based on your personal profile, past training volume, current lifestyle, goals, and response to training, as well as the number of weeks before your event.

- **Intensity** varies depending on each particular training block and the goal of the workout, much like duration and frequency. Training blocks can vary in length, but for the plans in this book, a block is typically three or four weeks long. There are myriad ways to measure intensity—heart rate, speed, power output, and perceived exertion, to name a few. These will be discussed in more detail later in this chapter. Training at the appropriate intensity minimizes the risk of injury while stressing the body enough to achieve the goal.

- The **specificity,** or mode, of training should vary over the course of the season. For athletes utilizing a year-round approach to training, aerobic crosstraining is most appropriate in the early training blocks. In northern latitudes, cyclists often use cross-country skiing workouts to bolster endurance. As the key event draws near, training that is specific to the sport becomes more important than generalized training.

- **Progressive overload** must be applied in order for you to achieve physiological improvement and bring about a training change. A widely accepted rule of thumb is to increase annual training hours or annual volume by 10 percent or less.

- **Rest and recovery** are critical training components. Performance gains are made when the body has a chance to repair itself and absorb the training workload.

- **Supercompensation,** sometimes also referred to as overcompensation, is a combination of overload (sometimes but not always progressive) and recovery: If you stress your body with increasing volume or intensity and then allow it to rest, your fitness level after the rest will be greater than before the workout. Supercompensation requires careful balancing. Under too much stress, the body breaks down, resulting in illness or injury. Under too little stress, the body makes no progress.

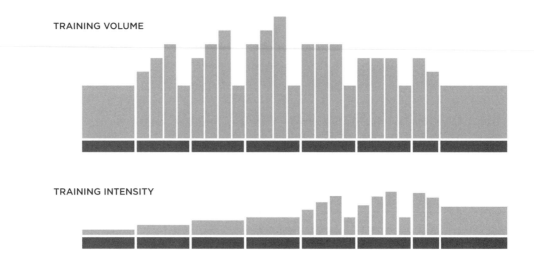

TRAINING VOLUME

TRAINING INTENSITY

FIGURE 2.1 Typical Interrelationship of Volume and Intensity

In many textbook models, training volume increases during early training periods and training intensity increases at modest rates. As training volume decreases or remains constant, training intensity increases. These graphs display how training volume and intensity might interrelate on the same training plan for the same periods of training.

Figure 2.1 shows a textbook model displaying the interrelationship between training volume and training intensity. Training volume begins at a steady rate, then increases in three-week blocks. After each three-week build of training volume, one week of reduced volume is included to allow for recovery. After three blocks of increasing volume, training volume is reduced and intensity begins to increase. Near the end of the plan, volume and intensity decrease before a race or a block of races. This is one example of a training strategy covering over 30 weeks of training appropriate for key races that are within a six-week block.

Now take a look at Figure 2.2. Notice how training volume builds near the end of the training plan. This is a training strategy that might be used by a cyclist racing long-distance events, such as a 100-mile mountain bike race. He or she might keep volume steady while including some higher-intensity training early in the plan. While this pattern can seem to be forced by weather, it can also work to the cyclist's advantage. As he or she gets closer to race day and the weather is more cooperative for long rides, volume builds to accommodate an event that will take over 10 hours to complete. This particular cyclist decreases intensity when volume starts to build and then holds the intensity level steady.

These figures are just two examples of the many periodization training strategies you can use to accomplish a particular racing goal. The most important thing is that your training plan be appropriate for your fitness, lifestyle, and race goals.

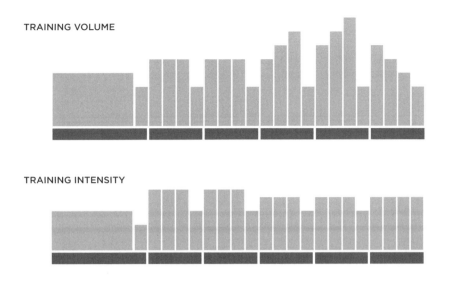

TRAINING VOLUME

TRAINING INTENSITY

FIGURE 2.2 Interrelationship of Volume and Intensity for Long-Distance Training
For some training circumstances, such as training for long-distance racing, training volume may increase while training intensity decreases.

Different books and magazines on fitness and training often use different terminology to refer to the same periodization concepts. Figure 2.3 shows how some of this popular terminology overlaps. The terms used in this book are closest to those used internationally across many sports. Let's take a closer look at these training phases.

General Preparation Phase

Some cyclists crosstrain during this phase, with the goal of building or maintaining cardio-vascular fitness. This phase can include several blocks, such as General Preparation 1, 2, and 3, and the training intensity throughout tends to be aerobic. Both General Preparation and Specific Preparation phases are often referred to as base training.

Specific Preparation Phase

The goal of this phase is to move toward sport-specific training, reducing or eliminating crosstraining. More race-paced training is added in this phase, but the race-paced work segments tend to be short with ample recovery at the beginning of the phase. The intention is to build neuromuscular movement patterns. As this phase continues, a greater percentage of the training resembles race pace. This phase can include several blocks, such as Specific Preparation 1, 2, and 3.

JOE FRIEL TERMINOLOGY

RECOVERY	GENERAL PREPARATION			SPECIFIC PREPARATION		COMPETITION	
PREPARATION	BASE 1	BASE 2	BASE 3	BUILD 1	BUILD 2	PEAK	RACE

TUDOR BOMPA TERMINOLOGY

PREPARATORY		COMPETITIVE	
GENERAL PREPARATION	SPECIFIC PREPARATION	PRE-COMPETITIVE	COMPETITIVE

GALE BERNHARDT TERMINOLOGY

RECOVERY	GENERAL PREPARATION		SPECIFIC PREPARATION		PRE-COMPETITIVE PREPARATION		COMPETITIVE
	GENERAL PREPARATION 1	GENERAL PREPARATION 2	SPECIFIC PREPARATION 1	SPECIFIC PREPARATION 2	PRE-COMPETITIVE PREPARATION 1	PRE-COMPETITIVE PREPARATION 2	RACE

FIGURE 2.3 Training Terminology
The terminology used in this book most closely resembles Tudor Bompa's terminology and is utilized across multiple sports worldwide.

Pre-competitive Preparation Phase

The goal of this phase is to prepare the cyclist for his or her specific race requirements. These requirements—race time and intensity—are quite different for a 30-mile event, a century ride, and a multiday tour. These requirements also vary with each individual athlete. An athlete who has minimal conditioning has different requirements from an athlete who is highly conditioned. This phase can include several blocks, such as Pre-competitive 1, 2, and 3. It can also include low-priority races used as training events.

Competitive Phase

This phase may include a series of races over the course of six to eight weeks, such as in a race series, or it may be a period of tapering volume in the lead-up to a single race, such as an ultra-distance event.

Recovery Phase

This phase allows you to recover from the rigors of training and racing. It has no specific parameters, just basic guidelines to maintain fitness, such as:

- **Recover weekly:** Take at least one to two days off from training each week.
- **Reduce intensity:** Keep your training intensity aerobic in nature. (See "Energy Production.")
- **Reduce duration:** Limit all your training sessions to two hours or less.

For a competitive athlete, this phase is often one to four weeks in length.

MEASURING INTENSITY

Getting into peak condition requires both science and art. Science helps you understand how the body responds to the stress of training. Art is knowing when to follow a plan and when to deviate from it. Each training plan in this book requires a basic understanding of the rationale or science involved so you can master the art, and I'll give you plenty of tips along the way. When you understand the demands placed on the body during exercise, you can more effectively balance the intensity in your training.

Energy Production

Your body requires a continuous supply of energy, even when you are asleep. Energy is supplied by complex chemical reactions. The end result of these reactions is a rich compound called adenosine triphosphate (ATP). The potential energy within the ATP molecule is utilized for all energy-requiring processes of the cells of your body.

> So the body relies more on anaerobic energy production as the pace increases.

Your body uses two basic methods to produce ATP. One method is aerobic (meaning with the presence of oxygen) and the second method is anaerobic (meaning without the presence of oxygen). The method of energy production your body uses depends on the rate of demand for energy (intensity) and the length of demand for energy (duration). Short bursts of high speed utilize the anaerobic system of energy production to fuel the muscles. For longer efforts, fat and glycogen are burned in the presence of oxygen to create ATP.

A small amount of energy is readily available to be utilized "on demand." For example, when you sprint to make it through an intersection before the light changes, a small amount of energy is needed instantly. The majority of the energy necessary for this sprint is created anaerobically. After you have made it through the intersection and resume a slower speed, energy is created mostly by aerobic means.

For short sprints, energy is primarily created anaerobically and uses ATP stored in the muscle cells to complete the work. ATP is stored in the cells in limited quantities. It is readily available but used quickly. Aerobically produced ATP, on the other hand, takes more time for the body to produce, but it is available in huge quantities. These large quantities of energy allow an athlete to exercise for several hours at easy to moderate speeds.

Although a cyclist may be riding at a moderate pace, some of the energy it takes to do so is produced anaerobically. In other words, both systems are working at the same time. As intensity or speed increases, energy production and utilization need to happen more rapidly. Remember, the aerobic system needs time to produce energy; it is not as quick as the anaerobic system. So the body relies more on anaerobic energy production as the pace increases.

Lactate

A by-product of the anaerobic energy production system is lactic acid. Lactic acid is often viewed negatively, but in fact it is an energy source for the body. When given enough time, the body can process and use lactic acid to produce ATP. Lactate (a salt of lactic acid) is present in the blood at rest. Even while you are sitting and reading this book, you have low levels of lactate circulating in your bloodstream.

At low levels, lactic acid is not a problem. However, as you continue to increase your workout intensity, your body increases energy production, relying more heavily on anaerobic metabolism. More reliance on anaerobic metabolism means the lactate level in your blood begins to increase. When your body can no longer process lactic acid fast enough, lactate begins to accumulate at an increasing rate in the blood—a condition called "onset of blood lactate accumulation" or "lactate threshold" (LT). This accumulation has a close correlation with heart rate and ventilatory rate (the rate at which air moves into and out of the lungs). Athletes can often tell when they have reached lactate threshold because their breathing becomes labored and they begin to feel a burning sensation in their muscles.

Because it is not possible for athletes to measure blood lactate accumulation and LT, heart rate and breathing rate can be used to estimate LT. Lactate threshold can be understood as the pace and correlating average heart rate that an athlete can sustain for approximately one hour while participating in a single sport. (See the test for "Finding Your Lactate Threshold" later in this chapter.) For example, the LT for a highly fit cyclist is approximately the pace and average heart rate that the athlete can maintain for a 40-kilometer time trial on the bicycle. The average heart rate that correlates with LT is known as the lactate threshold heart rate (LTHR).

If athletes exceed LT pace, they can sustain the increased pace for only a few minutes before the discomfort forces them to slow down. The margin by which LT is exceeded is inversely proportional to the time the athlete is able to sustain that pace. In other words, if an athlete's lactate threshold heart rate (LTHR) is 162 and heart rate is pushed to 172, he or she will be able to hold that pace for a shorter period of time than if working at a heart rate of 164.

In healthy, untrained people, LT typically occurs at 55 to 65 percent of VO_2max, the measure of aerobic capacity noted in Chapter 1. In highly trained endurance athletes, LT is often greater than 80 percent of VO_2max. As you might recall from Chapter 1, you can train your body to process lactate at higher percentages of VO_2max, which means you can reach increased levels of speed before the discomfort forces an end to the effort.

Studies have shown LT to be a reliable predictor of endurance race performance, and some methods of estimating your LT—and then determining your training zones—are discussed later in this chapter. VO_2max is not nearly as reliable. So if you have been tested for VO_2max and your numbers weren't stellar, don't panic.

> Lactate threshold (LT) has proven to be a reliable predictor for endurance race performance.

The training zones at the end of this chapter are approximations. If you were to test blood lactate levels daily for a period of time, you would find that a heart rate of 162 would produce some variation in the levels of lactate. The more experience you gain as an athlete, the more tuned in you will become to your personal exercise intensity levels.

Intensity Indicators

Perceived Exertion

The Borg scale, more commonly referred to as rate of perceived exertion (RPE), was originally designed to correlate with heart rate for young athletes and derived by dividing the heart rate by 10. For example, easy exercise at a perceived exertion value of 6 was intended to correlate with a heart rate of 60. Although the numbers do not always correlate exactly with heart rate, the perceived exertion scale can be very valuable and is still widely used. Table 2.1 (found later in this chapter) details the Borg scale and describes how your breathing will change from one intensity level to the next. If you are new to cycling, your breathing rate will be key to determining your initial LTHR, as detailed later in "10-Minute Time Trial for Beginners."

Heart Rate

Next to RPE, heart rate is the most economical measure of exercising intensity. Each workout in each training plan in this book has a specific purpose, and monitoring your heart rate and RPE helps you achieve the designed training effect. You can estimate your heart rate using RPE and breathing rates, or you can measure it using a heart rate monitor (see Chapter 4 for guidance on selecting a monitoring system).

Your heart rate is affected by your conditioning and present level of rest; the amount of stress you're experiencing; and heat, humidity, and fatigue. One indicator of improving fitness is the capability of increasing the speed you achieve for a given heart rate level. For example, when beginning a training plan, you may find you can ride 14 mph steadily while your heart rate stays around 140 beats per minute (bpm). As you improve your fitness, a heart rate of 140 corresponds with speeds greater than 14 mph.

If you have a heart rate monitor, you should wear it for most workouts. Whether or not you wear it during a race depends on your experience level and the event distance. Experienced athletes are more skilled at judging intensity and pace; whether or not they wear a monitor during a race depends on personal preference. Less experienced athletes can use a heart rate monitor during a race to keep them from starting out too fast and bonking before the end of an event. In general, I suggest that all cyclists—experienced or not—wear a heart rate monitor for events over about three hours.

Power Output

In recent years, training with power has become more widespread because power meters and power-estimating devices are more widely available and affordable for athletes. A cyclist riding based on power output is similar to a runner or a swimmer training in response to results from time-based intervals at the track or in the pool. Like the stopwatch at the track and the clock on the wall of the pool, a power meter provides an accurate measure of improvement. Cyclists who use average speed to measure or grade improved fitness know that average speed on any ride is influenced by factors like wind, hills, and other riders. So while an improvement or decrease in average speed during a ride can be deceptive, power output is a more reliable guide.

Some power meters measure the force you apply by using a strain gauge in the bike's bottom bracket, rear hub, or crankset. These strain gauges measure actual material displacement due to force. That is, mathematical formulas are used to calculate power output based on the force and velocity of the movement of the part to which the strain gauge is applied. Other power meters do not take a direct strain-gauge measurement, instead estimating velocity using other factors and mathematical calculations. (See Chapter 4 for more information on selecting and reading a power meter.) In short, you can increase your power output by pushing harder on the pedals, by pedaling faster, or through some combination of both.

Power is measured in watts. Cyclists produce different average wattages depending on the length of a time trial or measurement period and the effort level of the cyclist. For example, the average wattage you produce during a 30-minute easy ride will be lower than what you produce during a 30-minute all-out time trial. Similarly, the wattage you produce during the 30-minute time trial is lower than what you produce during an all-out effort for one minute. In addition to raw power numbers, an important measure is *watts produced per kilogram of body weight*. It takes more raw power output (watts) to propel a 220-pound cyclist at 20 mph than it takes to propel a 120-pound cyclist at 20 mph.

If you have a power meter, you can use power-based training zones rather than heart rate–based zones to complete the workouts in this book. By following the power meter testing protocol in this chapter (see "30-Minute, Individual Time Trial with a Power Meter"), you can define your lactate threshold power and then calculate your individual training zones. Average wattage information can also help you structure interval workouts.

To use power-based intervals in the training plans, try to train within the range of power in that zone. For example, if your LT power is 238 watts, the interval power range for zone 4 is 217 to 236 watts (91 to 99 percent of 238; see "Training Zones" and Table 2.1 later in this chapter). If a workout calls for "4 × 6 minutes at zone 4 intensity," it is best to begin the intervals on the low end of the wattage and plan to finish strong on the last interval, producing an average wattage that is at the high end of the zone.

Heart rate can be an inaccurate guide and difficult to monitor in estimating high-end speed training zones (4 to 5a). In fact, for short sprints, a heart rate monitor is useless; by the time your heart rate responds to the effort and the monitor displays the corresponding heart rate, your work bout is long over. For longer intervals, many cyclists ride the first couple of intervals too fast and fade at the end of the set. In this case, using a power meter allows the cyclist to maintain more consistent energy production, which usually leads to a strong finish and a higher average speed.

Even if you use a power meter, you should still monitor how your heart rate responds to power-based intervals. Combining RPE, heart rate, and power gives you the best of all worlds. In some cases, you may find that the three numbers don't match your past performances for a given situation. If this happens, evaluate possible causes. Your fitness, the weather, the course profile, and your current fatigue levels all affect the numbers.

TESTING

Finding Your Lactate Threshold

You can estimate your lactate threshold through several methods. The most precise method is a graded exercise test performed at a laboratory. In this test, the exercise workload is incrementally increased and blood samples are taken at specific intervals to measure the level of lactate in the blood. Also during this test, the ratio of oxygen to carbon dioxide being expelled from your respiratory system can be measured and used to estimate LT.

In the field, you can estimate LT and LTHR using the tests that follow. You will need a heart rate monitor. If you own a power meter, collect both heart rate and power data.

In order to get the most accurate results in these tests, you need to be rested and highly motivated. If you do a test when you are tired, you may end up understating your training zones. If you have concerns about doing such tests, seek the advice of a physician first. Also, it is not wise to conduct the tests during the first workouts you do after you've been inactive for a long period of time. (Please note that these tests are *not* intended to find maximum heart rate.)

For the most accurate results, complete tests when you are rested and highly motivated.

The testing methods outlined here will estimate your LT, and in my experience, they work well. Also record your rating of perceived exertion, breathing rate, and heart rate. Keep in mind that your LTHR can change. If the numbers seem off compared with your RPE, you can hone in on a more precise number by repeating the LT test periodically and by noting your heart rates during training and racing.

10-Minute Time Trial for Beginners

After reaching a level of base fitness, you can conduct a short time trial to estimate your LTHR. Warm up for 10 to 15 minutes at RPE zones 1 to 2 (see Table 2.1 later in this chapter). After the warm-up, ride for about 10 minutes, increasing your pace every minute. The increased pace should be sustainable for the full minute, and you will repeat this bump in intensity 10 times—this is not a sprint. Note your heart rate at the end of each minute. How do you feel? What is your breathing like?

At some point during the test, your breathing will become noticeably labored. Record your heart rate at this point; you will use this rate as your LTHR for now. A short while later, a burning sensation will begin to creep into your legs. Take a mental note of when you feel this sensation as well, because the two points are not the same.

If you were to use the burning sensation to estimate your LTHR, you might overestimate it. Overestimating threshold leads to overestimating all the training zones, which means you might be exercising anaerobically when you intend to work mostly aerobically. As a result, your aerobic system can end up overtrained and underdeveloped, so I encourage beginners to be more conservative with this first LT number. As you gain more training experience, your estimated LT can be further refined.

20- to 30-Minute Race

Typically, your LTHR equals your average heart rate during an all-out 60- to 90-minute cycling event. (Keep in mind that your average should be significantly higher for the shorter race.) If you are an experienced cyclist, you can estimate LTHR using your average heart rate during a 20- to 30-minute race, which will be about 104 percent of your LTHR. Use a heart rate monitor that calculates average heart rate over a selected interval or period. Once you have this average number, divide it by 1.04.

For example, assume you ride a local time trial and it takes you 25 minutes to finish. You calculate that the value of your average heart rate during the race, excluding warm-up and cool down, was 170 bpm. Your estimated LTHR is 170 divided by 1.04, or 163 bpm.

20-Minute Individual Time Trial

To conduct your own time trial, find a flat course with no stoplights and minimal distractions. After a good warm-up, start your heart rate monitor and then ride your 20-minute time trial as fast as possible. Meter your speed so you can produce the highest average and best effort for the full 20 minutes. The most common mistake cyclists make during this test is to break out with a fast 5-minute effort, then slowly fade.

Collect your heart rate average for the time trial and divide this value by 1.02. For example, if your average heart rate for the 20-minute time trial was 160 bpm, then your LTHR is 160 divided by 1.02, or 157.

30-Minute Individual Time Trial with a Power Meter

To estimate lactate threshold power, take the average power produced during the 30-minute time trial and subtract 5 percent. For example, if your 30-minute time trial average power is 250 watts, your lactate threshold power is approximately 238 watts—that is, 250 minus 12.5 (250×0.05). Also record your average heart rate for this test.

TRAINING ZONES

Once you have your estimate of lactate threshold heart rate or power in hand, you can use this number to define your individual training zones using the respective LT percentages in Table 2.1. What follows is a brief explanation of each zone.

Zone 1

Zone 1 is used to build fitness in beginning athletes and for recovery purposes in more experienced athletes. The energy production is primarily aerobic. Zone 1 is also used in conjunction with zone 2 to build exercise endurance for long-distance racing.

Zone 2

Zone 2 is used to build fitness and maintain current levels of fitness. Lactate begins to increase, but the accumulation tends to be linear and manageable by the body for very long periods

TABLE 2.1 TRAINING ZONES BASED ON RPE, HEART RATE, AND POWER

| ZONE | RATE OF PERCEIVED EXERTION (RPE) | | LACTATE THRESHOLD (LT) | |
	Original Borg Scale	New Borg Scale	Heart Rate (%)	Power (%)
1	6–9	1–2	<80	<55
2	10–12	3–4	81–88	56–75
3	13–14	4–5	89–93	76–90
4	15–16	6	94–99	91–99
5a	17	7	100–102	100–105
5b	18–19	8–9	103–105	106–120
5c	20	10	106+	121+

of time, such as training and racing for time periods of 6 to 12 hours, or more. Within this intensity zone is what many coaches call "aerobic threshold." Some scientists and coaches define the lactate measurement of 2 millimoles per liter (mmol/L) and the associated heart rate as aerobic threshold; there is disagreement about this value. (See "Zone 5a" for further discussion.)

Zones 1 and 2 are often used in conjunction with drills to improve athletic skills. Good form improves athletic economy, which translates to less oxygen needed for a given pace.

Zone 3

Zone 3 intensity is used for early-season tempo work and to begin LT improvement. Zones 1 through 3 are used by experienced athletes training for and racing in events that last longer than about three hours.

DESCRIPTION OF BREATHING AND PERCEPTION	COMMON TERMINOLOGY
Gentle rhythmic breathing. Pace is easy, legs feel relaxed, minimal pressure on the pedals. Easy spinning.	Easy Aerobic Recovery
Breathing rate and pace increase slightly. Many notice a change with slightly deeper breathing, although still comfortable. Legs remain comfortable and conversations possible.	Aerobic Extensive endurance Aerobic threshold endurance
Aware of breathing a little harder, pace is moderate. Legs begin to feel some stress and it is more difficult to hold conversation.	Tempo Intensive endurance
Starting to breathe hard, pace is fast and beginning to get uncomfortable, approaching all-out 1-hour ride pace.	Subthreshold Muscular endurance Threshold endurance Anaerobic threshold endurance
Breathing deep and forceful, many notice a second significant change in breathing pattern. Pace is all-out sustainable for 60 to 90 minutes. Mental focus required, legs are moderately uncomfortable, and conversation is undesirable.	Lactate threshold endurance Anaerobic threshold endurance Superthreshold Muscular endurance
Heavy, labored breathing. Pace is noticeably challenging but sustainable for 15 to 30 minutes. Leg discomfort is high but manageable.	Aerobic capacity Speed endurance Anaerobic endurance
Maximal exertion in breathing, pace is sprinting effort, legs experience high discomfort that is unsustainable for over 1 minute.	Anaerobic capacity Power

Zone 4

This zone is used in conjunction with intervals, hill work, and steady-state work to improve LT speed and muscular endurance. Intervals in this zone commonly have a work-to-rest ratio of 3:1 or 4:1 in cycling.

Zone 5a

The lowest heart rate value in zone 5a (100 percent of LTHR in Table 2.1) is most commonly called lactate threshold. As mentioned earlier, some coaches and scientists call this anaerobic threshold. Laboratories often associate a blood lactate value of 4 mmol/L with LT. Although the 4 mmol/L value is common for many athletes, LT can vary widely. It can be as low as 2 mmol/L or as high as 8 mmol/L for individual athletes. So the statement "anaerobic threshold is 4 mmol/L" may be incorrect for some athletes. Quality laboratories typically provide lactate curves and interpret the data for you, eliminating a "one-size-fits-all" value for both thresholds.

This zone is used in conjunction with intervals, hill riding, and tempo rides to improve LT speed and muscular endurance. It is often used in conjunction with zone 4.

Zone 5b

The major use for this zone is to improve anaerobic endurance. Intervals in this zone often have a work-to-rest ratio of 1:1. This zone is also used in hill workouts.

Zone 5c

Zone 5c is fast—really fast—or powerful cycling. For example, sprinting to grab a competitor's wheel or climbing hills out of the saddle elicits heart rates in zone 5c. Exercise in zone 5c cannot be maintained for long periods of time. Intervals in this zone commonly have a work-to-rest ratio of 1:2 or more.

The preceding comments for each zone are not all-inclusive, but they do give an idea of the uses for each particular training zone. Table 2.2 further helps you define your training zones.

This book uses the seven training zones to measure speed and help you avoid mediocre workouts. Remember that anyone can train and race hard, but not everyone is fast.

TABLE 2.2 CYCLING HEART RATE ZONES

ZONE 1 RECOVERY	ZONE 2 AEROBIC	ZONE 3 TEMPO	ZONE 4 SUB-THRESHOLD	ZONE 5a SUPER-THRESHOLD	ZONE 5b AEROBIC CAPACITY	ZONE 5c ANAEROBIC CAPACITY
90—108	109—122	123—128	129—136	137—140	141—145	146—150
91—109	110—123	124—129	130—137	138—141	142—146	147—151
91—109	110—124	125—130	131—138	139—142	143—147	148—152
92—110	111—125	126—130	131—139	140—143	144—147	148—153
92—111	112—125	126—131	132—140	141—144	145—148	149—154
93—112	113—126	127—132	133—141	142—145	146—149	150—155
93—112	113—127	128—133	134—142	143—145	146—150	151—156
94—113	114—128	129—134	135—143	144—147	148—151	152—157
95—114	115—129	130—135	136—144	145—148	149—152	153—158
95—115	116—130	131—136	137—145	146—149	150—154	155—159
97—116	117—131	132—137	138—146	147—150	151—155	156—161
97—117	118—132	133—138	139—147	148—151	152—156	157—162
98—118	119—133	134—139	140—148	149—152	153—157	158—163
98—119	120—134	135—140	141—149	150—153	154—158	159—164
99—120	121—134	135—141	142—150	151—154	155—159	160—165
100—121	122—135	136—142	143—151	152—155	156—160	161—166
100—122	123—136	137—142	143—152	153—156	157—161	162—167
101—123	124—137	138—143	144—153	154—157	158—162	163—168
101—124	125—138	139—144	145—154	155—158	159—163	164—169
102—125	126—138	139—145	146—155	156—159	160—164	165—170
103—126	127—140	141—146	147—156	157—160	161—165	166—171
104—127	128—141	142—147	148—157	158—161	162—167	168—173
104—128	129—142	143—148	149—158	159—162	163—168	169—174
105—129	130—143	144—148	149—159	160—163	164—169	170—175
106—129	130—143	144—150	151—160	161—164	165—170	171—176
106—130	131—144	145—151	152—161	162—165	166—171	172—177
107—131	132—145	146—152	153—162	163—166	167—172	173—178
107—132	133—146	147—153	154—163	164—167	168—173	174—179
108—133	134—147	148—154	155—164	165—168	169—174	175—180
109—134	135—148	149—154	155—165	166—169	170—175	176—181

CONTINUED

TABLE 2.2 CYCLING HEART RATE ZONES CONTINUED

ZONE 1 RECOVERY	ZONE 2 AEROBIC	ZONE 3 TEMPO	ZONE 4 SUB-THRESHOLD	ZONE 5a SUPER-THRESHOLD	ZONE 5b AEROBIC CAPACITY	ZONE 5c ANAEROBIC CAPACITY
109—135	136—149	150—155	156—166	167—170	171—176	177—182
110—136	137—150	151—156	157—167	168—171	172—177	178—183
111—137	138—151	152—157	158—168	169—172	173—178	179—185
112—138	139—151	152—158	159—169	170—173	174—179	180—186
112—139	140—152	153—160	161—170	171—174	175—180	181—187
113—140	141—153	154—160	161—171	172—175	176—181	182—188
113—141	142—154	155—161	162—172	173—176	177—182	183—189
114—142	143—155	156—162	163—173	174—177	178—183	184—190
115—143	144—156	157—163	164—174	175—178	179—184	185—191
115—144	145—157	158—164	165—175	176—179	180—185	186—192
116—145	146—158	159—165	166—176	177—180	181—186	187—193
116—146	147—159	160—166	167—177	178—181	182—187	188—194
117—147	148—160	161—166	167—178	179—182	183—188	189—195
118—148	149—160	161—167	168—179	180—183	184—190	191—197
119—149	150—161	162—168	169—180	181—184	185—191	192—198
119—150	151—162	163—170	171—181	182—185	186—192	193—199
120—151	152—163	164—171	172—182	183—186	187—193	194—200
121—152	153—164	165—172	173—183	184—187	188—194	195—201
121—153	154—165	166—172	173—184	185—188	189—195	196—202
122—154	155—166	167—173	174—185	186—189	190—196	197—203
122—155	156—167	168—174	175—186	187—190	191—197	198—204
123—156	157—168	169—175	176—187	188—191	192—198	199—205
124—157	158—169	170—176	177—188	189—192	193—199	200—206
124—158	159—170	171—177	178—189	190—193	194—200	201—207
125—159	160—170	171—178	179—190	191—194	195—201	202—208
125—160	161—171	172—178	179—191	192—195	196—202	203—209
126—161	162—172	173—179	180—192	193—196	197—203	204—210
127—162	163—173	174—180	181—193	194—197	198—204	205—211
127—163	164—174	175—181	182—194	195—198	199—205	206—212

Nutrition

In an interview about ten years ago, I spoke wistfully of a future time when optimum fitness and nutrition plans could be prescribed for an athlete based on his or her DNA. I concluded that until optimization could be guaranteed, we'd have to settle for a bit of science and art. As I write this book, a relatively new science called nutrigenomics is exploring the interplay between genetic makeup and the ways in which nutrients found in certain foods might assist in the prevention of specific diseases. Although scientists have not mastered DNA testing and subsequent individual nutritional prescriptions for health and athletic optimization, I have no doubt that one day this service will be available.

Until then, you are left to make nutritional decisions for yourself. At your local bookstore, you will find an overwhelming number of books about diet. A search of one of the popular online bookstores reveals nearly 7,000 relevant titles. If there were one golden diet that worked for everyone, the person who discovered it would be rich and famous. But based on all my research on nutrition for general health and athletic performance, I can say with certainty that no single nutrition plan works for everyone.

However, in the most general terms, perhaps there is one perfect diet: Eat and drink enough of the right foods to build and maintain a healthy body. It's simple, but not easy, especially when you want to know *exactly* what to eat. How many carbohydrates, how much fat and protein? How many calories? Precisely which foods should you eat each day to guarantee optimal health?

THE OPTIMAL DIET

The appropriate diet for any individual depends on:

- **Genetics:** Some people are born with faster metabolisms than others. Also, some people have inherited health issues that require medication. Some medications affect basal metabolism.
- **Gender:** Men have greater percentages of muscle mass than women, so they have greater basal metabolic rates.
- **Body surface area:** Given the same weight for two individuals, one tall and one short, the tall, thin person has a greater body surface area and therefore has a greater basal metabolism.
- **Daily routine activity level:** If your job has you sitting at a desk all day long with little movement, your caloric needs are different from the needs of someone who is in constant physical motion most of the day.
- **Lifestyle and personal preferences:** Some people have a lifestyle of eating only home-prepared foods, while others are dependent on food prepared by others. In both scenarios, selecting foods that build healthy bodies is a challenge. We all have foods we prefer and foods we simply do not enjoy.
- **Exercise activity level:** Duration and intensity of exercise burn calories and can affect basal metabolism.
- **Quality of foods:** Highly processed foods tend to have fewer nutrients than whole foods. Athletes who are concerned with health and performance should maximize the nutrient quality of their food.

If you take one message from this chapter, remember that you are a study of one. Your unique genetics, history, and lifestyle all contribute to your nutritional status. You need to take responsibility for your health and track your health status with the help of your health-care professional. When your health status markers are out of line with what you expect for optimal health, you need to take action and seek the advice of your family doctor and sports medicine specialists.

I share my own story with many of the athletes I coach because it illustrates many of the nutrition rules discussed in this chapter. You may be able to relate to many of the challenges I faced in my own struggle to find a good nutrition plan.

A Study of One

When I was racing competitively, I became convinced that if I could lose some weight, I could race even faster. I was well-read in diet and nutrition, and the prevailing advice (circa 1980) told me I could lose weight by exercising and following a low-fat diet of no fewer than 1,200 calories per day. So that's what I did.

I carefully monitored my caloric intake and opted for high-value foods, chock-full of vitamins and minerals but also low in fat. In other words, I ate predominately fruits and vegetables. I knew I needed protein, but I was well aware of statistics on the average American's overconsumption of protein. Most of my protein came from nonfat dairy products and an occasional piece of fish or poultry.

Season after season, I was unable to change my body weight. I was perplexed. I was exercising between 6 and 10 hours each week, working between 48 and 55 hours each week, and watching what I ate. Why didn't my body look like the body of a fit athlete? I also had no energy, and every year I found myself nursing one small, nagging injury that prevented me from improving my speed.

Finally, I sought the help of a registered dietician. I was asked to keep food logs for a week—an easy task for me, as I had been meticulously counting calories for years and could estimate portions without weighing or measuring them. The dietician's analysis found that my diet was very high in vitamins and minerals, low in fat (10 percent of total caloric intake), low in protein (10 percent of total calories), and high in carbohydrate (80 percent of total calories).

> You are a study of one: Your unique genetics, history, and lifestyle all contribute to your nutritional status.

My daily intake averaged around 1,300 calories, which seemed perfect to me for losing weight (if not 100 calories too high, by my estimate). However, my dietician told me that this caloric intake was far too low. Based on my work and exercise routine, she recommended that I increase my daily caloric intake to 2,300 calories. Not surprisingly, I wondered how I would ever lose weight this way.

She also told me that my fat and protein intake was too low, which was less surprising. I was familiar with the work that Barry Sears did with the Stanford swim team, implementing a diet for the team that was 30 percent fat, 30 percent protein, and 40 percent carbohydrates. It was a far cry from my own diet, but with my dietician's support, I was willing to give it a try. I agreed to increase the levels of fat and protein in my diet and lower the level of carbohydrates.

After one week, I had lost three pounds. I felt better physically, although I felt like I was eating a ton of food. With this added confidence in the plan, I continued eating more calories and maintaining a macronutrient split that included more fat and protein.

When I first made these changes, it was November. In the weeks and months that followed, I began to notice big changes. I had more energy. I was sleeping through the night rather than getting up three to five times as I had before—sometimes for a snack. My hair was growing faster. My menstrual cycles, which had been irregular for years, were once again regular. Put simply, I felt good.

By the time the next racing season arrived, in May, I was feeling better than ever and had made it through a winter of training with no injuries. The initial three pounds were all I had lost, but the numbers on the scale now meant less to me because I felt better and was racing faster.

During the race season, I found I could generally continue a daily diet with the 30-30-40 proportions, but I needed to make adjustments during races. I increased my carbohydrates during races lasting longer than one hour, as well as during the hours following a hard workout or race to speed my recovery.

My only lingering worry was my cholesterol level, which had been up around 195 for years. I decided that even if this new diet was good for my cycling, I wasn't willing to put myself at risk for heart disease. But fourteen months after changing my diet, my blood work showed my cholesterol to be vastly improved, at 160.

Two years later, I had dropped an additional seven pounds. I was still seeing faster race times, my menstrual cycle remained regular, I remained injury-free, and I felt great.

Although I no longer keep food logs, I try to balance my snacks and meals by eating some protein, fat, and carbohydrates. Fruits and vegetables are still a good portion of my diet, but I also consume plenty of lean meats and nuts and minimize my intake of highly processed foods.

> When athletes cut significant calories in order to lose weight, the results are often counterproductive.

The temptation to lose weight in the hope of increasing speed is all too common among cyclists, both women and men. First, they cut calories. No one wants to diet for any extended period of time, so they cut a lot of calories for a short period of time to get it over with. Unfortunately, when athletes cut significant calories in order to lose weight, the results are often counterproductive.

We can glean from my own experience that:

- Extreme calorie restriction and chronic dieting slow metabolism.
- Very low-fat and/or very low-protein diets are correlated with amenorrhea in women. Many studies further correlate amenorrhea in female athletes with loss in bone density.
- Inadequate nutrition will cause the body to break down. This can mean more frequent colds and flu, or it can mean more serious physical injuries. Athletes who are often ill or injured aren't likely to be competitive or to reach their full potential.

Scientific Support

A nutritional study examined the dietary habits of four male and two female elite triathletes by analyzing their seven-day diet records. Researchers found that the athletes' daily intake of calories and carbohydrates was insufficient to support their estimated requirements, and also that their diets were low in zinc and chromium. The researchers recommended diet changes to increase food intake. Follow-up seven-day diet records found the athletes had increased average daily calories, increased carbohydrate consumption, and met their daily requirements for zinc, chromium, and all other nutrients. Their race results also displayed an improvement in performance.

In a separate study on trained cyclists, a high-fat diet was found to increase endurance. Five trained cyclists followed either a high-fat diet (70 percent fat, 7 percent carbohydrate, 23 percent protein) or a high-carbohydrate diet (74 percent carbohydrate, 12 percent fat, 14 percent protein) for two weeks. Endurance at 60 percent of VO_2max was measured before and after the dietary changes, and the high-fat diet was associated with significant increases in endurance.

If performance is not your only concern—perhaps you want to live to be a hundred years old—consider the people who live in Lerik, Azerbaijan, a small mountain town near the Iranian border. This village is famous for people living a hundred years or more, and scores of old people live in the town. How do they do it?

The town is poorly served by medicine, most of the people are uneducated, and they eat very little and work hard. Vegetables, fruit, and sour cheeses make up the majority of their diet. When Azerbaijan was part of the Soviet Union, doctors visited the town and took numerous blood samples, looking for some secret to longevity. The tests were inconclusive. Researchers theorized the villagers' longevity was related to genetics and clean, stress-free living.

So how can we make sense of the differences between the people of Lerik and the trained athletes? Some of the athletes studied followed a 30-30-40 diet, others simply increased calories, still others followed a high-fat diet, and they all had performance increases. The Lerik "athletes" toil each day, outlive most people, and display sustained high performance. How is it that these groups can follow completely different diets and both have improved or sustained high performance? What *is* the perfect diet?

Most of us don't live the Lerik lifestyle, so perhaps it is not a fair comparison. People living in modern cities deal with pollution, job-related toxins, job- and family-related stress, and water and foods that have been processed. Given the variables, how do you figure out what your own optimal diet is? This chapter offers information you can use to evaluate and improve your diet. Although one chapter cannot cover all the information necessary to understand nutrition (and as technology develops, we will have new and more accurate

Nutrition Rules

Rule No. 1: Eat adequate calories.

Rule No. 2: Do not try to lose weight through extreme calorie restrictions.

Rule No. 3: Eat a balance of macronutrients.

Rule No. 4: Drink adequate fluids.

Rule No. 5: There are no "bad" foods; however, some foods should be consumed with discretion.

Rule No. 6: Fat is essential to optimal health.

Rule No. 7: A healthy diet should contain a wide variety of minimally processed foods.

information), it will give a good overview of macronutrients and micronutrients, some nutritional concerns common to athletes, and some tools to evaluate your own diet.

MACRONUTRIENTS

Depending on which expert you ask, there are either three or four macronutrients. The commonly agreed-upon macronutrients are carbohydrates, fat, and protein. Some sources consider water to be a fourth macronutrient. Let's take a look at water first.

Water

Between 40 and 60 percent of an individual's body weight is made up of water. Water is typically 65 to 75 percent of the weight of muscle and less than 25 percent of the weight of fat. Water is essential to a functioning body. A body can survive many days without food but only a few days without water.

A well-hydrated athlete performs better. Dehydration levels as low as 2 percent of body weight are thought to impair athletic performance—perhaps by as much as 20 percent.

> Dehydration levels as low as 2 percent of body weight can impair athletic performance by as much as 20 percent.

Many athletes do not adequately hydrate. Most literature recommends drinking 8 to 10 glasses of water each day. However, if you are drinking 8 to 10 glasses daily and your urine is dark yellow in color and foul-smelling, you are not drinking enough. Rather than aiming for a certain number of glasses of water per day, a better guideline is to drink enough water so that your urine is light in color and has minimal odor. Other signals of dehydration are constipation, fatigue, and headaches.

Caffeinated coffees, teas, and soft drinks can have a diuretic effect, which means they increase the normal urinary output, leaving less fluid in the body for normal functioning. Although individual responses to caffeine vary, routine caffeine consumption can increase tolerance and further influence caffeine's effect on individuals. Depending on caffeine's effect on you, limiting your daily intake of caffeine can help keep your body hydrated.

Carbohydrates

Carbohydrates are almost exclusively found in plants and their processed by-products. Fruits, vegetables, beans, peas, and grains are sources of carbohydrates. The only animal sources that have significant carbohydrates are milk and yogurt.

Carbohydrates are made of sugar molecules and are divided into two major groups: complex carbohydrates and simple carbohydrates. Complex carbohydrates consist of many sugar molecules linked together. Foods in the complex group include vegetables, whole grains, beans, and peas. These foods contain fiber and starches and are made of long complex chains of sugar molecules. They are more difficult than simple carbohydrates for the body to break down into fuel.

Simple carbohydrates, sometimes referred to as simple sugars, include fructose (fruit sugar), lactose (milk sugar), sucrose, and glucose. Note that all of these terms end in the suffix "-ose," which indicates something is a carbohydrate. A food product with several "-ose" ingredients listed separately on its label actually contains that many simple sugars or combinations of sugars of different origin.

The body absorbs sugars and eventually converts them into glucose, the body's usable form of sugar. Sugar is absorbed into the blood, heart, skeletal muscle, and liver—in that order. When blood sugars reach homeostasis, or a state of balance in the blood, the heart and skeletal muscles accept glucose. The always-working heart uses glucose for energy, and the skeletal muscles can also use it for energy. Skeletal muscles also have the capability to store glucose as glycogen, to use for work at a later time. The liver can also absorb glucose from the blood and convert it to glycogen. The glucose not immediately needed or stored by functioning body parts is converted to fat.

A food's glycemic index value indicates how quickly you digest its carbohydrates and how this affects the level of your blood sugar.

Insulin is a pancreatic hormone that regulates blood sugar, and its effects are most beneficial when it does so at a moderate pace. When insulin continuously spikes and dips or is produced in inadequate quantities, health problems arise, including hypoglycemia (low blood sugar), diabetes (high blood sugar), and some health issues related to coronary heart disease. Maintaining blood sugars and insulin response prevents such large peaks and valleys.

The rate at which carbohydrates in a food are digested, and their effect on the rise of blood glucose, are described by the food's glycemic index (GI). Foods that are easily digested and cause a pronounced rise in blood sugar have high GI values. This pronounced rise of blood sugar initiates an insulin surge and stimulates body cells to store glucose as fat.

Foods that are slowly digested have low GI values and do not cause the paired glucose and insulin spikes. The GI values of some common carbohydrates are shown in Table 3.1. Foods containing fats and proteins have lower GI values because fat and protein take more time to digest.

High-GI foods are most valuable during exercise and post-exercise recovery. Otherwise, they should be consumed in moderation or in combination with fat and protein. When high-GI foods are combined with fat and protein, their absorption rate is slowed. As Nutrition Rule No. 5 notes, there are no "bad" foods, but some foods should be consumed with discretion.

TABLE 3.1 GLYCEMIC INDEX FOR COMMON CARBOHYDRATES

HIGH (>80)	MODERATE (50–79)	LOW (30–49)	VERY LOW (<30)
Apricots	Baked beans	Apples	Cherries
Bananas	Beets	Apple juice	Grapefruit
Carrots	Bran cereal	Barley	Peanuts
Corn	Energy bars	Black-eyed peas	Plums
Corn chips	Garbanzo beans	Figs	Soybeans
Corn flake cereal	Navy beans	Grapes	
Crackers	Oatmeal	Lentils	
French bread	Oranges	Lima beans	
Honey	Orange juice	Milk	
Mangos	Pasta	Peaches	
Molasses	Pinto beans	Pears	
Muesli	Potato chips	Rye bread	
Oat bran	Yams	Sweet potatoes	
Pastries		Yogurt	
Potatoes			
Raisins			
Rice			
Rye crisps			
Shredded wheat			
Soda pop			
White bread			
Whole-grain cereal			
Whole-wheat bread			

Fat

Fat is essential for normal body functions. It also makes foods taste good, is enjoyable to eat, and makes us feel satisfied after we've eaten it. Fats are constructed of building blocks called fatty acids. The three major categories of fatty acids are saturated, polyunsaturated, and monounsaturated. The body can use all three kinds; but just as some carbohydrates should be consumed in moderation, so should certain fats.

Some of the fatty acids necessary for good health are called essential fatty acids (EFAs). EFAs contribute to a healthy body by improving hair and skin texture, reducing cholesterol and triglyceride levels, preventing arthritis, and contributing to healthy hormone levels. EFAs are found in large quantities in the brain, where they aid in the transmission of nerve impulses and overall brain function. EFAs are also essential for rebuilding and producing new cells.

The body cannot manufacture EFAs; they must be obtained through diet. Omega-3 and omega-6 fats are the two basic categories of EFAs. Omega-3 fats are found in cold-water fish like salmon, mackerel, menhaden, herring, and sardines. They are also found in canola, flaxseed, and walnut oils. Omega-6 fats are found primarily in raw nuts; seeds;

and grapeseed, sesame, and soybean oils. To supply essential fatty acids, omega-6 fats must be consumed in raw or supplement form or as pure liquid; they can't be subjected to heat in processing or cooking. Wild game, not subjected to chemical-laden, fatten-them-up, feedlot-style diets, is rich in both omega-3 and omega-6 fats.

Essential fatty acids (EFAs) improve hair and skin texture, reduce cholesterol and triglyceride levels, prevent arthritis, and contribute to healthy hormone levels.

Saturated fats should be consumed in moderation. Excess consumption of saturated fats can raise cholesterol levels, particularly LDL (low-density lipoprotein), or "bad" cholesterol. Saturated fats are found in animal products and some tropical oils, like coconut and palm. Also, when some unsaturated oils are partially hydrogenated (a process that turns a liquid fat into a solid one), the new fat is more saturated. Hydrogenated fats contain trans-fatty acids, which are not well digested by the body and are thought to contribute to coronary artery disease. Hydrogenated and partially hydrogenated fats are prevalent in many processed foods like crackers, cookies, and some canned products. Read the labels on your food products and look for uses of the word "hydrogenated."

Polyunsaturated fats are found in corn, safflower, soybean, canola, and sunflower oils. Consumption of the polyunsaturated family may actually lower total cholesterol. However, large amounts of polyunsaturated fats may also lower HDL (high-density lipoprotein), or "good" cholesterol. Some of the polyunsaturated oils do contain EFAs.

Monounsaturated fats are thought to positively influence health. They are found in nuts and some vegetables, and also in the oils of these foods, such as almond, avocado, olive, canola, and walnut oils.

Fat in the diet is essential to optimal health. This is Nutrition Rule No. 6.

Protein

Protein in the diet is absolutely necessary for growth and development of the body. Next to water, protein makes up the greatest portion of body weight. All body cells contain protein. Some protein sources are considered complete proteins because they include all of the amino acids the body cannot manufacture on its own (the "essential" amino acids). Complete-protein foods include meat, milk, eggs, poultry, fish, cheese, yogurt, and soybean products.

Complete proteins include the "essential" amino acids the body cannot manufacture on its own.

Vegetarians need to be well educated on combining foods to achieve complete proteins. Most plant products—with the exception of soybeans—are incomplete proteins, meaning they are missing one or more of the essential amino acids. If a diet consistently omits one or more of the essential amino acids, a deficiency will develop, resulting in illness or injury.

MICRONUTRIENTS

Vitamins and minerals are considered to be "micronutrients" because they are needed in smaller quantities than the macronutrients (water, carbohydrates, fat, and protein). Some vitamins and minerals are coenzymes, enabling the body to produce energy, grow, and heal.

Vitamins regulate metabolism and assist in the biochemical processes that release energy from digested food. Some vitamins are known for their antioxidant, cancer-prevention, and cardiovascular disease–protection properties. Vitamins E and C are two of the vitamins scientists believe we should supplement in our diet, because we probably do not get enough of these vitamins from our food. Some sources of vitamin E are nuts, seeds, whole grains, cold-pressed vegetable oils, and dark green leafy vegetables. Vitamin C is found in green vegetables, citrus fruits, and berries, to name a few sources.

Minerals are necessary for the correct composition of body fluids, the formation of blood and bone, the regulation of muscle tone, and the maintenance of healthy nerve function. Calcium and iron are two of the minerals of most concern. Adequate calcium is necessary to ward off osteoporosis. Calcium can be found in dairy products, tofu, fortified orange juice, soymilk, and canned fish with bones (such as sardines and salmon). Iron is incorporated in hemoglobin and myoglobin and aids in the oxygenation of red blood cells and muscle. It is found in the largest quantities in the blood. Women lose blood and iron each month due to menstruation. Care must be taken to consume adequate iron so as not to become anemic. The best dietary sources of iron are red meat, eggs, and beans.

While eating real food is the best way to consume vitamins and minerals, supplements can also be useful. I'll talk more about supplements later in this chapter.

ANTIOXIDANTS AND PHYTOCHEMICALS

Scientists have recognized for years that diets rich in fruits, vegetables, grains, and legumes appear to reduce the risk of a number of diseases, including cancer, heart disease, diabetes, and high blood pressure. Researchers have found these foods to contain antioxidants, which protect cells against oxidation. Oxidation is damage to cells, similar to rust on metal.

Phytochemicals are another group of health-promoting nutrients thought to prevent a number of diseases and to aid in the repair of cells when disease strikes. Phytochemicals give plants their rich color, flavor, and disease-protection properties. There are literally thousands of phytochemicals—tomatoes alone are thought to contain over ten thousand different varieties.

The relatively recent discovery of phytochemicals illustrates how science continues to discover more about whole foods and their valuable properties. Dietary supplements cannot replace the value of whole foods, because supplements represent only some of our current knowledge—and humankind's quantity of knowledge is still quite small. Therefore, as Nutrition Rule No. 7 states, a healthy diet should contain a wide variety of minimally processed foods.

> Dietary supplements cannot replace the value of whole foods

HOW MUCH OF WHAT

Now things get sticky. We need carbohydrates, fat, and protein to sustain good health, but how much of each? How many calories are enough? How can you lose weight without compromising health? Should you take vitamin and mineral supplements? Long bouts of exercise need calorie supplementation, but how much and from what kind of foods? Long or exhausting exercise requires quick recovery. How is that best accomplished? The answer to all of these questions is "Well, it depends."

If you first establish your dietary and fitness goals, prioritize those goals, and determine how to measure them, then the answers become clearer. Consider the following goals, listed here in order of importance to long-term wellness. Your optimal diet will:

- Build and maintain a healthy body in the short term and minimize the risk of disease in the future
- Allow you to feel good physically and mentally
- Consider your genetic makeup
- Take into account your lifestyle, fitness, and activity level
- Enhance your athletic capabilities

If you eat with the main goal of building a healthy body, chances are good you will live a full and active life.

Before changing your diet, you should assess your nutritional needs and evaluate your current diet. A good place to start is the Health Questionnaire in Appendix A. This questionnaire considers your genetic background, helps you recognize the shortfalls and the successes in your diet, and brings attention to other aspects of your health that might speak to the needs of your body.

If you consult a registered dietician, he or she will ask you to keep a food diary. If you decide to evaluate your diet on your own, you will need to do the same thing. Use a reference book (such as *The NutriBase Nutrition Facts Desk Reference*) to measure the calories and macronutrients in your current diet. Log what foods you eat, how much, and when. Begin with tabulating just calories or log the grams of carbohydrate, fat, and protein as well. Record your information honestly and try not to change your eating behaviors just because you're keeping a food log. It may turn out you have been maintaining a healthy weight while eating 3,000 calories per day, and you have no reason to change anything. Or you may constantly feel weak and tired while eating 3,000 calories per day; in this case, something needs to change. If you are not as healthy as you'd like to be, consider changing your diet or lifestyle or both, in consultation with a registered dietician who specializes in sports nutrition.

BENCHMARK NUTRITION FORMULAS

So far, we have established a set of nutrition rules, prioritized the goals of a healthy diet, determined what you are currently eating, and recorded your current health status on the Health Questionnaire. You know where you are and, in general, where you want to go. Now how do you get there?

If you are satisfied with your current diet, if it meets both your needs and the goals of a healthy diet, celebrate! If you think your diet needs fine-tuning, or if you just want more information about measuring your intake of micro- and macronutrients, read on.

Some people prefer general dietary guidelines, while others want numbers. What follows is a bit of each.

Daily Caloric Intake

One of the common formulas used to determine the daily caloric intake you need to maintain body weight is 30 calories per kilogram of body weight. To find your weight in kilograms, divide your weight in pounds by 2.2. For example, if your weight is 140 pounds, your weight in kilograms is 140 divided by 2.2, or 63.6 (rounded to 64) kilograms. Your daily caloric needs are calculated by multiplying 64 kilograms by 30, to get a total of 1,920 calories.

At 140 pounds, you will need roughly 80 calories per hour (1,920 calories per 24 hours) to fuel your body. Of course, the exact value changes depending on if you are awake and active or sleeping, but 80 calories per hour is a good start.

Modify the formula for daily caloric intake as appropriate:

Add more calories (about 100 to 300) to the daily total if you lead a highly active lifestyle.

The following modifiers are gross values that include resting energy expenditure and exercise expenditure.

Add about 0.15 to 0.17 calorie per minute, per kilogram of body weight, for cycling. (*For example*: 0.17 calorie per minute × 60 minutes × 64 kilograms = 653 calories needed for an hour of fast cycling.)

Add about 0.14 to 0.29 calorie per minute (roughly the range from an 11-minute pace per mile to a 5-minute, 30-second pace per mile), per kilogram of body weight, for running, for the multisport athletes reading this book. (*For example*: 0.2 calorie per minute × 60 minutes × 64 kilograms = 768 calories needed for an hour of fast running.)

Add about 0.1 calorie per minute, per kilogram of body weight, for strength training. (*For example*: 0.1 calorie per minute × 60 minutes × 64 kilograms = 384 calories needed for an hour of strength training.)

Subtract calories (about 100 to 300) from the daily total if your lifestyle or job is sedentary.

So, if you (as our hypothetical 140-pound person) are not doing any exercise but are moderately active, you need to consume 1,920 calories. If your lifestyle is sedentary, you need about 1,620 calories (1,920 − 300). Adding a couple of hours of fast cycling to your moderately active day drives your needs for that day to 3,066 calories (1,920 + [2 × 653] − [2 × 80]) to maintain weight. (Average calories per hour are subtracted because the exercise calories include resting metabolic rate.) On days when your exercise level increases, you need more calories, and on days you aren't exercising, you need to decrease calories accordingly.

> To maintain body weight, your daily caloric intake should be 30 calories per kilogram of body weight.

If you keep track of estimated caloric intake and energy expenditure for a period of time, you will learn what values work for you.

Weight Loss

When I first began my coaching career, I seldom heard men talk about body weight issues. Women were the ones concerned about weight. Times have changed, and now I hear as many men as women talk about maintaining and losing weight.

Before you head into your weight-loss program, understand that severe caloric restrictions can decrease resting metabolic rate by 45 percent. Decreasing your metabolism is the last thing you want to do when you are trying to lose weight. One of the most commonly suggested ways to lose weight is to decrease your daily caloric intake by 200 to 300 calories, without dropping your total caloric intake below 1,500. You can determine how many calories it takes to maintain your current weight from your food log, assuming your weight has been constant. This slow approach to weight loss, through reduced food intake, reduces the risk of compromising health.

The strategy I recommend to athletes is to begin eating now the way you plan to eat at your new weight. This is a long-term strategy for success. Athletes who go on a diet to lose weight and then return to old eating habits will not keep the lower weight for long.

To illustrate how easy it is to eat for your new weight, let's look at an example. If you currently weigh 175 pounds and want to weigh 165 pounds, what is the difference in daily

> To lose weight, decrease your daily caloric intake by 200 to 300 calories, without dropping your total caloric intake below 1,500.

calories you'll need to maintain body weight, without looking at exercise? At 175 pounds (79.5 kilograms) your maintenance level is 2,385 calories per day (79.5 × 30). At your goal weight of 165 pounds (75 kilograms), you'll need 2,250 calories per day (75 × 30). Yes, that's right; it amounts to a difference of only 135 calories per day.

Good Sources for Calories

Current research shows a range for macronutrient consumption that will maintain or improve health and athletic training. See Figure 3.1.

Exactly how much of each macronutrient each person should eat depends on the individual's health risks, dietary goals, and current mode of training. Health and athletic training needs are constantly changing, so diet must also change. Nutrition needs on a heavy training day are not the same as on a day of rest or very little exercise. Consider four suggested diet modifications specific to your training:

1. Carbohydrate consumption should be on the higher end of the range when your training includes fast miles (zones 4 and 5) or long miles (90 minutes or more).
2. Carbohydrate consumption should be in the middle range when you're training in zones 1 to 3.
3. Carbohydrate consumption should be on the lower end of the range when you're trying to lose weight. (Do not try to lose weight and race at the same time. This can result in emotional instability or decreased performance.)
4. Protein consumption should be between 1.5 and 2.0 grams per kilogram of body weight. Use values on the higher end when training hard, trying to build muscle mass, exercising for very long periods (over three hours), or trying to maintain muscle mass while dieting.

Calorie and nutrient needs can be estimated in different ways.

Some sources refer to macronutrient consumption as a percentage of calorie intake, whereas other authorities talk about consuming a certain number of grams of each macronutrient. These measuring systems can seem confusing when they are talked about interchangeably. It helps to know that not all types of food grams have equal energy values:

- 1 gram of carbohydrate contains about 4 calories
- 1 gram of protein contains about 4 calories
- 1 gram of fat contains about 9 calories
- 1 gram of alcohol contains about 7 calories

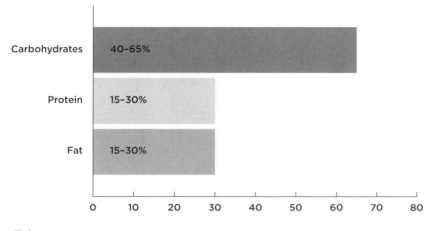

FIGURE 3.1 Macronutrient Consumption

Energy Needs During Exercise

Your fuel can come from either fluid or solid sources or both when you are training and racing. For exercise longer than an hour, consume—at minimum—30 to 60 grams of carbohydrates per hour of intense or long-term exercise. For exercise lasting less than three hours, many athletes find that consuming 150 to 250 carbohydrate calories works just fine. For exercise lasting over three hours, anecdotal evidence says many athletes need a minimum of 300 calories per hour and, on rare occasions, more than 500 calories per hour. Athletes who compete in events that take 6 to 17 hours to complete will tell you that nutrition can significantly influence the outcome of a race. Nutrition, in effect, becomes an event within the event.

Some of these ultra-endurance athletes prefer to include fat and protein in their exercise nutrition. The exact macronutrient proportions necessary for optimum performance varies by individual. How much you need to consume depends on your body size, pace, pre-event muscle glycogen storage, and metabolism.

Hydration needs to be maintained at 4 to 8 ounces every 15 to 20 minutes. Individual sweat rates vary significantly, with some individuals losing more fluid than they can replace or absorb. Fitness, environmental conditions, acclimatization to heat, and genetic differences are some of the factors influencing individual fluid losses. One way to estimate your individual sweat rate is to weigh yourself, in the nude, before and after a one-hour cycling session. Each pound of weight loss is roughly 15 ounces of fluid. Repeat the test for different environmental conditions, such as cool winter training and hot summer training. For each test, note the amount of fluid you lost and your exercise intensity during the session. From these tests, you can estimate your sweat rate and therefore attempt to ingest fluids at a pace equal to your sweat rate to keep your body in balance.

Excessive hydration with water can cause a dangerous condition called hyponatremia, in which the sodium content of the blood is diluted. High levels of hyperhydration and dehydration are both undesirable conditions; your body seeks balance.

During long exercise sessions or due to excessive sweat rates, your body loses electrolytes. Lost electrolytes are a concern because the sodium lost needs to be replaced. Once again, individuals vary in how much sodium they lose and how much needs to be ingested to keep their bodies in balance. For long exercise sessions, a rule of thumb is to include between 250 and 500 milligrams of sodium per hour along with your fluid replacement strategy. Some ultra-endurance athletes may need to supplement sodium at rates higher than 500 milligrams per hour. It is best to begin on the low end of supplementation and make gradual adjustments as needed.

Other electrolytes of note are potassium, magnesium, and calcium. Many energy drinks include a combination of one or more of these electrolytes. You will need to experiment to determine the fluid and electrolyte replacement strategy that works best for you.

Energy Needs During Recovery

To speed recovery after long or exhausting workouts, consume liquid or solid fuel within 20 to 30 minutes after exercise. This fuel should contain 1.5 to 1.6 grams of carbohydrates per kilogram of body weight and 0.4 to 0.5 gram of protein per kilogram of body weight. To further enhance recovery after such workouts, during the 24 hours after exercise consume liquid or solid fuel that contains 6 to 8 grams of carbohydrates per kilogram of body weight.

Recovery foods include milkshakes, chocolate milk, bagels with cottage cheese or lean meat, fruit and protein powder smoothies, yogurt smoothies with fruit, and beef jerky combined with a sports drink. Some studies indicate that regular snacks of approximately 50 grams of carbohydrates, eaten every two hours, may optimize recovery. Of course, an evening meal containing adequate carbohydrates would be necessary to get you through a night's sleep. In other words, do not try to set an alarm to wake up every two hours to eat.

Putting It Together

Let's say you are a 64-kilogram cyclist doing a long ride of three hours. When you calculate the total calories you'll need for a three-hour ride day, remember that the exercise rates include resting energy expenditure.

Using the nutrition formulas discussed earlier, the total calories you'll need today should be about 3,523:

When fueling training sessions lasting 1 to 3 hours, an athlete has the following energy needs.

Energy Source	Hourly Intake
Carbohydrates	30–60 g
Hydrating fluids	12–24 oz.
Sodium	250–500 mg

Note: For some athletes, exercise lasting more than about three hours may require a higher hourly intake of fuel. Anecdotal evidence suggests that a range of 300 to 500 calories per hour may be more appropriate. Practice fueling during long training sessions to find what works best for you.

When fueling for recovery, an athlete has the following energy needs.

Recovery Period	Carbohydrates
20–30 minutes post-workout	1.5–1.6 g/kg body weight
24-hour period post-workout	6–8 g/kg body weight

Note: Some athletes find their recovery improved by including some protein in their post-workout fuel. A ratio range of 4:1 to 7:1 of carbohydrate grams (or calories) to protein grams (or calories) appears to work best. In other words, your recovery fuel should have four to seven times the carbohydrate calories as it has protein calories.

1,920 (calories needed daily)

– 240 (i.e., 3 hours × 80 calories per hour resting rate,
removed because the exercise calories include resting metabolic rate)

+ 1,843 (i.e., 0.16 calorie per minute for the exercise time
× 64 kilograms × 60 minutes per hour × 3 hours)

= 3,523 calories needed for a 3-hour ride day

This moderately tough group ride requires 1,843 calories of total energy, including resting metabolic needs. If today's caloric needs are about 3,523 and you break down the macronutrients by percentages, due to the long ride, you'll place 60 percent of the calories as carbohydrates, or

3,523 × 0.60 = 2,114 carbohydrate calories

At 20 percent of the calories for fat

3,523 × 0.20 = 705 fat calories

At 20 percent of the calories for protein

$$3{,}523 \times 0.20 = 705 \text{ protein calories}$$

On the long ride, you will consume 350 carbohydrate calories per hour (1,050 calories total). Then you will consume a post-ride recovery food containing 1.6 grams of carbohydrate per kilogram of body weight, totaling about 102 grams of carbohydrate (1.6 × 64). Because 1 gram of carbohydrate contains about 4 calories, your post-recovery food will give you 408 more carbohydrate calories (102 × 4). With this nutrition strategy, your total ride calories and post-ride recovery calories consumed will equal 1,458 (1,050 + 408). But this total falls short of meeting your cycling energy requirements of 1,843. If you expect to maintain weight, you'll need to make up the calories in other snacks or meals, which you can do over the next few days.

After this moderately fast group ride, you'll need to consume 6 to 8 grams of carbohydrate per kilogram of body weight over the next 24 hours to restore your glycogen levels. At the 6-gram rate, you would need 384 grams of carbohydrate (including the post-ride recovery drink); at the 8-gram rate, you would need 512 grams of carbohydrate. If you choose the 512 grams, you'll need to consume about 2,048 carbohydrate calories (512 × 4 calories per gram of carbohydrate) over 24 hours to restore glycogen. Some of those calories can be consumed today and the remaining calories tomorrow.

Recall that you were aiming to consume 2,114 carbohydrate calories today, race day. So, subtracting the 1,458 carbohydrate calories associated with riding and post-ride recovery, you need to consume an additional 656 carbohydrate calories today.

You may notice that the two sets of formulas provided for estimating macronutrient needs don't always mesh. If you were to consume 20 percent of the 3,523 calories as protein, those 705 calories (0.20 × 3,523) translate to

$$705 \text{ calories} \times 1 \text{ gram of protein per 4 protein calories}$$
$$\div \ 64\text{-kilogram athlete}$$
$$= 2.75 \text{ grams of protein per kilogram of body weight}$$

The perfect diet and nutrient breakdown depends on many factors. The best place to start is to simply log what you are doing now and review your current health and performance status. If your diet is not meeting your needs, consider a change.

A HEALTHY PERSPECTIVE

Now that you have formulas to estimate caloric needs, macronutrient breakdowns, fuel needs for a long ride, and post-ride fueling strategies, here are some words of caution:

- **The word "estimate" is critical.** Don't worry about exact numbers when consuming calories. Food product labels include margins of error and so should estimates of personal nutrition needs. If you have determined you need 100 grams of carbohydrate and 33 grams of protein for post-ride recovery and a food source has 115 grams of carbohydrates and 25 grams of protein, it will work fine—don't worry.

- **Don't become a food log addict.** Use food logs to establish good eating behaviors or to spot-check your diet strategies. You can drive yourself nuts weighing and counting everything. Let food logs serve their purpose; then let them rest.
- **Just because you exercise doesn't mean you can eat unlimited quantities of food.** Every body has an energy balance system. You need to learn to manage your own body and its special needs.
- **Body weight is just a number.** Don't weigh yourself every day and look for changes. In fact, if you lose several pounds from one day to the next, it is probably due to dehydration. Remedy that situation by drinking additional fluids. At most, weigh yourself weekly. Your overall health is a better measure of nutritional success than numbers on a scale.

SUPPLEMENTS

The *American Heritage Dictionary* defines a supplement as "something added to complete a thing or to make up for a deficiency." Note that it does not say "a substitute for . . ." No amount of vitamin and mineral supplementation will make up for an inbalanced diet—something people often do not seem to understand. As a case in point, once when I was talking with a young person sacking my groceries, the young man inquired about the volume and variety of vegetables I was purchasing. "Are you a vegetarian or something?" he asked.

"No, at our house we eat lots of different vegetables because they taste good and their vibrant colors make an exciting plate," I replied.

"Oh, I don't like vegetables, so I just eat meat and potatoes and take vitamins. Anyway, one vitamin pill has all the stuff I really need, so I don't have to worry about it. I'm training to be a boxer, so I need all the vitamins."

His thought process is all too common. While he continued sacking the groceries, I explained about fiber, phytochemicals, and the unknown, healthy substances that are also likely contained in real food. I explained how recent the discovery of phytochemicals was and that although we humans are pretty smart, we are a long way from knowing everything; the study of nutrition is still a young science. I further explained that supplements are meant to complement a diet high in whole foods but that no supplementation plan will make up for a diet high in processed foods, saturated fat, sugar, and salt and low in fiber and variety. The young man carried my groceries to the car just so he could ask more questions, which I was glad to answer. I don't know if he went on to change his habits, but at least he was thinking about it.

Researchers are continually finding out more information about vitamin and mineral supplementation. A survey asked top researchers what they took for vitamin and mineral supplementation, and the answers were not uniform. Some of the supplements that continue to receive attention among scientists are multivitamin-plus-mineral supplements, vitamin C, vitamin E, calcium, and iron.

Multivitamins with Minerals

Most experts recommend a multivitamin-plus-mineral supplement. Some experts still hold a strong belief we should be able to meet all of our vitamin and mineral needs from food, but more research is telling us it does not happen for most folks. U.S. Department of Agriculture data indicate that at least 40 percent of people in the United States routinely consume a diet containing only 60 percent of the recommended daily allowances (RDAs) of 10 selected nutrients. We would likely fare worse if more nutrients were evaluated.

> Controversy continues over whether or not athletes need more vitamins and minerals than the average population.

Controversy continues over whether or not athletes' requirements for vitamins and minerals exceed those of the average population. If athletes are consuming a balanced and varied diet and taking some supplements, perhaps that is enough.

Vitamins C and E

The current recommendation is to supplement a multivitamin with 500 to 1,000 milligrams of vitamin C and 400 IU of vitamin E. Both of these are antioxidants, substances that block oxidative damage to the cells of the body. To maintain constant concentrations of vitamin C in the blood, it is best to take two doses, 8 to 12 hours apart.

Calcium

The current recommendation is to consume between 1,000 and 1,500 milligrams of calcium daily. In order for calcium to be absorbed well, protein and vitamins C, D, E, and K all play key roles. Several minerals also play important roles in calcium absorption. For example, too much magnesium, sodium, and/or phosphorus (found in many soft drinks and processed foods) can inhibit the absorption of calcium.

Just supplementing the diet with calcium is not the cure-all. Weight-bearing exercise is also important. More is not necessarily better, however. Even men, who seem less prone to bone loss, can suffer when exercise levels are excessive. One study of University of Memphis male basketball players found they were losing about 3.8 percent of their bone mass from pre-season to mid-season of a single year. Bob Klesges, the head scientist, determined the ballplayers were losing substantial amounts of calcium in their sweat. He concluded this by collecting the sweaty T-shirts of the players and carefully wringing out their contents to be analyzed. (Yuck!)

He found the players gained back 1.1 percent of their bone mass during summer, but they lost an additional 3.3 percent when practices resumed, making their total losses now about 5.8 percent. With supplemental calcium, they were able to regain the lost amounts.

You should try to get 1,000 to 1,500 milligrams of calcium *from your diet* (an 8-ounce glass of milk contains 290 milligrams of calcium). If you are not getting enough through your diet, consider a supplement on days your food consumption does not give you the recommended requirements. A superior supplement is calcium citrate malate, found in many calcium-enriched juices. On average, people absorb 35 percent of the calcium in calcium citrate malate, compared to 30 percent of the calcium in other supplements.

> For athletes serious about wellness and competition, an annual blood test is an excellent source of information.

Iron

As noted earlier in this chapter, iron is an essential component of hemoglobin and myoglobin and functions in the oxygenation of red blood cells and muscle. Women especially can have problems with low levels of iron, developing anemia. One of the common causes of anemia is excessive menstrual flow. Aggravating this deficiency due to blood loss, some women consume inadequate dietary iron. Good food sources of iron are fish, meat, beans, whole grains, enriched breads, and enriched cereals. Iron supplements should not be self-prescribed but taken only on the advice of a physician.

Constant fatigue is a common symptom of anemia, which can be diagnosed through a simple blood test. In fact, blood tests can detect many problems associated with diet, health, and wellness. For athletes serious about wellness and competition, an annual blood test—during recovery or in the off-season—is an excellent source of information. This baseline test can then be used to diagnose changes to blood chemistry when a competitive season seems to have gone awry.

ERGOGENIC AIDS

The items I receive the most questions about are ergogenic aids—things that can increase muscular work capacity—such as sport drinks, energy bars, and caffeine.

Sport Drinks

The simple rule of thumb for sport drinks is to use the one that tastes best to you and does not cause extra potty stops or stomach-content reversal. If you select a drink that tastes good and you use it for any workout over an hour long, it will generally be beneficial. Be aware that some athletes have gastrointestinal problems with fructose-based sport drinks. If you are having difficulties caused by a specific sport drink, check to see if fructose is one of the main ingredients.

Some sport drinks include protein. Common carbohydrate-to-protein ratios range from 4:1 to 7:1. In general, for short, fast events, I recommend sticking to a product that contains only carbohydrates. For events longer than about three hours, many athletes find that some protein seems to help. The amount of protein athletes can tolerate varies by individual. Some do fine with a 4:1 mix, while others experience gastrointestinal distress at this level. Test your sport drinks during training events.

Energy Bars

Energy bars are useful for long rides, as pre- and post-workout snacks, and as pre-race snacks. They are not, however, one of the major food groups. Some athletes use them as a major source of calories, choosing them over fruits and vegetables because they are easy to acquire and eat. But you should use them only as supplements for sporting activities; they are not appropriate as meals. Eat minimally processed foods and, whenever possible, choose whole foods over highly refined foods—including energy bars.

Caffeine

Caffeine may be the most widely used drug in the world. It stimulates the central nervous system, the adrenal system, the metabolic system, and the muscular system. Although some studies have shown that caffeine influences the metabolic system by stimulating fat metabolism and sparing glycogen during aerobic exercise, the research on this theory is not conclusive. For example, some studies show that glycogen sparing is limited to the first 15 to 20 minutes of exercise. Additional studies, focusing on the measurement of free fatty-acid metabolism (which spares glycogen), show the response to fat-burning may not be optimal until three to four hours after ingestion.

Another theory is that caffeine lowers the level of perceived pain at a given pace, so athletes have the ability to produce more work or work for longer periods of time with the use of caffeine. When caffeine is used in conjunction with exercise, several studies support the notion that it appears not to have the diuretic effect that it has when consumed in a non-exercise situation.

Whether or not regular caffeine users need to abstain from caffeine use for some period of time prior to an important event in order to optimize the effects of caffeine is, again, uncertain. At least one study suggests that people who don't use caffeine and people who are regular users respond similarly to caffeine when it is taken before exercise, so it may not be necessary for regular users to abstain from caffeine before important events. A second study

TABLE 3.2 COMMON SOURCES OF CAFFEINE

PRODUCT	SERVING SIZE	CAFFEINE CONTENT (mg)
Excedrin	2 tablets	130
Coffee	8 oz.	100–250
No-Doz, regular	1 tablet	100
Mountain Dew	12 oz.	55
Pocket Rocket, chocolate	1 packet	50
Cola	8 oz.	38–46
Espresso	1 oz.	35–60
Cappuccino	8 oz.	35–60
Caffe latte	8 oz.	35–60
Mountain Dew	12 oz.	55

gave doses of 5 milligrams of caffeine per kilogram of body weight to regular caffeine users and non-users, and results showed that the ergogenic effect was greater in non-users who exercised one and three hours after ingestion than in users who did the same.

Some studies show that ingesting caffeine in the form of coffee is ineffective compared with ingesting pure caffeine. The reason for this is not clear. Major sources of caffeine are listed in Table 3.2.

A dose of 5 to 7 milligrams of caffeine per kilogram of body weight, taken one hour prior to exercise, has been the typical protocol for most studies; however, doses as low as 3.3 to 4.4 milligrams of caffeine per kilogram of body weight have been shown to be effective.

Caffeine consumption can produce negative side effects for some individuals. Some people do not tolerate it well and become shaky, jittery, and unable to focus. Caffeine also bothers some people's gastrointestinal systems, resulting in stomach pain, abdominal cramps, and diarrhea. The U.S. Olympic Committee once banned caffeine at levels measuring 12 micrograms per milliliter of urine, but this restriction was removed in January 2004. To reach this level would require ingesting nearly 1,200 milligrams of pure caffeine.

Although the exact mechanisms that cause caffeine to be an ergogenic aid are unclear, I did not find a single study that concluded that caffeine is ineffective.

If you decide to use caffeine, experiment with it during training sessions. It is best not to wait until a race or big event to test your tolerance and advantage levels. For racing, consume the caffeine approximately 30 minutes to one hour before the race start.

A faulty nutrition plan can derail even the best athlete. Good athletes—including good cyclists—need to be as serious about fueling and hydration as they are about training. Use the information in this chapter to help you establish an effective and healthy nutrition plan.

Equipment

Equipment has a significant impact—whether positive or negative—on your cycling experience. While the best equipment cannot make up for poor conditioning, poor equipment choices can cause short-term and chronic pain.

For a cyclist, the most important piece of equipment is, of course, the bike. Ten years ago, most bicycles were manufactured to meet the needs of the average rider, and that rider was assumed to be an average-sized male. Since that time, some fantastic changes have taken place. The cycling population has grown dramatically, creating a greater demand for recreational and high-performance bicycles for people of all sizes. Because a wider variety of bikes and other equipment to make cycling more comfortable are available, more people are attracted to cycling—an excellent synergistic relationship.

This chapter covers some of the most common bike designs and proper bike fit, as well as clothing, gear, and equipment you can use to measure performance. The tips and information here can help you choose the most effective equipment and setup for you.

FRAME GEOMETRY AND BIKE DESIGN

Different types of bicycles accommodate different purposes. A bicycle designed for the road, often called a road bike, has skinny tires and frame geometry intended for road riding (Figure 4.1). The frame geometry measurement that separates different types of bicycles—and the one people talk about most often—is the seat-tube angle (see dimension E in Figure 4.2). This

FIGURE 4.1 Road Bike
A road bike has skinny tires, handlebars with drops, and fingertip shifters. It may or may not have aerodynamic wheels.

angle affects both the handling of the bike and the position of the body on the bike, ranging from 73 to 75 degrees.

Hybrid and mountain bikes usually have tires wider than those on a road bike and seat-tube angles that range from just over 71 to as steep as 75 degrees. The lower seat-tube angles found on these bikes are considered a more relaxed frame geometry. Hybrid bikes are designed for road and light off-road riding, such as on dirt roads with few technical obstacles (see Figure 4.3). This type of bike is also a good option for commuting and for riding on city bike trails. Some riders will use it for longer bike rides and tours, but most long-distance cyclists prefer road bikes.

Mountain bikes are designed for heavy off-road riding and single-track trails, for going over rocks and other trail obstacles (see Figure 4.4). Even within the mountain bike category, you will find several different designs for different purposes. Hardtail mountain bikes (mountain bikes without a rear shock) are designed for trails with minimal technical obstacles. These bikes tend to be lighter than cross-country mountain bikes. A cross-country mountain bike is designed for a mix of mountain terrain and with racing in mind. A downhill mountain bike is designed for bombing downhill at high speeds and dropping off of high obstacles. Because these bikes are built for rough riding, they are heavier than the other mountain bike styles.

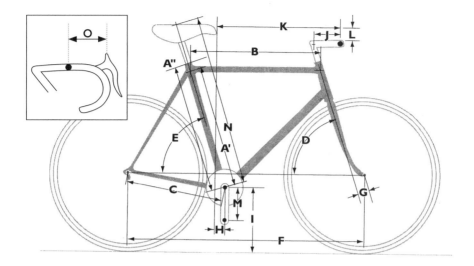

FIGURE 4.2 Road Bike Anatomy

A' Seat-tube length, measured center to center
A" Seat-tube length, measured center to top
B Top-tube length
C Chainstay length
D Head-tube angle
E Seat-tube angle
F Wheelbase

G Fork offset
H Seat setback
I Bottom bracket height
J Stem length
K Saddle to transverse centerline of handlebar
L Seat to handlebar drop
M Crank

N Seat height, measured from bottom bracket centerline (also shown in Figure 4.7)*
O Transverse centerline of handlebar to brake hood

Note: This illustration displays common terms used to describe the anatomy of a road bike. These terms are also used to describe measurements on other types of bicycles, but bike types differ in ways both subtle and marked. All of the anatomical dimensions described here also vary from bike to bike.
* Seat height can also be measured from pedal spindle as shown in Figure 4.8.

Cyclocross bikes usually have lightweight frames so that they are easy to carry over obstacles. These frames have wider stays—the parts of the frame that surround the tires—to allow clearance for the wide, knobby tires and the mud that the tires pick up from the course (see Figure 4.5). Traditional road brakes are replaced by cantilever brakes for better stopping power. The frame's bottom bracket is higher for additional clearance over obstacles and for pedaling around corners.

FIGURE 4.3 Hybrid Bike
Hybrid bikes have wider tires and steeper seat-tube angles than road bikes, and they are designed for road and light off-road riding.

FIGURE 4.4 Mountain Bike
Mountain bikes have tires that are wider than those on a road bike and designed for heavy off-road use, handlebars that are straight across (no drops), shocks on the front wheel, and sometimes rear shocks as well.

FIGURE 4.5 Cyclocross Bike

Cyclocross bikes are designed for lighter off-road use. Compared with road bikes, cyclocross bikes usually have wider tires and more frame clearance for mud and obstacles. The components are also usually lighter than on mountain bikes and do not have shocks or disc brakes.

FIGURE 4.6 Time Trial Bike

Time trial bikes often have frames and wheels that are aerodynamic. The handlebars are extended and have elbow pads so the rider can rest in an aerodynamic (aero) position. When riding in an aero position, shift levers are at the rider's fingertips. The brake levers are located about halfway between the elbow pads and the bar-end shifters.

Cyclocross racing is growing in popularity. The races are typically 30 to 60 minutes in length. Their multiple-lap courses usually include a mix of terrain, often both on- and off-road areas. Many races feature some mud on the course, and all include obstacles that force riders to dismount and run while carrying the bike. Riders can use modified road or mountain bikes, but cyclocross-specific bikes are the norm for intermediate and hard-core racers.

Time trial–specific or triathlon frames have skinny tires like road bikes and are intended for road use. One of the most noticeable differences between a time trial or triathlon bike and a road bike is the use of aerobars instead of regular handlebars. Aerobars are extended handlebars with elbow pads that allow the rider to rest in an aerodynamic (aero) position. Also, many time trial or triathlon bike models include specially shaped frame tubing and special wheels (see Figure 4.6), and the bikes have steep seat-tube angles that range from about 75 to 80 degrees. These design features are intended to minimize drag and increase speed (more on this later).

So as you might expect, geometry and design affect the handling and comfort of a bike. A bicycle created for time trial purposes handles differently from a bike designed for off-road use. A bike designed to tour across the country, carrying panniers, or packs, on both sides of the back wheel, needs different features from a bike designed for racing criteriums. (Criteriums are short-course road races with multiple corners to be taken at high speeds in a group or pack-riding situation.) Understanding these differences can help you choose the best type of bike for your cycling needs.

CHOOSING A BIKE

Here are some questions you should answer before purchasing your next bike:
- Where will I do most of my riding? (Road, bike path, trails, single track.)
- Which bike best suits my cycling goals? (Pleasure rides; bike tours; organized century rides; gentle off-road rides on dirt roads; off-road, single-track rides; aggressive off-road ride with difficult obstacles; triathlons; cyclocross or other races; and so on.)
- How many hours per week or per year do I plan to ride?
- Am I concerned about performance? (Riding fast, either for racing or recreational purposes; having equipment that is built to endure heavy use; or a combination of both.)

If you are just taking up cycling and you want your bike to serve multiple purposes, I recommend a road bike. The geometry of a road bike is much better suited for multipurpose riding, including bike tours, hilly courses, and maybe even an occasional triathlon. A road bike will maximize comfort and performance. Plus the geometry of the frame is better suited for cycling in a group and climbing hills, and the drop bars offer more hand positions to make riding comfortable.

If you live in an area with limited roads for riding but plenty of dirt roads and trails, you may be better off with a mountain bike. Mountain bike design falls into two general categories: hardtail and full suspension. A hardtail design is usually lighter and is less forgiving on technical trails. Full-suspension bikes have front and rear shocks. The amount of shock travel, or the distance the shocks can compress, varies by bike design. Generally, more shock travel is intended for aggressive riding, such as chucking yourself off major drops or into the air off big jumps.

> The geometry of a road bike is much better suited for multipurpose riding.

Depending on your riding goals, a specialty bike might be just what you need. If you plan to own only one bicycle and your passion is mountain bike riding, cyclocross racing, or triathlon, purchase the bike to fit your passion. You can change the tires on these bikes and use them on the road as well; just be aware that your ride quality will be compromised by the less-than-ideal body position.

If you have the luxury of owning more than one bicycle, first get a road bike and then a goal-specific bike. The road bike can be used for some training and group-riding situations. The other specialty bikes can be used to develop skills and fitness in mountain biking, cyclocross, or time trial skills.

In all bicycle categories, you can encounter a wide range of prices for a new ride. Price increases come from one or more of the following customizations: lightweight frame material, special aerodynamic frame design, aerodynamic wheels, lightweight components, high-quality components that resist wear with higher volumes of training, or new technical advances in design. Keep in mind that the most expensive bike in the world is useless if it does not fit.

AERODYNAMICS

Making yourself more aerodynamic means taking measures that allow you to slip easily through the air while cycling. You want to reduce drag, or the resistance to forward progress. The bike's design and components and your position—especially your hand positions, which directly affect your body position—have the greatest effects on drag.

The two most common hand positions for road riding are on the brake hoods and on the top of the handlebars. These positions, though not aerodynamic, put the rider upright and are comfortable for many people. Many cyclists prefer riding with their hands on the brake hoods because this position also gives them easy access to the brakes.

Changing your hand positions from on top of the brake hoods to on aerobars makes you more aerodynamic. Riding in an aerodynamic position while on a flat or rolling course considerably reduces your required power output. For an elite cyclist pedaling at

25 mph, moving to the aerobars will reduce the power required to maintain the same speed by 20 percent—a significant difference. The cyclist can either conserve energy, riding the same speed at a lower power output, or maintain the same power output and ride faster. This is why time trial bikes are superior for speed events.

Full aerobars, complete with elbow pads and fingertip shifters, are the best aerodynamic option for speed events such as road-racing time trials and triathlons. Elbow pads provide comfort, and with the shifters at your fingertips, you can minimize the number of times you sit up and create a "sail" with your chest, which catches the wind.

> The right bike means comfort, reduced likelihood of injury, and more power—which translates to more speed.

If aerobars make such a big difference, why not just add them to a road bike? Indeed, putting short, clip-on aerobars on a road bike offers an aerodynamic advantage for long, solo pulls. But some of the short aerobars do not have elbow pads, and they are not the most comfortable option for long-distance racing.

Also, while full aerobars can be successfully added to a road bike, this option doesn't work for most cyclists. One problem is that this configuration compromises your comfort, handling, and performance as a result of your entire body moving forward on the bike to rest on the elbow pads. Even moving your seat all the way forward and installing the shortest stem to hold the aerobars (see "The Elements of Bike Fit" for information on adjusting bike components) is sometimes not enough to prevent you from stretching out too much on the bike. The elbow pads often end up at the centers of your forearms, which is definitely uncomfortable. When you are stretched out like this and the support point is under the midsections of your forearms, you may experience arm, neck, and shoulder pain. In short, this compromised position reduces your power output, makes your bike handling dangerous, and can result in injury.

THE ELEMENTS OF BIKE FIT

Finding a bike that fits is critical to optimum performance, handling, and comfort. The only type of discomfort you should ever feel while riding your bicycle is the self-induced muscular discomfort that comes from riding fast or the overall muscular fatigue that comes from riding long distances. Cycling should not cause you pain in the neck, shoulders, hands, crotch, back, hips, knees, or feet. You may feel some short-term discomfort in these areas when you are building endurance for your long rides, but that discomfort should disappear quickly as your fitness level increases. The right bike means comfort, reduced likelihood of injury, and more power—which translates to more speed.

A rule of thumb for selecting a road bike frame is to stand over the bicycle in stocking feet and lift the bicycle until the top tube is snug in your crotch; the clearance between the tires and the floor should be one to two inches. However, creating the perfect fit requires attention to many more details. Let's look at the important considerations for determining whether a bike fits you.

Frame Size

Road Bike, Regular Geometry

Figure 4.2, found earlier in this chapter, shows some of the anatomy and geometry of a standard bicycle. Bicycle size is typically given in centimeters and refers to the length of the seat tube. A 54-centimeter (cm) bike has a 54 cm seat tube. Frames are measured in two ways: center-to-top and center-to-center. Center-to-top measures the distance from the center of the bottom bracket to the top of the top tube or seat lug. Center-to-center measures from the center of the bottom bracket to the center of the top tube at the seat lug. The center-to-center measurement is often 1.0 to 1.5 cm smaller than the center-to-top measure. (Remember this distinction when you are comparing frames.)

Frame sizes in the 50 to 60 cm range are easy to find. Several manufacturers make 49 cm, 48 cm, and down to 43 cm. Small frames often have 650 cm wheels. These smaller wheels keep your foot and the front tire from interfering with each other on tight turns.

As noted previously, different bike styles may have different seat-tube angles. On a road bike, the most common range of 73 to 75 degrees allows the average-sized cyclist to position his or her knee over the pedal axle with minor adjustments in the fore and aft position of the saddle.

The next consideration when selecting a frame size is the length of the top tube. Top tubes typically measure within 2 cm of the seat-tube length. If you are an average-sized rider, one guideline to follow is to divide your height by your inseam length, measured as shown in Figure 4.7. If that value is 2.0 to 2.2, you are considered average, and a bike frame with a top-tube length equal to its seat-tube length will fit you. If the value is greater than 2.2, you have a long torso and may need a longer top tube. A value of less than 2.0 indicates your torso is short in comparison to your legs, and you are better off with a top tube that is shorter than the seat tube.

For example, if your inseam is 32.5 inches and your height is 64.5 inches, your ratio is 1.98 (64.5 ÷ 32.5). You are just under the 2.0 guideline and may be able to ride an average

Custom Frames

There is no easy way to determine whether you need a custom frame or not. That formula, yet undeveloped, is a function of your overall height in addition to the ratio of your leg length, torso length, and arm length to height. Custom frame maker Lennard Zinn suggests that cyclists on the low and high ends of the height spectrum might consider custom frames. Generally speaking, cyclists under 5'3" or over 6'4" with an inseam longer than 36" are good candidates. Also, riders who have torsos that are much shorter or longer than average may want to consider going custom.

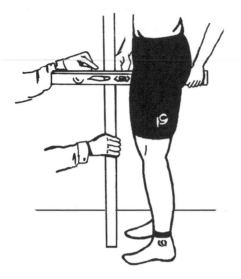

FIGURE **4.7** Inseam Measurement with a Level

Using a carpenter's level that is 2 to 3 feet long, stand without shoes on a flat, hard surface and snug the level into your crotch. The pressure between the level and your crotch (how much force you apply upward) should be similar to the pressure between a bicycle seat and your crotch. Have an assistant tell you when the level is parallel to the floor and have him or her measure the distance from the floor to the top of the level. This value is inseam length.

frame, depending on the length of your arms. If your arms are not longer than average, you may be more comfortable on a frame with a top tube that is shorter than its seat tube.

Custom frame builder Lennard Zinn finds that "smaller riders always need top tubes longer than the seat tube, and vice versa for very tall riders. This is because the top-tube length is a proportional measurement, whereas the seat-tube length is produced by subtraction and is dependent on crank length, seat-post extension, and saddle dimensions, which are similar regardless of the rider."

Top-tube and seat-tube lengths vary among manufacturers and within the product line of a single manufacturer. Additionally, the ratios for regular-geometry bicycles—on which the top tube is parallel to the ground—do not apply to compact-geometry bicycles.

Road Bike, Compact Geometry

Compact-geometry bicycles have top tubes that angle toward the ground. Some manufactures make compact bikes in small, medium, and large sizes. Other manufacturers size according to seat-tube, center-to-top measurement. You may have more stand-over clearance between your crotch and the top tube on these bikes. Check manufacturer catalogs for seat-tube, top-tube, and effective-top-tube measurement differences. Effective-top-tube measurement refers to the length of an imaginary parallel-to-the-ground top tube.

Hybrid Bike, Mountain Bike, and Cyclocross Frames

Selecting a hybrid or mountain bike frame size is similar to selecting the frame size of a road bike. From there, how you set up your hybrid or mountain bike depends on the terrain you plan to ride, your riding experience, and your riding style. Most hybrid riders will have seat-height setups similar to those for road frames, but the handlebars will be set higher than for traditional road setups. For a mountain bike, if your off-road terrain contains a minimal number of obstacles and your riding style is similar to road riding, your setup will also be very close to that of your road bike. For cyclocross riding, your bike frame size should be the same as for your road setup.

Seat Height

Estimating Seat Height

You can estimate the correct height for your seat (also called a saddle) in several different ways. If you currently have a bike and you know the seat height is correct, take that measurement with you to the bike shop. If you aren't sure what the correct seat height is, you can estimate it by taking your inseam measurement (as shown in Figure 4.7) and multiplying it by 0.883. The product of those two numbers is the distance from the center of the bottom bracket to the top of the saddle, which can also be measured as shown in Figure 4.8. Yet another type of seat-height measurement, this time from the top of the pedal spindle to the top of the saddle, is shown in Figure 4.9.

Your crank length, pedal, and shoe combination influences seat height. If you use toe clips, the methods of estimating seat height noted in the previous paragraph are close to what you need. If you use clipless pedals, you may have to adjust the seat-height measurement around 3 millimeters. How much you adjust the value depends on your shoe, cleat, and pedal combination and how far that combination stacks your foot above the pedal axle.

FIGURE 4.8 Seat Height Measured from the Center of the Bottom Bracket
The distance from the center of the bottom bracket to the top of the saddle is measured along a line that would connect the bottom bracket to the point where the rider's crotch would rest on the saddle.

FIGURE 4.9 Seat Height Measured from the Top of the Pedal Spindle
The distance from the top of the pedal spindle to the top of the saddle is measured along a line that would connect the spindle to the point where the rider's crotch would rest on the saddle. This particular method is helpful when changing crank lengths or saddles. The distance from the saddle rails to the top of the saddle varies from saddle to saddle. When changing saddles or cranks, be certain the saddle height remains the same; otherwise discomfort or injury may result.

Seat height is also affected by muscle flexibility. If you're not very flexible, you may require a lower seat. If you decide to change your current seat height, make changes slowly—only about an eighth- to quarter-inch adjustment per week.

Another easy way to estimate seat height is to sit on the bike while it is mounted in a stationary trainer. A quality bicycle shop will help you do this. With your bike on the trainer, pedal while sitting at a seat height that seems comfortable. Unclip your cleats from the pedal system, put your heels on the top of the pedals, and pedal backward. The seat height should allow you to keep your heels on the pedals while pedaling backward, and it should not allow your hips to rock from side to side.

> Your crank length, pedal, and shoe combination influences seat height.

When you are clipped into the pedals and pedal forward again, you should have a slight bend in your knee, about 25 to 30 degrees, when your foot is at the bottom of the pedal stroke. Pedal for a few moments until you are settled and comfortable with your position. Then, continue to pedal and have someone look at your hips from the rear. Your hips should have a slight, but not excessive, rocking motion. Excessive rocking, as if you are straining to reach the bottom of every pedal stroke, indicates your seat is too high.

While you are pedaling, a view of you from the front should reveal your knees tracking in a straight line from your hips to the pedals. Minimal side-to-side motion of your knees is normal. If your knees travel far outside a straight line from the hip to the pedal, the seat may be too low. If the seat height is correct, excessive side-to-side movement of the knees may indicate a need for orthotics. Also, if you are bowlegged, take this condition into consideration when assessing your knee tracking.

Adjusting for Anatomy

Some athletes have anatomical features that may need special adjustments. People with very wide hips may need spacers added to their pedal spindles to move their feet more in line with their hips. Others may have a pedaling motion that when viewed from the rear seems uneven, or as though they are "limping" on the bike, which may indicate a difference in leg length. Bike modifications can be made to accommodate leg-length differences, including adding spacers in shoes or on the cleats and adjusting fore-aft positioning of the cleats on the pedals.

If you suspect you have some anatomical issues that are causing you problems on the bike, your best bet is to seek the help of a qualified professional, such as a sports medicine physician who can take X rays and physical measurements and give you a physical examination to determine if you have anatomical abnormalities.

> Many mountain bike and cylocross riders prefer a seat height that is slightly lower (by 1 to 2 cm) than on a road setup.

Adjusting for Mountain Biking or Cyclocross

If you ride mountain bike courses that are very technical or you ride cyclocross, you may spend a fair amount of time out of the saddle, mounting and dismounting your bike. To make such movements easier, many mountain bikers and cyclocross riders prefer a seat height that is slightly lower—by 1 to 2 cm (0.4 to 0.8 inch)—than on a road setup.

Pedals

Clipless pedals are the pedals of choice for competitive cyclists. Pedals that allow some rotation may prevent or minimize your risk of injury by allowing your foot to "float" instead of being "fixed."

No matter which type of pedal you use, a general guideline for alignment is to position the ball of your foot over the pedal axle. If you have problems with tightness in your Achilles tendons or calf muscles, you can consider moving the ball of your foot ahead of the axle. In this position, the lever arm from your ankle to the pedal axle is shortened, which puts less stress on your Achilles and calf muscles. This position also requires less force to stabilize your feet. Time trial specialists use this position because it allows the production of more force while using larger gears.

If the ball of your foot is behind the pedal axle, it lengthens the ankle-to-pedal-axle lever arm. Some track cyclists prefer this position because it allows a higher cadence during fixed-gear events.

Saddles

Saddle Position

To estimate your optimum saddle position, start by pedaling the bicycle on a stationary trainer until you feel settled. Then stop pedaling and put the crank arms horizontal to the ground, in the three and nine o'clock positions, as shown in Figures 4.10 and 4.11. Your feet should be horizontal, or as close to horizontal as your flexibility allows. A neutral foot position lines up the front of your knee with the front of the crank arm. The position can be measured with a common yardstick, a wooden dowel, a sturdy piece of one-by-one-inch lumber, or a carpenter's level. Whatever you use, be certain the measuring tool remains perpendicular to the ground and does not bend beneath the measuring pressure.

Some time trial specialists prefer to have the knee slightly forward of the neutral position. Remember that if you slide the seat forward on the rails, you are, in effect, lowering seat height. If you adjust the saddle forward, fine-tune the seat height up or increase the measurement taken (as shown in Figures 4.8 and 4.9). A rule of thumb: For every centimeter forward you move the seat, raise the seat post half a centimeter.

The saddle should be level, or parallel to the ground, for general riding purposes. You can use a carpenter's level to help you position the saddle correctly. Check seat tilt while your bike is held in the riding position by an assistant or on a stationary trainer. If you use a trainer, make sure it is level and both bike tires are raised equally above the ground.

Riding with your saddle nose pointed downward may cause you to put more pressure on your upper body to keep from sliding forward. If you find that you need to point the nose of your saddle downward, your seat may be too high or your handlebars too low. If you intentionally decide to tilt the nose of your saddle downward a degree or two, be sure you are not constantly pushing yourself back onto the saddle. This constant body adjustment is a recipe for loss of power and speed—in addition to sore and bruised body parts.

A very few cyclists prefer to tilt the nose of the saddle up. If you do this, be certain the saddle doesn't put pressure on your genital area, which can cause pain, saddle sores, or numbness.

Saddle Style

Saddle style is probably the most intimate and frustrating part of bike fit. No saddle is going to make up for an ill-fitting bicycle. Also, an ill-fitting bicycle seat can make you feel miserable on an otherwise well-fitting bicycle.

Saddles come in various styles, lengths, and widths to accommodate individual anatomies. Whether your anatomy finds more comfort with a wide or narrow seat, minimal padding or a gel insert, or a solid seat or seat with a cutout will depend on your riding style, the

FIGURE 4.10 Knee in Relation to the Crank Arm
The yardstick should touch the knee and align with the end of the crank arm. The assistant can make certain the yardstick is perpendicular to the ground.

FIGURE 4.11 Knee in Relation to the Crank Arm
When a plumb line is looped around the leg and dropped from the front of the knee, the line should touch the end of the crank arm. A plumb line can be constructed with lightweight nylon string and a nut, available at hardware stores.

length of time you spend in the saddle, and your personal preferences. The saddles touted as "women's models" tend to be wider and shorter than standard saddles. In recent years, due to publicity about some research linking bike seats and male impotence, many men have begun investigating different saddles. Some men have found that the wider saddles suit their anatomy just fine and eliminate genital numbness. (This numbness is the first indication of undue pressure that, if left unchecked, can lead to more problems.) Be aware that some women's saddles are limited in their range of fore-aft adjustment.

A number of saddle discomfort issues are due to fitness and riding style. Novice cyclists do not have the strong leg and gluteus muscles that prevent experienced cyclists from using the saddle as a chair. That is, novice cyclists who have not yet developed strong leg muscles tend to sit on the saddle and move their legs, while experienced cyclists are somewhat suspended by their legs. As you build cycling miles, which you should do gradually, you will build leg strength and saddle time. Even experienced cyclists need to rebuild saddle time after being off the bike for a while.

Saddle padding is important for comfort. However, too much padding or padding that is very pliable can still cause numbness. Over the course of a ride, the padding can get reshaped and move into the perineum, which is the area between your "sit bones." This area contains arteries and nerves that, when compressed, can cause pain.

> An ill-fitting saddle can make you feel miserable on an otherwise well-fitting bike.

Unfortunately, saddles have no easy, fool-proof sizing system. One manufacturer has designed a device that allows you to sit down and indent a gel pad with your sit bones, which can help with the sizing process. Good bicycle shops will mount your bike on a stationary trainer and let you try a few saddles before you buy one. Even after you've carefully selected a saddle, you may find it feels different on the road. Some trial and error is usually in order for new cyclists.

If you ask around, you're likely to find saddle styles are a bit like ice cream flavors: Everyone has a different favorite for a different reason.

Stem

The position of your knee over the pedal is important. Do not compromise this position in an attempt to compensate for components that aren't set up correctly. A common mistake is to move the seat forward to accommodate a short arm reach or the addition of aerobars to an otherwise well-fitting road bike. If your reach is short, in most cases the stem on the bicycle can easily be changed.

Along the same lines, do not use a longer stem to compensate for a frame size that is too small. If you need a stem length longer than about 140 millimeters (mm) or shorter than 60 mm, your top-tube length is incorrect. The sizes most often used are 110 to 130 mm.

One method to determine if your stem length is correct is to have a friend drop a plumb line from your nose to the ground, while you look forward, settled in your comfortable riding position. The plumb line should intersect the center of your handlebar.

The amount of stem post visible affects the height of your handlebars. This distance can be measured by using the same yardstick or other tool you used to measure your knee position over your crank arm. Lay the straightedge across your saddle and have someone measure the distance from the straightedge to the top of your handlebars, as shown in Figure 4.12. Typically, handlebars are about one to two inches below the top of the saddle. Some cyclists who are tall or have long arms set their handlebars as much as four inches below the top of the saddle.

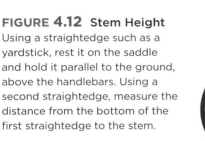

FIGURE 4.12 Stem Height
Using a straightedge such as a yardstick, rest it on the saddle and hold it parallel to the ground, above the handlebars. Using a second straightedge, measure the distance from the bottom of the first straightedge to the stem.

Typically, lowering the stem puts your body in a more aerodynamic position. To be comfortable in a lower position, you need flexible hamstrings and an ability to rotate your pelvis. Signs that your stem may be too low include pain or numbness in the genital area; quadriceps hitting your torso on each pedal stroke; neck, shoulder, or arm pain; and hand numbness.

Raising the stem puts you in a more upright riding position and can take some pressure off the body areas just mentioned. A high stem, however, opens your chest area to catching more wind and is less aerodynamic. On the threadless systems, height adjustment is made with spacers that vary in width. Typical widths are 5 and 10 mm. The stem can also be rotated 180 degrees to affect handlebar height.

Handlebars and Brake Levers

Your setup for the previous bike components will largely determine your handlebar height. Handlebar widths are different and can be changed to suit your anatomy; your handlebar width should be roughly the same as your shoulder width. Typically, handlebars are either level with the road or rotated slightly up, so the handlebar ends point toward the rear hub.

Most of the time, bikes come equipped with standard brake levers. If you happen to have small hands, consider "short-reach" brake levers available from some bike component manufacturers. Some women-specific bike designs include short-reach levers, but that is not always the case.

Crank Length

Most beginning cyclists purchase stock frames, which come with standard crank arms. If the speed bug bites you and you begin researching ways to ride faster, crank-arm length is one subject that will continue to surface. Crank-arm length is a much-debated topic when it comes to optimizing performance.

Longer cranks have a mechanical advantage and are good for pushing larger gears, as you would do in time trial riding. This advantage can translate to more power and speed. Keep in mind, however, that crank-arm length affects cadence and saddle height and can cause extra stress on the knees. A switch to longer cranks may mean you need to lower your seat in order to keep your hips from rocking at the bottom of the pedal stroke. But once your seat height is properly adjusted to longer cranks, the change may cause interference between your quadriceps and torso, which is certainly not ideal.

> Longer cranks have a mechanical advantage and are good for pushing larger gears.

Optimizing crank-arm length is not covered in detail in this book. Some good resources for information on cranks and other bicycle topics come from Lennard Zinn, an equipment expert and legendary frame builder. You can find crank information on his Web site, www.zinncycles.com. He has also written several books—including *Zinn's Cycling Primer*, which features extensive information on bicycle fit.

BIKE FIT FOR TIME TRIALS

For optimum time trial performance, you want to ride in an aero position, or a position that keeps your body low on the bike and reduces drag. As mentioned earlier, using the aero position in a road time trial (or a non-drafting triathlon) can result in a 20 percent energy savings, compared with riding in an upright position. Your time trial bike fit should maximize aerodynamics without sacrificing safety or comfort.

One aerodynamic design feature of a time trial bike is the steep seat-tube angle of about 75 to 80 degrees, which allows you to get into an aero position with a flatter back but without sacrificing pedaling power. This seat-tube angle rotates you forward with the crank as a fixed point of rotation, allowing your hip and knee angles to remain open rather than cramped. This rotation is also less stressful on back and hamstring muscles that are not as flexible in a flat-back time trial position.

Some cyclists seek the help of knowledgeable professionals to help them set up a time trial bike, and others prefer to do it themselves. If you decide to evaluate and make changes to your body position on your own, a good tool to use is a camera. Set up your bike on a trainer and ask a willing assistant to take photos—or better yet, movies—of you pedaling. You'll want to have shots of the front, both sides, and the back.

Position your body low on the bike. From a front view, your arms should be about shoulder-width apart. While you're pedaling, your knees should be in line with your feet and hip joints. In other words, your knees shouldn't protrude outward or inward on a pedal stroke. From a rear view, your knees, ankles, and hips should all track in a line perpendicular to the ground.

From a side view, while you are in the aero position, your back should look relatively flat. (If you have a natural hump in your back, as some people do, your back will never appear totally flat.) While you are pedaling and looking straight ahead in a riding position, an imaginary line drawn from your ear down through your elbow should be perpendicular to the ground.

The ability to ride in an aerodynamic position using aerobars may take some time to develop. Resting on your forearms affects steering responsiveness and balance. Riding with a flat back requires flexible back and hamstring muscles and a rotation of the pelvis forward. This forward rotation and new position may put added pressure on genitals. A seat that has a portion of the nose relieved or has gel padding on the nose may help relieve pressure.

> Using full aerobars on a time trial-specific bike is more effective than adding short aerobars to a road bike.

BIKE FIT AND GENDER

In 1998, when I began work on my first book, *The Female Cyclist: Gearing up a Level*, the common knowledge in popular cycling literature was that women have shorter torsos than men do. I did not find a single document about cycling that contradicted this belief, so assuming it was a fact, I thought it would be fun to include anatomical drawings of male and female bodies in the book to display the differences. But when I began searching for data to support the notion that women have shorter torsos than men, I found none.

What I found instead was little difference between male and female ratios of torso or leg length to overall height. When looking at the gross data—compiled by NASA and reprinted in the books *Ergonomic Design for People at Work,* volumes 1 and 2—I saw that, given a male and a female of equal height and relatively equal leg length, the major fit concerns were arm reach to the hoods (or drops) and hand size, affecting reach to the brake levers. Comparing the gross data for a male and a female who were each 64 inches tall showed that the arm length for women was, on average, shorter by two inches. In addition, women tended to have smaller hands than men of the same height.

Comparing a 64-inch man and to a 64-inch woman works well to examine the differences between the genders; however, the average male derived from the original data set used was 69 inches, compared with the average female at 64 inches.

While writing this book, I reexamined anthropometric data using *The Measure of Man and Woman* (Henry Dreyfuss Associates, 2002). What I found in more recent data is that differences between the average U.S. male and the average U.S. female, in dimensions critical for cycling, are very small. Proportional to height, male and female dimensions of leg, hand, and arm length are very close.

Figures 4.13 and 4.14 show the average dimensions from these data. The average female measures 64 inches and the average male measures 69.1 inches in height. The rest of the dimensions in the figures are expressed as a proportion of height. For example, in Figure 4.14, the female's femur (thigh) length is 0.241 multiplied by her height (H) of 64 inches. So her femur measures 15.42 inches (0.241 × 64).

Table 4.1 shows the differences in body dimensions for a male and a female of equal height. You can see the female's key dimensions for bike fit are slightly shorter than those of the male, except for grip-to-shoulder length.

Because bicycles are not fitted by overall height, Table 4.2 shows the differences in key body dimensions affecting bike fit for a male and a female with equal leg lengths. People within this data set have very little difference in leg-length dimensions. The differences in torso length and grip-to-shoulder length are each less than half an inch.

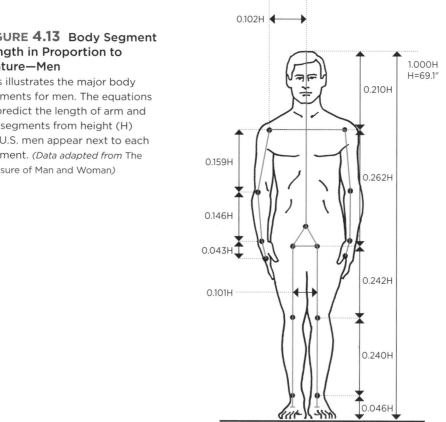

FIGURE 4.13 Body Segment Length in Proportion to Stature—Men
This illustrates the major body segments for men. The equations to predict the length of arm and leg segments from height (H) for U.S. men appear next to each segment. (*Data adapted from* The Measure of Man and Woman)

So while U.S. men are, on average, five inches taller than U.S. women, the proportions of their limb dimensions (expressed as percentages of height) are very similar. When viewing these data, however, remember that we are not all carbon copies of the data set, with all our proportions exactly equal and to scale. Your proportions may fall near this average range, or your measurements may fall outside the average measurements on one or more dimensions.

One female cyclist I know is the average height, 64 inches tall. Her arm, leg, and femur lengths, however, are longer than the averages, and her shoulders are wider than average. Her torso length is shorter than average and hands are smaller than average. This knowledge helps her find, and modify, bicycles and clothing to fit her individual proportions.

Consider, too, anatomical differences based on ethnic background. For example, the average Japanese male has a seated height (measured from the seat to the top of the head) equal to the average U.S. male's. Measured from that same seated position, the Japanese male has a leg length 3.6 inches shorter than the average U.S. male. This is a significant difference.

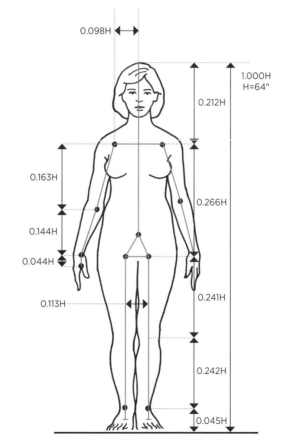

FIGURE 4.14 Body Segment Length in Proportion to Stature—Women
This illustrates the major body segments for women. The equations to predict the length of arm and leg segments from height (H) for U.S. women appear next to each segment. (Data adapted from The Measure of Man and Woman)

TABLE 4.1 COMPARATIVE BODY MEASUREMENTS FOR A MALE AND A FEMALE OF EQUAL HEIGHT

	MALE 64 IN		FEMALE 64 IN		DIFF*
Femur Length	.242H	15.49 in	.241H	15.42 in	-0.07 in
Tibia Length	.240H	15.36 in	.242H	15.49 in	0.13 in
Leg Length	.528H	33.79 in	.522H	33.40 in	-0.39 in
Torso Length	.262H	16.77 in	.266H	17.02 in	0.25 in
Grip-to-Shoulder Length	.348H	22.27 in	.351H	22.46 in	0.19 in
Total Arm Length	.414H	26.50 in	.414H	26.50 in	0 in
Shoulder Width	.102H	6.53 in	.098H	6.27 in	-0.26 in

*H = height in decimal inches. Difference between female and male data, in inches. Positive numbers indicate the female dimension is greater than the male dimension. Negative numbers indicate the female dimension is lower than the male dimension. Measurements have been rounded to the nearest hundredth.

TABLE 4.2 COMPARATIVE BODY MEASUREMENTS FOR A MALE AND A FEMALE HAVING EQUAL LEG LENGTHS

	MALE 63.26 IN		FEMALE 64 IN		DIFF* 0.74 IN
Femur Length	.242H	15.31 in	.241H	15.42 in	0.11 in
Tibia Length	.240H	15.18 in	.242H	15.49 in	0.31 in
Leg Length	.528H	33.40 in	.522H	33.40 in	0 in
Torso Length	.262H	16.57 in	.266H	17.02 in	0.63 in
Grip-to-Shoulder Length	.348H	22.01 in	.351H	22.46 in	0.45 in
Total Arm Length	.414H	26.20 in	.414H	26.50 in	0.30 in
Grip Length	.043H	2.72 in	.044H	2.82 in	0.10 in

*H = height in decimal inches. Difference between female and male data, in inches. Positive numbers indicate the female dimension is greater than the male dimension. Negative numbers indicate the female dimension is lower than the male dimension. Measurements have been rounded to the nearest hundredth.

The more you know about your body dimensions, the more you'll understand how to optimize your bike fit.

Physical dimensions vary among individuals, as do cycling goals. Just because you might be an "average" height does not mean your legs are of average proportion. Two people of similar physical dimensions may have completely different cycling goals and, therefore, different bike needs. In any case, a bicycle should be reasonably comfortable to ride over a gradual buildup of mileage, and that bike should suit your purpose.

When you shop for a new bicycle, or any cycling equipment, be a smart shopper: Know bicycle geometry and the rules of thumb for bike setup. Go to a reputable bike shop where the personnel are willing to help you and to spend time answering your questions. A shop with good mechanics who are willing to teach you about a bicycle and other equipment is a place worthy of your business.

ESSENTIAL CLOTHING

One of the best investments you can make for cycling comfort is to buy padded cycling shorts. These shorts are designed to be worn without underwear and protect your under regions from pressure and friction. Wearing underwear with cycling shorts is likely to cause chafing and pressure-point problems, so don't do it.

Cycling shorts come in two basic designs: the baggy style and the tight-fitting Lycra style. Which style you choose depends on your personal preference, riding style, and cycling goals.

The padded portion of cycling shorts is called a chamois. In the early days of cycling, the chamois was made from animal hide. Now, most cycling shorts have synthetic chamois manufactured from performance-oriented materials intended to wick moisture away and reduce pressure and friction. The major variables for chamois include the material, size, shape, thickness, and placement within the shorts. Shorts and a chamois that are comfortable for one rider may not be comfortable for the next rider, so try on a few different pairs. For hygiene purposes, wear underwear when you try on shorts and always wash the shorts before wearing them for the first time.

Bike Shorts

Bike shorts come in many styles, and it's helpful to consider which style best suits your cycling.

Get Rolling: Some riders are more comfortable in baggy-style shorts. Others like the compressive feeling of tight-fitting cycling shorts. Well-fitting and inexpensive cycling shorts in either style are easy to find. All the seams should be free of raised areas and thread knots.

Intermediate: Mid-range cycling shorts are typically made of more expensive materials than get-rolling versions. They also tend to have longer life spans.

Hard Core: High-priced shorts and bibs are made from fabrics boasting the current technology for wicking, comfort, and style. Some styles feature aerodynamic qualities, while others tout the latest "in" fashion. The seams are flat or hidden.

Some cyclists feel that shorts dig into the waist and are uncomfortable, so they prefer bibs. A bib is a cycling short that includes upper-body material, similar to suspenders. By eliminating the elastic waistband, bibs eliminate restrictions around the waist and can keep your torso more comfortable. The downside to bibs is that if you need to use the restroom, you will need to strip off all of your upper body garments. Also, cyclists who prefer shorts often complain that bib straps dig into their shoulders. No matter which style you prefer, you'll find a number of choices.

After you finish a ride, get out of your cycling shorts or bib and shower as soon as possible. If it is not possible to shower at the end of your ride, at least get out of your cycling shorts or bib. You can use disposable towelettes or carry a damp washcloth in a baggie for a quick cleanup. Showering or cleaning soon after the ride helps reduce the likelihood of saddle sores caused by bacteria.

> One of the best investments you can make for cycling comfort is to buy padded cycling shorts.

After cycling shorts, padded gloves are your next best clothing investment. Gloves can help prevent numb or sore hands, and they also keep your hands protected in the unfortunate event of a crash.

Cycling jerseys are typically close-fitting to reduce wind drag and are made of wicking materials to keep you dry. They have pockets in the rear panels to carry food, extra clothing, or flat-repair materials. While cycling jerseys are not mandatory for comfortable cycling as cycling shorts are, jerseys provide added storage.

COLD-WEATHER GEAR

Most of the time, new cyclists head indoors when the temperature drops below a certain mark on the thermometer. Intermediate riders have slightly higher thresholds, and hard-core riders are found cycling in all kinds of weather and temperatures.

When the weather is cold—say, 20 or 30 degrees (Fahrenheit)—you know it's cold and you can prepare for it. Problems can occur when the temperature is in the range of 40 to 50 degrees and you are unprepared for sudden weather changes, such as an unexpected storm that makes conditions wet and/or windy. For example, an ambient temperature of 40 degrees changes to 34 degrees on your skin with the addition of a 10 mph headwind. Add a cycling speed of 20 mph into that headwind and the windchill takes the temperature to—*brrr*—28 degrees.

You can increase the fun factor on these long rides by protecting yourself from outside elements like wind and rain and by keeping sweat off your skin. Also, consider finding a group to ride with in the cooler conditions. Cycling with a group is much easier and more enjoyable than facing chilly temperatures on your own.

EQUIPMENT TO MEASURE PERFORMANCE

Heart Rate Monitors

A heart rate monitor system is a good investment; it allows you to monitor your body's response to exercise intensity—and at a reasonable cost. It's like having a tachometer for the body, similar to the one on a sports car. (See Chapter 2 for information on how monitoring heart rate benefits your training and racing.) Basic systems are available for well under $100. The more features a monitor has, the more expensive it is.

Gearing up for the Cold

From toe to head, here are some gear suggestions to get you started:

- Wear socks that give your toes enough room to move. Cramped toes are cold toes. Be sure your socks are made of moisture-wicking material.

- Wear booties to keep the wind off your toes. For cool temperatures, try the wind-stopper booties. For colder temperatures, neoprene materials are great.

- Keep your legs warm by wearing tights or leg warmers, with or without wind protection on the front.

- Wrap your torso with a base layer that wicks moisture away from your body, a second layer to insulate, and a third layer that provides wind protection yet allows moisture to escape.

- Keep your hands protected with gloves or lobster-claw mittens with wind-stopper material on the outside and moisture-wicking material next to your hands.

- Use an oil-based moisturizer on your face. Water-based lotions wet the skin, increasing the likelihood of frostnip or frostbite. Or consider a balaclava to cover your face. If you have asthma, a balaclava can slow moisture loss and help preheat cold air before you suck it into your lungs.

- Keep your head warm. Consider a favorite combination of many cyclists: a helmet cover and ear warmers. If you get too hot, you can easily peel off the helmet cover or pull down the ear warmers. Other cyclists prefer skullcaps that fit under cycling helmets.

- Fill your insulated water bottles or a backpack hydration bladder with hot energy drink. A good apple flavor mimics hot apple cider.

- Carry small heat packs in your pocket. These are little packages that produce heat once the outer wrapping is opened—good for warming fingers and hands that have changed a flat tire in cold conditions.

- Carry a cell phone in case you need to call for help. While you are waiting for your ride, keep warm by putting the chemical heat packs in your shoes or gloves.

- Find buddies who are willing to ride with you, so you can look forward to riding in the cold rather than worry about or dread going it alone.

A basic heart rate monitor consists of a transmitter belt worn strapped around the chest, just below the breasts, and a receiver worn on the wrist or mounted on the handlebar of a bike. The transmitter belt picks up electrical impulses from the heart and relays the information to the receiver via an electromagnetic field. The receiver then displays the heart rate.

Advanced models can store several hours' worth of data, which you can then download to a computer for analysis. These models may include features such as lap timers, individual heart rate zone settings and alarms, interval timers, data collection and analysis tools, speed and distance monitoring, and power monitoring.

> Most beginning cyclists who use a heart rate monitor need only the basic displays of heart rate and total exercise time.

Most beginners need only the basic displays of heart rate and total exercise time. If desired, an inexpensive heart rate monitor can be used in conjunction with an inexpensive cycling computer that displays speed, distance, average speed, maximum speed, and ride time. Additional features are included on various computers and, in general, cost increases with more features.

Power Meters

Power meters utilize various technologies to directly measure or scientifically estimate the power (in watts) that a cyclist generates while riding a bicycle. Because of an increased interest among cyclists in training with power, several power meter companies compete for business, and the cost to the consumer is decreasing. (You can find more information in Chapter 2 on how to train with power.)

Some power meters display estimated calories (kcal) burned during a workout, while others only display a measure called kilojoules (kJ). If you are interested in the number of calories burned, you can use a one-to-one conversion from kJ to kcal.

The actual conversion factor is 1 kJ equals 0.239 kcal, but to use that we would have to assume that our bodies can convert 100 percent of the food energy (chemical energy, thermal energy) into work at the power meter (mechanical energy). By happy coincidence, our bodies are only about 22 to 25 percent efficient. I assume that we are 23.9 percent efficient (a tidy recommendation from Race Across America rider Pete Penseyres), so the conversion nicely becomes one-to-one. If you wonder where the other 75 percent or so of our energy goes, it is given off as heat, which is why we sweat so much. Training can improve our efficiency and fat-burning percentages somewhat, but for all practical purposes, the one-to-one conversion is close enough.

If you own or have access to multiple power systems, keep in mind that your power output on one system (let's call it System 1) is relative only to System 1, and your power output on another system (let's call it System 2) is relative only to System 2. Your power output as measured by System 1 may not match your power output as measured by System 2.

PART II

EVENT
TRAINING PLANS

30-Mile Ride

Level I

You've probably heard it before: To move toward any goal, you have to take that first step. You've got to start somewhere. Start here!

PROFILE

If you want to get into cycling—or get back into cycling after a long break—this plan is designed for you. Right now, you are not cycling or doing any aerobic exercise. You can devote only three days per week to training. You need to see results quickly or you tend to get discouraged.

GOAL

Your six-week goal is to go from fitness hibernation to the ability to complete a 30-mile ride. Your event can be self-designed or you can enter a sponsored event. This plan assumes your average speed is 12 to 14 mph for the 30 miles, resulting in an event ride time of between 2:10 and 2:30.

THE PLAN OVERVIEW

Success depends on consistency. In this plan, you ride three times per week for six weeks. You can do it!

Take a look at the full plan in Table 5.1. If the days you can exercise are different from the ones shown, you can adjust the training days to fit your schedule. If possible, alternate the days you exercise with days off.

Note that a 30-minute ride is scheduled for every Tuesday. The ride is intended to be aerobic and the first step in building your endurance. In addition, you are looking to improve your pedaling cadence. If you have a cyclometer that measures cadence, you're set.

If you do not have a cyclometer that measures cadence, you can periodically check your cadence during the ride by counting pedal strokes. For example, using a watch to track time, aim to have your right (or left) pedal arrive at the bottom of the pedal stroke 22 to 23 times in 15 seconds. (While you're counting pedal strokes, be sure to watch the road and not your feet!)

The second workout of each week will continue to increase your endurance. These rides include short accelerations, to work on leg speed, and small increases in power. The rides in this plan will serve as the foundation for your future fitness. These types of rides are in nearly all of the plans in the book.

PLAN DETAILS

Explanations of the workout codes used throughout this plan can be found in Chapter 21. Here, let's break down the plan by week.

Week 1

Look at the workout on Thursday in Week 1. Your total ride time is 30 minutes. After some warm-up time, incorporate 4 acceleration intervals of 30 seconds each. During the 30 seconds, gradually increase your speed so that you finish faster than you began. Between the 30-second intervals, spin at an easy pace for 90 seconds. Every Thursday workout will include some intervals; however, the interval workout in Week 6 focuses more on muscular endurance.

Your long rides are shown on Saturdays. If it works better for you to do these rides on Sundays, you can switch the days. Each Saturday shows a range of riding time, and you can ride for any length of time within this range. If you're feeling good, strive to ride for the longer periods. If you're feeling tired or you're pinched for time, stick to the shorter end of the range.

For the long ride in Week 1, don't ride at zone 1 to zone 2 intensity for more than about an hour. (Use the rate of perceived exertion [RPE] column in Table 2.1 in Chapter 2 to gauge your exercise intensity.) Be sure you are consuming appropriate amounts of fuel and fluid. See Chapter 3 for more details on fueling and hydration.

Week 2

In Weeks 2 through 4 and Week 6, you can ride anywhere between 30 and 45 minutes on Thursdays. In Week 2, keep the intensity for your long Saturday ride at zone 1 to zone 2, but if possible, increase the length of your ride by 30 minutes over your ride time in Week 1.

Week 3

In Week 3, the long ride includes some zone 3 intensity. If you are gauging your intensity with RPE instead of using a heart rate monitor or power meter, you'll find it tough to know exactly how much time you are accumulating in zone 3. The goal for this ride is to accumulate 15 to 20 minutes in zone 3.

Week 4

During the Week 4 Saturday long ride, accumulate 20 to 30 minutes in zone 3.

Week 5

The weekend ride time in Week 5 is shorter to allow you to rest and absorb the benefits of your training. Within this 1:00 ride, incorporate 5 to 6 cruise intervals of 3 minutes each. Between the intervals, allow 1 minute of very easy spinning to recover.

Week 6

The Thursday workout in Week 6 is the final tune-up before your event. The acceleration intervals in this workout are increased to 90 seconds, but the duration of the rest intervals has also increased.

The grand finale for this training plan is the 30-mile ride, shown here on Saturday. Enjoy your ride!

After you've successfully completed your event, remember to celebrate your success. To maintain your fitness, you can repeat this plan or look at other chapters in this book to plan for your next event.

TABLE 5.1 LEVEL I 30-MILE RIDE

WEEK	MONDAY	TUESDAY	WEDNESDAY	THURSDAY
1	Day off	S5	Day off	S1a
				4 × 30 sec. (90 sec. RI)
		0:30		0:30
2	Day off	S5	Day off	S1a
				6 × 30 sec. (90 sec. RI)
		0:30		0:30–0:45
3	Day off	S5	Day off	S1a
				6–8 × 30 sec. (90 sec. RI)
		0:30		0:30–0:45
4	Day off	S5	Day off	S4
				4 × 20 sec. (100 sec. RI)
		0:30		0:30–0:45
5	Day off	S5	Day off	S1a
				4 × 30 sec. (90 sec. RI)
		0:30		0:30
6	Day off	S5	Day off	M7
				2–4 × 90 sec. (3 min. RI)
		0:30		0:30–0:45

FRIDAY	SATURDAY	SUNDAY	WEEKLY TOTAL
Day off	E2a	Day off	
			1:30–2:00
	0:30–0:60		
Day off	E2a	Day off	
			2:00–2:45
	1:00–1:30		
Day off	E3	Day off	
	15–20 min. z3		2:30–3:15
	1:30–2:00		
Day off	E3	Day off	
	20–30 min. z3		3:00–3:45
	2:00–2:30		
Day off	M2 (z3)	Day off	
	5–6 × 3 min. (60 sec. RI)		2:00
	1:00		
Day off	Ride 30 mi	Day off	
	z1–3		3:10–3:45
	2:10–2:30		

100K or 50-Mile Ride
Level I

A 100K ride (62 miles), also known as a metric century, is a benchmark accomplishment for many cyclists. Those new to long-distance rides may find it useful to begin with a 100K or 50-mile ride before tackling a full century (100 miles). Often, 100K and 50-mile events are offered in conjunction with century rides. If you are a fit cyclist looking for a new challenge, the 100K or 50-mile race might be just what you need.

PROFILE

This plan is designed for a cyclist who is currently riding three days per week. Your rides might be outdoors or indoors on a stationary bike, solo or in a class. Two of those rides are 45 to 60 minutes long. The third ride is at least 60 minutes and maybe as long as 90 minutes. At minimum, you are able to commit to cycling three days per week.

This plan includes the option of one day of strength training per week. If you currently have a strength training program, you can continue that program on your days off from cycling. If you are not strength training but want to begin a routine, this chapter includes information to get you started.

GOAL

Your goal is to complete a 100K or 50-mile ride at the end of 8 weeks of training. Your event can be self-designed or you can enter a sponsored event. The plan assumes your average speed is 12 to 15 mph for the ride, resulting in a 100K ride time of between 4:08 and 5:10 or a 50-mile ride time of between 3:20 and 4:10.

THE PLAN OVERVIEW

Take a look at the full plan in Table 6.1. Note that the plan has cycling scheduled for Tuesdays, Thursdays, and Saturdays. If other days of the week work better for you, move the rides accordingly. It is best if these rides are separated by at least one day.

A fourth, optional ride is included on each Sunday in five of the weeks. If your current level of fitness is low and your goal is the 50-mile ride, you can train to comfortably complete the event by doing the three assigned workouts for the minimum times noted on the plan. You can eliminate the optional Sunday rides.

If you are aiming for the 100K, have a high level of fitness and good recovery from workouts, and have the time to devote to cycling, you can consider doing the highest volumes suggested on the plan.

Most Mondays and Wednesdays are scheduled as "day off or strength train." As noted earlier, if you are already strength training, you can keep your current routine. You may find that you need to modify the routine, reducing sets, repetitions, or weight so that strength training does not negatively impact your cycling.

If you are not yet strength training but would like to incorporate a weight room routine in your workout plan, see Chapter 22. I suggest beginning with the anatomical adaptation phase of strength training and keeping the weight relatively light for the first two weeks.

As your body adapts to the routine, you can slightly increase the weight and reduce the number of repetitions to 12 to 15 (from the 15 to 20 suggested in Chapter 22). You can maintain this reduced range for both your strength training days, or you can do 12 to 15 reps on one day and 15 to 20 reps with less weight on the other day. You might have to experiment to see which routine works best for you.

PLAN DETAILS

Explanations of the workout codes used throughout this plan can be found in Chapter 21. Here, let's break down the plan by week.

Week 1

Your first Tuesday workout is an endurance workout that focuses on cadence. Ride between 45 and 60 minutes total.

The Thursday workout is an endurance workout that challenges you to increase your cadence beyond a normal comfort zone. The workout includes 6 repeats of 20-second spin-ups. Try to spin your legs fast while staying seated (without bouncing).

The Saturday long ride starts the process of building your event endurance. Ride between 1:30 and 2:00 on a rolling course in zones 1 to 2. Be sure to carry fluids and fuel for all Saturday long rides.

Sunday's workout is the optional, easy ride mentioned earlier. Any other Sunday rides throughout the plan are structured the same way.

Week 2

In Week 2, the Tuesday ride works on leg-to-leg imbalances in strength and coordination, and the Thursday spin-ups increase to 30 seconds long.

The Saturday ride increases in length and includes some zone 3 training. Try to accumulate about 20 minutes of zone 3 intensity during the ride. You do not have to ride *steadily* at zone 3 for 20 minutes, and I recommend that you don't in this particular plan. By breaking up the time you spend in zone 3, you will likely produce a higher average power output for that 20 minutes than if you were to ride a steady 20 minutes. Save the bigger time trial–type efforts for after you've built some fitness.

Week 3

The Week 3 Tuesday workout is the same as in Week 2. The Thursday workout changes to a spin step-up workout with longer fast-cadence intervals.

The long ride this week is 2:30 to 3:00 and falls into zones 1 to 3. Accumulate 20 to 30 minutes of zone 3 intensity throughout the ride.

Week 4

Week 4 is for recovery. You should strength train only one day this week, if at all. Although the plan schedules the optional strength training on Monday, you can train on either Monday or Wednesday. Just be sure you decrease the weight to allow your body to recover.

Tuesday's workout is the same cadence workout you did in Week 1, only slightly shorter. On Thursday is a fartlek (speed play) workout, which allows you to add in the speedy portions as the mood strikes you.

Saturday is your first day of structured cruise intervals, at zone 3 intensity. During this 1:30 to 2:00 ride, complete 4 or 5 intervals that are each 5 minutes long.

Week 5

This week builds on the fitness you have achieved to this point. The Tuesday and Thursday workouts are variations of past workouts. Your Saturday long ride is between 3:00 and 3:30 and you accumulate between 30 and 40 minutes in zone 3.

TABLE 6.1   LEVEL I 100K OR 50-MILE RIDE

WEEK	MONDAY	TUESDAY	WEDNESDAY	THURSDAY
1	Day off or strength train (see text)	S5 0:45–1:00	Day off or strength train (see text)	S1a 6 × 20 sec. (100 sec. RI) 0:45–1:00
2	Day off or strength train (see text)	S2 0:45–1:00	Day off or strength train (see text)	S1a 6 × 30 sec. (90 sec. RI) 0:45–1:00
3	Day off or strength train (see text)	S2 0:45–1:00	Day off or strength train (see text)	S1 0:45–1:00
4	Day off or strength train (see text)	S5 0:30–0:45	Day off	S4 0:30–0:45
5	Day off or strength train (see text)	S5 0:45–1:00	Day off or strength train (see text)	S1a 6 × 30 sec. (90 sec. RI) 0:45–1:00
6	Day off or strength train (see text)	E2a 0:45–1:00	Day off or strength train (see text)	S1a 8 × 30 sec. (90 sec. RI) 0:45–1:00
7	Day off or strength train (see text)	S5 0:30–0:45	Day off	S4 0:30–0:45
8	Day off	M7 3–4 × 90 sec. (3 min. RI) 0:45–1:00	Day off	S4 0:30

FRIDAY	SATURDAY	SUNDAY	WEEKLY TOTAL
Day off	E2a	E1a	
	(z1/2)		3:30–4:45
	1:30–2:00	0:30–0:45	
Day off	E3	S5	
	-20 min. z3		4:00–5:15
	2:00–2:30	0:30–0:45	
Day off	E3	E1a	
	-20–30 min. z3		4:45–6:00
	2:30–3:00	0:45–1:00	
Day off	M2 (z3)	Day off	
	4–5 × 5 min. (2 min. RI)		2:30–3:30
	1:30–2:00		
Day off	E3	E2a	
	-30–40 min. z3		5:15–6:30
	3:00–3:30	0:45–1:00	
Day off	E4	S5	
	-20 min. z4		6:00–7:00
	3:30–4:00	1:00	
Day off	M2 (z3)	Day off	
	4–5 × 5 min. (2 min. RI)		2:30–3:30
	1:30–2:00		
Day off	50 mi. or 100K	Day off	
	(mostly z1/4)		5:15–6:45
	4:00–5:15		

Week 6

The biggest change introduced in Week 6 is in the long ride on Saturday, which is between 3:30 and 4:00 and includes some zone 4 intensity. Accumulate about 20 minutes of zone 4 intensity throughout the ride.

Week 7

Week 7 is for recovery, with reduced training and volume. The routine is exactly the same as in Week 4.

Week 8

Week 8 is your event week. Limit your training volume to no higher than the guidelines shown in the plan. Your goal is to be well rested by Saturday.

This week includes only one new workout, on Tuesday. Just enough intensity is included in this workout to keep your legs feeling fresh for event day.

For your 100K or 50-mile event, relax and ride the event as you have ridden your recent long rides. Plan to ride stronger as the event progresses: Control intensity for the first half of the event, and fuel and hydrate appropriately throughout (see Chapter 3).

Week 9

Although no Week 9 is shown in Table 6.1, cyclists often wonder what to do during the week after an event. I recommend you ride two or three times, keeping your intensity levels mostly at zone 1 to zone 2. After you have a chance to recover from your event, you can move on to a new goal.

Century Ride
Level I

For many cyclists, completing a century ride (100 miles) is a significant milestone. Organized century rides can be found in many locations and are occasionally fundraisers for charities. Regardless, a portion of the entry fee usually goes toward event support.

Organized events have rider-aid stations staffed by cheerful volunteers or paid help, as well as portable restrooms at regular mileage intervals. Aid stations may be minimally stocked with fruit or piled high with a variety of culinary goodies. All aid stations provide water, and often they will also stock electrolyte drinks.

For the safety of the riders, event organizers obtain road permits and hire police and medical personnel. Most events have sag wagons to pick up fatigued cyclists who wish to stop before reaching the finish line. Also, most events have mechanical support to help riders with equipment problems. Event directors spend a great deal of time and money to put on top-shelf events.

Although it might be tempting to tag along with an organized event, without paying the event fee (or consuming the goodies at the aid stations), don't do it. Participating in an event when you don't pay the fee is basically theft. If you are interested in completing a century ride without the support of other riders and an event organizer, map out your own ride.

A self-designed century ride can be fun for a small group of friends or family. The ride can be a looped design or a one-way destination route. If you design a one-way route, you might ask willing, non-cycling family or friends to pick you up at the completion of your goal or to be sag support if needed.

PROFILE

This plan is designed for a Level I cyclist, who is currently riding two or three days per week. You may or may not be strength training or participating in other sports. For the next 12 weeks, you can commit to riding at least three days per week, which includes a long ride that builds from one to four hours.

The plan sets out options to help you fit the training to your personal profile needs. For instance, the weekday rides can be outdoors or indoors on a stationary bike or trainer. Other options are detailed throughout this chapter.

If you currently have a strength training program, you can continue that program on your days off from cycling. You may find you need to reduce the weight, sets, repetitions, or some combination of these so that strength training doesn't negatively affect your cycling. If you are not strength training but want to begin a routine, this plan will get you started.

GOAL

Your goal is to complete a 100-mile ride at the end of 12 weeks of training. Your event can be self-designed or organized by a group. The plan assumes your average speed will be 12 to 15 mph for the 100 miles, resulting in a ride time of between 6:40 and 8:20.

THE PLAN OVERVIEW

Take a look at the full plan in Table 7.1. The basic layout of the plan includes days off or optional strength training days on Mondays and Wednesdays. Rides are shown on Tuesdays, Thursdays, Saturdays, and Sundays. Fridays are days off. If it works better for you to ride on Mondays and Wednesdays, you can ride on these days and strength train or take the day off on Tuesdays and Thursdays. Plan options:

Minimalist: You need to know the minimum time you can train and still comfortably complete the event. Other obligations keep you from devoting more time to cycling. If this description fits you, plan to ride three days per week and cut out the strength training. Keep the Sunday workouts and two other cycling days. If you give up the Tuesday or Thursday rides, your overall endurance will suffer less than if you give up the Saturday rides. If you minimize endurance training, your century ride will be less comfortable and slower than you are capable of riding, and the event will require more effort.

Few modifications: If you need to modify the plan on occasion, first reduce the training time of the shortest ride of the week or eliminate the easiest ride of the week. If you are pinched for time in Weeks 9 and 10, make the Saturday rides two hours long. Do not try to make up the time elsewhere.

As is: If you follow the plan as it is shown in Table 7.1, you will comfortably complete the event. Strength training is not mandatory but complements your on-bike training.

Strength training: As mentioned earlier, if you are currently strength training, you can keep your current routine—though you may find that you need to modify it. If you are not currently strength training but would like to incorporate a weight room routine in your workout plan, I suggest beginning with the anatomical adaptation phase of strength training described in Chapter 22. Keep the weight relatively light for the first two weeks. As your body adapts to the routine, you can slightly increase the weight and reduce the number of repetitions to 12 to 15 (from the 15 to 20 suggested in Chapter 22). You can maintain this reduced range for both your strength training days, or you can do 12 to 15 reps on one day and 15 to 20 reps with less weight on the other day. You might have to experiment to see which routine works best for you.

PLAN DETAILS

The overall structure of the plan includes rides to improve your cycling economy with skill building and drills, rides to improve or maintain endurance, and rides to improve your average speed. Explanations of the workout codes used throughout this plan can be found in Chapter 21. Here, let's break down the plan by week.

Week 1

Your first Tuesday workout, about 30 minutes total, is an easy one that focuses on cadence. The Thursday workout continues this focus and includes slightly higher intensity. The Saturday ride is an easy, fun ride, and the Sunday ride starts the process of building your endurance.

Week 2

The Tuesday and Thursday rides repeat the formats of those in Week 1, but both are now slightly longer. The Saturday ride is a negative-split ride that helps you learn how to pace yourself so you can finish rides strong. A negative-split is a workout or interval in which you finish the second half faster than the first. This format is directly opposite of, for instance, blasting out of your garage at rocket speed and having your speed and energy fade as your ride continues.

The Sunday ride is a repeat of that in Week 1.

Week 3

The Tuesday and Thursday workouts are new skill workouts, aimed at increasing your cadence. As you found during the Week 1 workouts, typical pedaling cadences range from

TABLE 7.1 LEVEL I CENTURY RIDE

WEEK	MONDAY	TUESDAY	WEDNESDAY
1	Day off or strength train (see text)	E1a 0:30	Day off or strength train (see text)
2	Day off or strength train (see text)	E1a 0:45	Day off or strength train (see text)
3	Day off or strength train (see text)	S1a 6 × 20 sec. (100 sec. RI) 0:45–1:00	Day off or strength train (see text)
4	Day off or strength train (see text)	E1a 0:30	Day off
5	Day off or strength train (see text)	S1a 6–8 × 30 sec. (90 sec. RI) 0:45–1:00	Day off or strength train (see text)
6	Day off or strength train (see text)	S2 0:45–1:00	Day off or strength train (see text)
7	Day off or strength train (see text)	S1a 6–10 × 30 sec. (90 sec. RI) 0:45–1:00	Day off or strength train (see text)
8	Day off or strength train (see text)	E1a 0:45	Day off
9	Day off or strength train (see text)	M2 (z4/5a) 5–6 × 3 min. (60 sec. RI) 0:45–1:00	Day off or strength train (see text)

THURSDAY	FRIDAY	SATURDAY	SUNDAY	WEEKLY TOTAL
S5	Day off	E1b	E2a	2:45
0:45		0:30	1:00	
S5	Day off	E2c	E2a	3:00-3:45
0:45-1:00		0:30-1:00	1:00	
S4	Day off	E2c	E2a	3:30-4:15
0:45		0:30-1:00	1:30	
E2a	Day off	S4	E3	4:00
			~15-20 min. z3	
0:30		1:00	2:00	
M2 (z3)	Day off	E2a	E3	4:30-5:15
5-6 × 3 min. (60 sec. RI)			~20 min. z3	
0:45		1:00	2:00-2:30	
M2 (z3)	Day off	E2c	E3	5:00-6:00
4-5 × 4 min. (60 sec. RI)			~20-30 min. z3	
0:45-1:00		1:00	2:30-3:00	
M2 (z3)	Day off	E2a	E3	6:30-7:30
4-5 × 5 min. (2 min. RI)			~30-40 min. z3	
0:45-1:00		2:00	3:00-3:30	
M6 (z1/3)	Day off	S4	E2a	4:30
0:45		1:00	2:00	
S1a	Day off	E4	E2a	7:30-8:30
6-8 × 30 sec. (90 sec. RI)		~20 min. z4/5a		
0:45-1:00		2:30	3:30-4:00	

CONTINUED

TABLE 7.1 LEVEL I CENTURY RIDE CONTINUED

WEEK	MONDAY	TUESDAY	WEDNESDAY
10	Day off or strength train (see text)	M2 (z4/5a) 4–5 × 4 min. (60 sec. RI) 0:45–1:00	Day off or strength train (see text)
11	Day off strength train (see text)	M6 (z1/5a) 0:30–0:45	Day off
12	Day off 	M7 4 × 90 sec. (3 min. RI) 1:00	Day off

80 to 100 revolutions per minute (rpm). Elite cyclists have sustainable pedaling cadences of 110 rpm and higher.

The Saturday workout is a negative-split workout, and the Sunday ride increases in length by 30 minutes.

Week 4

Week 4 is for recovery. You should strength train only one day this week, if at all. Although the plan schedules the optional strength training on Monday, you can train on either Monday or Wednesday. Just be sure you decrease the weight to allow your body to recover.

Tuesday's workout is the same cadence workout you did in Week 1. Thursday's workout is a maintenance spin, and Saturday is a fartlek (speed play) workout, which allows you to add in the speedy portions as the mood strikes you.

Sunday is your first workout that includes some zone 3 intensity. Accumulate no more than 20 minutes of zone 3 time. Be sure to pay attention to your nutrition and hydration needs as outlined in Chapter 3.

Weeks 5 through 7

Tuesday workouts in this training block continue to work on your cycling form and skills. The Thursday workouts begin structured interval training, aimed at improving your muscular endurance.

THURSDAY	FRIDAY	SATURDAY	SUNDAY	WEEKLY TOTAL
S2	Day off	E4	E2a	
		-20-30 min. z4/5a		8:30-9:00
0:45-1:00		3:00	4:00	
S4	Day off	E2a	E4	
				5:30-6:00
0:30-0:45		1:30	3:00	
S4	Day off	S7	Century ride	
				9:15
0:45		0:30	7:00	

The weekend workouts continue to focus on building your overall endurance. The Saturday rides keep intensity limited to zones 1 and 2, while the Sunday rides include more intensity. Gently build the accumulated volume of zone 3 intensity over the course of Weeks 5 through 7.

Glance at your heart rate monitor, if you have one, during the rides to get a sense of how much time you are spending in each zone. If you have a heart rate monitor or power meter that includes a download feature, you can check the time spent in each training zone post-ride. As you gain more experience, you'll find it easier to estimate the time spent in each zone.

As before, keep on top of your fueling and hydration needs during the longer rides and maintain your post-ride recovery routine.

Week 8

Week 8 is a recovery week, with reduced training volume to allow your body to adapt and get stronger.

Weeks 9 through 11

You will note a change in this training block. Your interval work moves to Tuesdays, and the intensity moves into zones 4 to 5a. This shift allows you a little more recovery from the interval session before you head into a weekend of high-quality work. These threshold workouts continue to focus on increasing your ability to sustain higher average speeds. The Thursday workouts in this block are the skills and drills workouts.

The weekend workouts also change slightly. The Saturday rides include higher intensities, and the Sunday rides help you build event endurance. The plan is designed this way so that you can give the Saturday rides a higher-quality effort on rested legs.

Note that your highest training volume comes in Week 10. Week 11 decreases the training volume and begins your taper process. Training is reduced, or tapered, before the century ride, so that you can be rested. This process gives you the best opportunity for a strong and fast ride on event day.

Week 12

In Week 12, do not hesitate to decrease training volume further if you feel tired. Extra training this week will not add to your endurance and will likely leave you feeling tired for the event.

For the century ride, remember to aim for a negative-split event. Due to the particular course profile for this ride, your actual time may not be lower in the second half of the ride, but your intensity should be higher than during the first half of the event.

Enjoy the ride!

CHAPTER

8

12 WEEKS

Century Ride
Level II

You have ridden at least one century ride, and now you're looking to do more than complete the event. You want to compete. You want to improve your performance and ride faster.

If you compare this training plan with the one in Chapter 7, the main differences are in the volume of training and intensity. To accommodate experienced cyclists, this training plan includes more total training volume and more intensity.

PROFILE

This plan is designed for a Level II cyclist, who rides three to four days per week and has a solid aerobic base. Your long ride is typically 2:00, and during most weeks, you can complete two weekday rides that are 1:00. You may or may not be strength training. For the next 12 weeks, you can commit to riding four days per week, which includes a long ride that builds from 2:00 to between 4:30 and 5:00.

In addition to your commitment to training, you have a commitment to recovery. You know that improved performance is accompanied by improved recovery techniques and high-density nutrition. In short, just as you must complete the training sessions, you need to get adequate rest and eat nutritious foods that fuel a high-performance body (see Chapter 3).

GOAL

Your goal is to ride a better, faster century at the end of 12 weeks of training. This plan assumes your average speed for the 100 miles will be 16 to 18 mph on a hilly course, resulting in a ride time of between 5:30 and 6:15. If your course is flat or rolling, your average speed will be higher and your final ride time better.

THE PLAN OVERVIEW

Your training plan is in Table 8.1. The basic layout of the plan includes days off or optional strength training days on Mondays and Wednesdays. Rides are shown on Tuesdays, Thursdays, Saturdays, and Sundays. Fridays are days off. If it works better for you to ride on Mondays and Wednesdays, you can adjust the rides to these days and move strength training days or your days off to Tuesdays and Thursdays.

If you currently have a strength training program, you can continue that program on your days off from cycling. You may find that you have to modify the routine, reducing sets, repetitions, or weight so that strength training doesn't negatively impact your cycling.

If you are not strength training but would like to incorporate a weight-room routine in your workout plan, I suggest beginning with the anatomical adaptation phase of strength training described in Chapter 22. Keep the weight relatively light for the first two weeks.

As your body adapts to the routine, you can slightly increase the weight and reduce the number of repetitions to 12 to 15 (from the 15 to 20 suggested in Chapter 22). You can maintain this reduced range for both your strength training days, or you can do 12 to 15 reps on one day and 15 to 20 reps with less weight on the other day. You might have to experiment to see which routine works best for you.

PLAN DETAILS

The overall structure of the plan includes a form workout on Tuesday, a high-intensity interval workout on Thursday, an endurance workout on Saturday, and a combination workout on Sunday. The Sunday rides are multifaceted, building endurance, hill-climbing strength, and lactate threshold speed. These rides also provide you with opportunities to iron out your nutrition and hydration plans. Explanations of the workout codes used throughout this plan can be found in Chapter 21. Here, let's break down the plan by week.

Week 1

Your first Tuesday workout is a 60-minute isolated leg workout to help you work out any dead spots from your pedal stroke.

The Thursday workout begins the process to improve your lactate threshold power and speed. You can find a review on lactate threshold in Chapter 2. (You can also review training zones there.) After a good warm-up, complete four or five 4-minute intervals at zone 3 intensity for each interval. Spin easy for 60 seconds between the repeats to recover. Aim to be in zone 1 during this recovery period. Be sure to leave enough time at the end of the workout to spin easy and cool down.

On Saturday, ride a rolling course for 60 to 90 minutes. The Sunday ride is more difficult; it includes more intensity. Try to accumulate between 20 and 30 minutes of zone 3 intensity during this ride.

Begin practicing good nutrition techniques on the Sunday ride, fueling and hydrating during and after. You may need to experiment with different fuels to find the fuel, or combination of fuels, that works best for you.

Week 2

The Tuesday ride in Week 2 focuses on leg speed and includes several 20-second acceleration intervals. These are not powerful sprints, but rather periods of gradual building of leg speed. The Thursday workout is similar to that in Week 1, but the work and rest intervals are both longer. The weekend rides are also similar to those in Week 1. The main change here is the accumulation of 30 to 40 minutes at zone 3 intensity during the Sunday ride.

Week 3

This training plan is structured with two-week periods of "work" weeks, each followed by a week of rest and recovery. In other words, this plan has three-week cycles. Week 3 is a rest week, with reduced training volume. Remember that the recovery period is equal in importance to the work period. You will not become a stronger cyclist if your body is constantly fatigued.

You should strength train only one day this week, if at all, lifting less weight than usual. You may also want to reduce the number of repetitions, sets, or both. Although the plan schedules the optional strength training on Wednesday, you can train on either Monday or Wednesday.

The Tuesday and Thursday workouts are form workouts that stay in aerobic training zones. After a day off on Friday, complete an all-out time trial on Saturday. Do the trial in a location where you will be able to repeat it later in the training plan. The Sunday ride is an easy aerobic maintenance ride. Ride for 1:30 to 2:00 anywhere in zone 1 to 2 intensity.

Weeks 4 and 5

These two weeks are similar in structure to Weeks 1 and 2. Tuesday is a form workout, and Thursday is an interval day. The change for Weeks 4 and 5 is that the Thursday intervals are done at zone 4 to 5a intensity, for you to work on your lactate threshold speed.

TABLE 8.1 LEVEL II CENTURY RIDE

WEEK	MONDAY	TUESDAY	WEDNESDAY
1	Day off or strength train (see text)	S2 1:00	Day off or strength train (see text)
2	Day off or strength train (see text)	S1a 6 × 20 sec. (100 sec. RI) 1:00	Day off or strength train (see text)
3	Day off	S4 0:45	Day off or strength train (see text)
4	Day off or strength train (see text)	S1 1:00	Day off or strength train (see text)
5	Day off or strength train (see text)	S2 1:00	Day off or strength train (see text)
6	Day off	S4 0:45	Day off or strength train (see text)
7	Day off or strength train (see text)	S5 1:00	Day off or strength train (see text)
8	Day off or strength train (see text)	S1 1:00	Day off or strength train (see text)
9	Day off	S2 0:45	Day off or strength train (see text)

THURSDAY	FRIDAY	SATURDAY	SUNDAY	WEEKLY TOTAL
M2 (z3)	Day off	E2a	E3	
4–5 × 4 min. (60 sec. RI)			~20–30 min. z3	5:00–6:00
1:00		1:00–1:30	2:00–2:30	
M2 (z3)	Day off	E2a	E3	
4–5 × 5 min. (2 min. RI)			~30–40 min. z3	5:30–6:30
1:00		1:00–1:30	2:30–3:00	
S5	Day off	T2	E2a	
				4:00–4:30
0:45		1:00	1:30–2:00	
M2 (z4/5a)	Day off	E2a	E3	
4–5 × 4 min. (60 sec. RI)			~30–40 min. z3	6:00–6:30
1:00		1:30	2:30–3:00	
M2 (z4/5a)	Day off	E2a	E4	
4–5 × 5 min. (2 min. RI)			~20 min. z4/5a	7:00–7:30
1:00		2:00	3:00–3:30	
S5	Day off	E2a	A1d	
				4:30
0:45		1:00	2:00	
M3 (z4/5a)	Day off	E2a	E4	
5–7 × 3 min. (60 sec. RI)			~20–30 min. z4/5a	7:30–8:30
1:00		2:00–2:30	3:30–4:00	
M3 (z4/5a)	Day off	E2a	E4	
5–7 × 3 min. (60 sec. RI)			~30–40 min. z4/5a	8:00–9:00
1:00		2:00–2:30	4:00–4:30	
S5	Day off	T2	E2a	
				4:30
0:45		1:00	2:00	

CONTINUED

TABLE 8.1 LEVEL II CENTURY RIDE CONTINUED

WEEK	MONDAY	TUESDAY	WEDNESDAY
10	Day off or	S1a	Day off or
	strength train	6 × 20 sec. (100 sec. RI)	strength train
	(see text)	1:00	(see text)
11	Day off or	S4	Day off
	strength train		
	(see text)	1:00	
12	Day off	S4	Day off
		1:00	

The Saturday ride stays an aerobic ride, in zones 1 and 2. The Sunday rides get longer, and the ride in Week 5 includes zone 4 to 5a intensities.

Week 6

Week 6 is for recovery; training volume is reduced so that your body gets stronger and faster. Tuesday and Thursday are form workouts. The Saturday ride is an aerobic ride on a rolling course. The Sunday ride is only two hours, but it is the first ride in which the intensity is opened up. Ride as fast as you feel like riding. If you're feeling strong, push the pace. If you are still feeling tired, keep the ride easy.

Weeks 7 and 8

These weeks follow the structure of previous work weeks. Tuesday is a form workout, and Thursday is an interval day. The Thursday intervals in this block are uphill or hill repeats and are done at zone 4 to 5a intensity. Start each repeat in the same location and use the downhill portions to spin easy and recover. Don't worry if coasting and spinning downhill back to your starting point take longer than the designated rest time. If the interval specifies *more* rest than you get on the downhill portion, just spin easy until it's time to begin the interval again. In other words, take your full rest time.

The Saturday ride is an aerobic ride. The length of the Sunday ride continues to build, reaching 4:00 to 4:30 at the end of Week 8. The volume of intensity is also building during these weeks.

THURSDAY	FRIDAY	SATURDAY	SUNDAY	WEEKLY TOTAL
A2	Day off	E2a	E4	
3-4 × 3 min. (3 min. RI)			-30-50 min. z4/5a	8:00-9:00
1:00		2:00-2:30	4:00-4:30	
A7	Day off	M2 (z4/5a)	A1d	
4 × 90 sec. (3 min. RI)		4-5 × 4 min. (60 sec. RI)		6:00
1:00		1:00	3:00	
A7	Day off	S7	Century ride	
3 × 90 sec. (3 min. RI)				8:15-8:30
0:45		0:45-1:00	5:45	

If you find that the weekend training is too much, first cut the time of the Saturday workout to no more than 2:00. Keep the Sunday rides at the low ends of the ranges given for time and intensity. If it is still too much, reduce the volume of the intensity down more.

Week 9

Week 9 is a much-deserved, and -needed, week of rest. As in Week 3, you have two 45-minute form workouts. Saturday is the repeat time trial mentioned in Week 3. (Are you faster?) Sunday is an easy aerobic ride. If you're tired, cut this workout down.

Week 10

Week 10 is the toughest training week of the plan in terms of training volume and intensity. After this week, the program is tapered; that is, volume decreases. Some intensity remains in the plan.

The Tuesday workout is one you have completed in past weeks. The Thursday workout includes very fast intervals. As always, be sure to eat nutritious foods and drink plenty of fluids to help your recovery.

The Saturday ride is aerobic, and the Sunday ride is long and includes some high-intensity riding. This is a great ride to put the final touches on your eating and drinking strategy for event day.

If possible, schedule any pre-event maintenance for your bike for this week or next.

Week 11

If you have been strength training, reduce your program to only one day this week and keep the weight light. Thursday, Saturday, and Sunday workouts all include some intensity. Be cautious with your energy. If you are feeling run-down, halve the intensity on each of those days. If you are feeling tired Sunday or you need the extra recovery, cut this ride to 2:00.

Week 12

The workouts in Week 12 need to be short, as you lead up to the event. Don't be afraid to reduce or halve the workout times. Eliminate all strength training workouts this week.

For the event, ride at the intensities you have practiced in your long rides. Plan to ride the second 50 miles with greater effort than the first 50 miles. In other words, rein yourself in and do not start too fast. Keep yourself at a steady rate of fueling and hydration. By monitoring and controlling your nutrition and intensity, you will have a solid finish. Ride strong!

PART III

TOURING
TRAINING PLANS

Three-Day Tour
25–30 MILES PER DAY
Level I

One of the best ways to enjoy the countryside is to tour it by bicycle. In recent years, bike tours that suit individual needs have been much easier to find. Several companies offer tours designed for all levels of tour cyclists, from new to experienced.

The plan in this chapter is perfect for a first-time tour rider with very limited fitness. In just 10 weeks, you can be ready to enjoy a long weekend or three consecutive days on your bike, riding 25 to 30 miles per day.

PROFILE

This plan is designed for a Level I cyclist or someone who currently goes to the gym and participates in group fitness activities a couple of times per week. Optimally, you are already riding your bike (or a spinning bike) at least once a week for 45 to 60 minutes.

If you are currently inactive, you can use this plan if you include two preparation weeks before Week 1. Ride your bike three days per week, 30 to 45 minutes per day at zone 1 to 2 intensity, before beginning the plan.

For the next 10 weeks, you can commit to riding four days per week, which includes a long ride that builds to 2:30. Take a look at Table 9.1 to see if the plan looks manageable for your lifestyle.

In addition to your commitment to training, you have a commitment to recovery. You know that improved performance is accompanied by improved recovery techniques and high-density nutrition. In short, just as you must complete the training sessions, you need to get adequate rest and eat nutritious foods that fuel a high-performance body (see Chapter 3).

GOAL

Your goal is to ride on three consecutive days, 25 to 30 miles each day, averaging 12 to 15 mph, after 10 weeks of training.

THE PLAN OVERVIEW

The basic layout of the plan in Table 9.1 includes a day off or an optional strength training day on Mondays and Wednesdays. On most weeks, rides are shown on Tuesdays, Thursdays, Saturdays, and Sundays. Fridays are usually days off.

Notice that Weeks 7 and 8 schedule rides on Fridays. This design is to help you build the ability to ride three consecutive days and is part of your final preparation for the event.

If you currently have a strength training program, you can continue that program on your days off from cycling. You may find that you have to modify the routine, reducing sets, repetitions, or weight so that strength training doesn't negatively impact your cycling.

If you are not strength training but would like to incorporate a weight-room routine in your workout plan, I suggest beginning with the anatomical adaptation phase of strength training described in Chapter 22. Keep the weight relatively light for the first two weeks.

As your body adapts to the routine, you can slightly increase the weight and reduce the number of repetitions to 12 to 15 (from the 15 to 20 suggested in Chapter 22). You can maintain this reduced range for both your strength training days, or you can do 12 to 15 reps on one day and 15 to 20 reps with less weight on the other day. You might have to experiment to see which routine works best for you.

PLAN DETAILS

The overall structure of most of the plan features form workouts on Tuesday and Thursday and endurance-building workouts on Saturday and Sunday. The rides are mostly aerobic until Week 4, when you begin work on building lactate threshold speed. Explanations of the workout codes used throughout this plan can be found in Chapter 21. Here, let's break down the plan by week.

Weeks 1 and 2

On Mondays and Wednesdays, the plan notes "day off or strength train." As mentioned earlier, you can keep a current strength training routine or begin one; strength training, however, is not mandatory.

The Tuesday workouts are 30 to 45 minutes long and include accelerations to help you work on leg speed. The Thursday sessions include isolated leg training to help remove any dead spots from your pedal stroke.

The Saturday rides are 30 to 45 minutes long and are easy, zone 1 endurance rides that focus on cadence. The Sunday rides increase the intensity into zone 2.

Week 3

This training plan is structured in three-week cycles: two-week periods of "work" followed by a rest week. Week 3 is a rest week, with reduced training volume to allow your body to recover. Remember that the recovery period is equal in importance to the work period. You will not become a stronger cyclist if your body is constantly fatigued.

The Thursday workout is new this week. It is a fartlek (speed play) workout, which is mostly aerobic with a few accelerations, inserted as you please.

On Sunday of this week, do a 5-mile aerobic time trial. Full instructions are found in Chapter 21.

Weeks 4 and 5

These two weeks have the isolated leg workouts on Tuesdays, and they are now 45 minutes in length. The acceleration workouts move to Thursdays and are each an hour long. The Saturday endurance rides are each an hour long at zone 1 to 2 intensity, while Sunday rides begin to include some zone 3 work. Try to keep the accumulated volume of zone 3 intensity to 15 minutes or less. The Week 5 Sunday ride is 1:30 and a good opportunity to practice the fueling and hydration techniques discussed in Chapter 3.

Week 6

Week 6 is a recovery week, similar to Week 3. The major difference is that instead of an aerobic time trial on Sunday, you have your first interval session. You use these intervals to begin working on lactate threshold speed.

Weeks 7 and 8

The Tuesday workouts in these two weeks are negative-split workouts that help you learn how to control your intensity and pace your speed. These skills are critical and become even more important as you improve your cycling speed.

This two-week block includes no Thursday workouts but features Friday workouts instead. The Friday, Saturday, and Sunday combination helps you prepare for three consecutive days of bike touring. The Friday workouts are zone 3 intervals, which help build the volume of zone 3 intensity your body can tolerate. Saturday rides are endurance rides, and Sunday rides are mixed-hill rides that include lactate threshold training.

TABLE 9.1 LEVEL I THREE-DAY TOUR, 25–30 MILES PER DAY

WEEK	MONDAY	TUESDAY	WEDNESDAY	THURSDAY
1	Day off or strength train (see text)	S3 4–6 0:30	Day off or strength train (see text)	S2 0:30
2	Day off or strength train (see text)	S3 4–6 0:45	Day off or strength train (see text)	S2 0:45
3	Day off	S2 0:30	Day off or strength train (see text)	S4 0:30
4	Day off or strength train (see text)	S2 0:45	Day off or strength train (see text)	S3 6–8 1:00
5	Day off or strength train (see text)	S2 0:45	Day off or strength train (see text)	S3 6–8 1:00
6	Day off	S2 0:30	Day off or strength train (see text)	S4 0:45
7	Day off or strength train (see text)	E2c 0:45	Day off or strength train (see text)	Day off
8	Day off or strength train (see text)	E2c 1:00	Day off or strength train (see text)	Day off
9	Day off	S4 0:30	Day off or strength train (see text)	M7 3–4 × 90 sec. (3 min. RI) 0:45
10	E2c 0:30	Day off	S4 0:30	Day off

Tours

FRIDAY	SATURDAY	SUNDAY	WEEKLY TOTAL
Day off	E1b	E2a	2:30
	0:30	1:00	
Day off	E1b	E2a	3:15
	0:45	1:00	
Day off	Day off	T1	2:00
		1:00	
Day off	E2b	E3	3:45
		-15 min. z3	
	1:00	1:00	
Day off	E2a	E3	4:15
		-15 min. z3	
	1:00	1:30	
Day off	Day off	M2 (z3)	2:15
		5–6 × 3 min. (60 sec. RI)	
		1:00	
M2 (z3)	E2b	E3	5:15
4–5 × 4 min. (60 sec. RI)		-20–30 min. z3	
1:00	1:30	2:00	
M2 (z3)	E2a	E3	6:30
4–5 × 5 min. (2 min. RI)		-20–30 min. z3	
1:00	2:00	2:30	
Day off	Day off	T1	2:15
		1:00	
Ride	Ride	Ride	6:00–8:30
25–30 mi.	25–30 mi.	25–30 mi.	
1:40–2:30	1:40–2:30	1:40–2:30	

Week 9

Week 9 is your recovery week before the bike tour. Tuesday is a fartlek ride, and Thursday includes three or four 90-second intervals that build intensity into zone 3. The Sunday ride is a repeat of your original aerobic time trial, to see how much you have improved over the past several weeks. It should be fun to see your fitness gains!

Week 10

This week is bike-tour week. Short, 30-minute workouts are shown on Monday and Wednesday. These workouts help keep your legs feeling fresh for the tour while you are resting. For most cyclists, completing short workouts is better than not riding at all, which can leave legs feeling heavy and slow.

On the bike tour, enjoy yourself and remember the pacing skills you learned in the training plan. Keep yourself fueled and hydrated during the ride. Most of all, have fun and enjoy the scenery!

Three-Day Tour
40–50 MILES PER DAY
Level I

Several charity rides and bike tours are three-day rides with ride distances of 40 to 50 miles per day. These tour packages are within reach of many busy people. With planning and a 12-week commitment, a healthy person with minimal fitness can be ready to spend three to four hours per day, for three days, on a bike tour.

Want to build your fitness, experience scenery you can't see or feel from inside a car, and enjoy a bike tour? Read on.

PROFILE

This plan is designed for a Level I rider who is, ideally, riding three or four days per week for 30 to 60 minutes—whether in an indoor cycling class or outdoors. If you are currently inactive, consider completing Weeks 1, 2, and 5 of the plan in Chapter 6 before beginning this plan.

For the duration of this 12-week training plan, you can commit to riding four days per week. Your longest rides build to approximately three and four hours, on Saturdays and Sundays in Weeks 9 and 10 (see Table 10.1).

Due to the volume of training in this program, you need to focus on recovery as much as on the training. Improved performance is accompanied by recovery techniques and high-density nutrition. In short, just as you need to complete the training sessions, you need to get adequate rest and eat nutritious foods that fuel a high-performance body (see Chapter 3).

GOAL

Your goal is to ride on three consecutive days, 40 to 50 miles each day, averaging 12 to 15 mph, after 12 weeks of training.

THE PLAN OVERVIEW

Take a look at the plan in Table 10.1. Due to everyday, noncycling commitments, many people find it easier to exercise early in the week. For this reason, Friday is always a day off.

You can see how the training volume for weekends builds through Week 10, except for during your recovery weeks. Also, although it may not be obvious at first glance, several weeks of the plan include rides on three consecutive days—Saturday, Sunday, and Monday. This format prepares you physically and mentally for riding three days of a bike tour.

Tuesdays and Thursdays are optional strength training days. If you currently have a strength training program, you can continue that program on your days off from cycling. You may find that you have to modify the routine, reducing sets, repetitions, or weight so that strength training doesn't negatively impact your cycling.

If you are not strength training but would like to incorporate a weight-room routine in your workout plan, I suggest beginning with the anatomical adaptation phase of strength training described in Chapter 22. Keep the weight relatively light for the first two weeks.

As your body adapts to the routine, you can slightly increase the weight and reduce the number of repetitions to 12 to 15 (from the 15 to 20 suggested in Chapter 22). You can maintain this reduced range for both your strength training days, or you can do 12 to 15 reps on one day and 15 to 20 reps with less weight on the other day. You might have to experiment to see which routine works best for you.

PLAN DETAILS

The overall structure of the plan begins with a form workout on Monday, an endurance workout on Wednesday, an easy ride on Saturday, and an endurance-building ride on Sunday. The Sunday rides build in length on every non-rest week, so you are riding 4:00 by the end of Weeks 9 and 10. Explanations of the workout codes used throughout this plan can be found in Chapter 21. Here, let's break down the plan by week.

Weeks 1 through 4

This training plan begins with a four-week block to get you jump-started on your fitness. Monday workouts are intended to improve your cycling efficiency. Each workout is either an acceleration session to improve your leg speed or an isolated-leg workout to improve pedaling economy.

On Tuesdays and Thursdays, the plan notes "day off or strength train." As mentioned earlier, you can keep a current strength training routine or begin one; strength training, however, is not mandatory.

Wednesday workouts are zone 1 to 2 intensity to build your overall endurance. In Week 4, you have your first negative-split workout, which is critical for learning how to pace yourself.

Saturday rides begin at 0:45 and build to 1:30 at an easy, zone 1 intensity. Sunday rides begin at 1:00 and build to 2:30 by the end of Week 4. To be successful in using this plan, you need to stay on track with the long rides. Try to keep your durations close to the designated times. If you find you need to reduce the intensity some, that's fine. The volume is more important than the intensity.

Because you are accomplishing long rides early in the plan, be sure to establish your fueling and hydration regimen early on as well. Find fuels that you enjoy and a pacing routine that is easy for you to keep.

Week 5

The plan includes three major blocks of training, and the next two blocks are each three weeks long. Week 5 is a reduced-volume week to help you recover and get ready for the next block. Be sure to reduce your training this week and do not be tempted to do more than is shown in the plan.

On Saturday, you have another negative-split workout. Whereas the Week 4 workout was only 1:00, now the workout is 2:00 and requires more discipline. A disciplined pace is a valuable tool that will help you far into the future.

Weeks 6 and 7

Week 6 begins with your first session of intervals, which begin to build your lactate threshold speed. The intervals are placed early in the week so you can give them a high-quality effort after your Week 5 rest.

Saturdays are zone 1 to 2 endurance rides. You can ride up to 30 minutes more than shown in the plan if you have the time and energy to do so. The Sunday rides in this block include more zone 3 intensity than the last block. As in Weeks 1 to 4, if you find the intensity is too much, reduce it and try to keep the ride lengths as assigned in the plan. For the Monday ride in Week 7, if you have the time and energy, ride for up to 90 minutes.

Week 8

This is a rest week similar to Week 5, with training volume reduced to allow for sufficient recovery before the next training block. The only new workout is on Wednesday, and details can be found in Chapter 21.

TABLE 10.1 LEVEL I THREE-DAY TOUR, 40–50 MILES PER DAY

WEEK	MONDAY	TUESDAY	WEDNESDAY	THURSDAY
1	S3 4–6 0:30	Day off or strength train (see text)	E2a 0:30	Day off or strength train (see text)
2	S2 0:45	Day off or strength train (see text)	E2a 0:45	Day off or strength train (see text)
3.	S3 6–8 1:00	Day off or strength train (see text)	E2a 1:00	Day off or strength train (see text)
4	S2 1:00	Day off or strength train (see text)	E2c 1:00	Day off or strength train (see text)
5	S3 4–6 0:45	Day off	E2a 0:45	Day off or strength train (see text)
6	M2 (z3) 4–5 × 4 min. (60 sec. RI) 1:00	Day off or strength train (see text)	E1b 1:00	Day off or strength train (see text)
7	E2c 1:00	Day off or strength train (see text)	M2 (z3) 3–4 × 5 min. (2 min. RI) 1:00	Day off or strength train (see text)
8	S3 4–6 0:45	Day off	M7 4 × 90 sec. (3 min. RI) 0:45	Day off or strength train (see text)
9	M2 (z3) 3–4 × 6 min. (2 min. RI) 1:00–1:30	Day off or strength train (see text)	S4 1:00	Day off or strength train (see text)

FRIDAY	SATURDAY	SUNDAY	WEEKLY TOTAL
Day off	E1a	E2a	
			2:45
	0:45	1:00	
Day off	E1a	E2a	
			3:45
	0:45	1:30	
Day off	E1a	E3	
		<15 min. z3	5:00
	1:00	2:00	
Day off	E1a	E3	
		-15–20 min. z3	6:00
	1:30	2:30	
Day off	E2c	Day off	
			3:30
	2:00		
Day off	E2a	E3	
		-20–30 min. z3	6:30
	1:30	3:00	
Day off	E2a	E3	
		-30–40 min. z3	7:30
	2:00	3:30	
Day off	E2c	Day off	
			3:30
	2:00		
Day off	E4	E2a	
	<15 min. z4/5a		8:30–9:30
	2:30–3:00	4:00	

CONTINUED

Tours

TABLE 10.1 LEVEL I THREE-DAY TOUR, 40–50 MILES PER DAY CONTINUED

WEEK	MONDAY	TUESDAY	WEDNESDAY	THURSDAY
10	M2 (z3) 2–3 × 8 min. (2 min. RI) 1:00–1:30	E2c 0:30	S4 1:00	Day off or strength train (see text)
11	S3 1:00	Day off	S4 0:45	Day off or strength train (see text)
12	Day off	M7 4 × 90 sec. (3 min. RI) 0:45	Day off	Day off

Weeks 9 and 10

These weeks provide the last push of training before your event. You have zone 3 intervals on Mondays, and you can ride for either 60 or 90 minutes, depending on your time and energy. Wednesday rides are fartlek rides, for some form work and recovery.

The combination of long and intense rides for this block moves from Sunday to Saturday. The Saturday rides include more intensity than those on Sunday. You can also increase these Saturday rides by up to 30 minutes.

The Sunday rides are kept in intensity zones 1 and 2 but are 4 hours in length. The toughest three-day block of this plan is the end of Week 9 to the beginning of Week 10. Accomplishing this three-day block is a significant milestone in your fitness. If you can successfully complete the block, you will be ready for your tour.

Week 11

Training volume is reduced this week to allow you to absorb the benefits of the last two weeks of training. The last workout of Week 11 opens up the intensity. Although the instructions in Chapter 21 are to "ride as you feel," be smart. Limit the zone 5 training to a manageable level, keeping it well under 20 accumulated minutes.

FRIDAY	SATURDAY	SUNDAY	WEEKLY TOTAL
Day off	E4	E2a	
	~20-30 min. z4/5a		9:30-10:30
	3:00-3:30	4:00	
Day off	A1d	Day off	
	<20 min. z5a		3:45
	2:00		
Ride	Ride	Ride	
40-50 mi.	40-50 mi.	40-50 mi.	8:45-13:15
2:40-4:10	2:40-4:10	2:40-4:10	

Week 12

Week 12 is your event week. If you have been strength training, eliminate it completely this week. On the first day of the tour, you may be tempted to tear out because you are rested and feel great. But hold back some and plan to ride your strongest on the last day of the tour.

How strong you ride on all three days will depend on how consistent you were with your training and how well you take care of yourself during the tour. Pacing your intensity, fueling, and hydrating are critical components of your success. Ride smart, ride fast, and have a blast!

Three-Day Tour
40–50 MILES PER DAY
Level II

Often, regular cyclists look for three-day events as great fitness getaways. Riding your bike and seeing the countryside for three solid days is a nice way to get rid of daily stress, enjoy your health, and enjoy riding with other people. Cycling with a group can provide the motivation to ride a little longer and a little faster than you would normally. Or perhaps your fitness can motivate others!

PROFILE

This plan is designed for a Level II rider who is currently riding two weekdays for an hour each, whether outdoors or in an indoor spinning class. These weekday rides already include some intensity; you push the speed from time to time.

Your long weekend ride is about two hours, and perhaps you take a second weekend ride that lasts about an hour. The two-hour ride includes some intensity as well. In other words, from time to time, you are pushing yourself for a stronger and faster performance.

If you are currently inactive, consider using a few weeks of one of the other plans to build up your cycling volume, so you can comfortably do the first week of the plan shown in Table 11.1.

For the duration of this 12-week training plan, you can commit to riding four days per week. Your longest rides build to approximately three and two hours, on Saturdays and Sundays in Weeks 7 and 8.

Due to the volume of training in this program, you need to focus on recovery as much as on the training. Improved performance is accompanied by recovery techniques and high-density nutrition. In short, just as you need to complete the training sessions, you need to get adequate rest and eat nutritious foods that fuel a high-performance body (see Chapter 3).

GOAL

Your goal is to ride three consecutive days, 40 to 50 miles each day, averaging 16 to 18 miles per hour, after 12 weeks of training. You want to push yourself and be one of the stronger riders on the tour.

THE PLAN OVERVIEW

Take a look at the plan in Table 11.1. The pattern is two weeks of training and one week of recovery, or three-week cycles. These cycles are grouped into three major blocks of training and one block of tapering volume to get you rested and ready for your event. Volume does not build significantly throughout the plan, but training intensity builds.

The Monday workouts are power intervals. These short intervals are intended to build your cycling power with short, high-intensity sprints that focus on leg speed with a load. Wednesday workouts are interval sessions dedicated to improving your speed at lactate threshold. Fridays are optional riding days that focus on leg speed *without* a load. For all Friday workouts except in Week 11, you can ride anywhere between 30 and 60 minutes. If you have more energy and feel great, ride longer.

Saturdays are big days on the bike. The long ride builds from two to three hours and its intensity increases throughout the plan. The Saturday ride in Week 3 is a time trial (TT). Alternatively, you can conduct the TT before beginning the plan; if you do, just make the Saturday ride in Week 3 a mixed-terrain ride with intensities into zone 3 and accumulate no more than 20 minutes in zone 3. The Sunday rides are aerobic, with no intensity higher than zone 2.

Although it may not be obvious at first glance, several weeks of the plan include rides on three consecutive days—Saturday, Sunday, and Monday. This format prepares you physically and mentally for riding three days of a bike tour.

The plan shows optional strength training days on Tuesdays and Thursdays. If you currently have a strength training program, you can continue that program on your days off from cycling. You may find that you have to modify the routine, reducing sets, repetitions, or weight so that strength training doesn't negatively impact your cycling.

If you are not strength training but would like to incorporate a weight-room routine in your workout plan, I suggest beginning with the anatomical adaptation phase of strength training described in Chapter 22. Keep the weight relatively light for the first two weeks.

As your body adapts to the routine, you can slightly increase the weight and reduce the number of repetitions to 12 to 15 (from the 15 to 20 suggested in Chapter 22). You can maintain this reduced range for both your strength training days, or you can do 12 to 15 reps on one day and 15 to 20 reps with less weight on the other day. You might have to experiment to see which routine works best for you.

PLAN DETAILS

Explanations of the workout codes used throughout this plan can be found in Chapter 21. Here, let's break down the plan by week.

Weeks 1 and 2

Monday workouts get you ready for higher-intensity sprints later in the plan. You are beginning with 10 seconds of effort: You build power output throughout the entire 10 seconds, so you are going nearly all-out at the end. You should feel strong and fast and should produce high speeds by the end of each 10-second effort.

On Tuesdays and Thursdays, the plan notes "day off or strength train." As mentioned earlier, you can keep a current strength training routine or begin one; strength training, however, is not mandatory.

The Wednesday sessions work on your lactate threshold speed, or the ability to hold a high intensity for a long period. This training block begins work on this skill using zone 3 intervals.

The Friday sessions are form workouts and, again, they are optional. Depending on your personal time constraints, you can ride from 30 to 60 minutes. Friday rides can also be floating rides for you: Ride when you can, and skip riding when you are too busy or too tired.

The Saturday rides in this block are two hours long and include a specified amount of zone 3 training. If your bike tour will be hilly, ride a hilly course on this day, and you may want to ride with a group of friends. Depending on the group, you may have to push the intensity to get the training effect noted in your plan, or you may have to sit in the back of the group to keep from going too hard. Be sure the ride meets your needs.

The Sunday ride in this block is an aerobic endurance ride. Keep the intensity at zone 2 or lower for this ride.

Week 3

Week 3 is a reduced-volume week to help you recover and get ready for the next block of training. The Monday and Wednesday workouts are 45 minutes long.

The Saturday ride in this block is a 20-minute TT, if you did not do one before beginning the plan. This TT is a benchmark of fitness. You repeat the TT in Week 9. (As noted earlier, if you did a TT before the plan, make this Saturday ride a mixed-terrain ride with intensities into zone 3 and accumulate no more than 20 minutes in zone 3.)

TABLE 11.1 LEVEL II THREE-DAY TOUR, 40–50 MILES PER DAY

WEEK	MONDAY	TUESDAY	WEDNESDAY
1	P1 4–6 × 10 sec. (4 min. 50 sec. RI) 1:00	Day off or strength train (see text)	M2 (z3) 4–5 × 3 min (60 sec. RI) 1:00
2	P1 4–6 × 10 sec. (4 min. 50 sec. RI) 1:00	Day off or strength train (see text)	M2 (z3) 4–5 × 4 min. (60 sec. RI) 1:00
3	S4 0:45	Day off or strength train (see text)	E2b 0:45
4	P1 5–7 × 20 sec. (4 min. 40 sec. RI) 1:00	Day off or strength train (see text)	M2 (z4/5a) 4–5 × 3 min. (60 sec. RI) 1:00
5	P1 5–7 × 20 sec. (4 min. 40 sec. RI) 1:00	Day off or strength train (see text)	M2 (z4/5a) 4–5 × 4 min. (60 sec. RI) 1:00
6	S4 0:45	Day off or strength train (see text)	E2b 0:45
7	P2 4–6 × 10 sec. (4 min. 50 sec. RI) 1:00	Day off or strength train (see text)	M2 (z4/5a) 3–4 × 6 min. (2 min. RI) 1:00
8	P2 5–7 × 10 sec. (4 min. 50 sec. RI) 1:00	Day off or strength train (see text)	M2 (z4/5a) 2–4 × 8 min. (2 min. RI) 1:00
9	S4 0:45	Day off or strength train (see text)	E2b 0:45

THURSDAY	FRIDAY	SATURDAY	SUNDAY	WEEKLY TOTAL
Day off or	S3 (optional)	E3	E2a	
strength train	4-8	~15-20 min. z3		5:30-6:00
(see text)	0:30-1:00	2:00	1:00	
Day off or	S3 (optional)	E3	E2a	
strength train	4-8	~20-30 min. z3		6:00-6:30
(see text)	0:30-1:00	2:00	1:30	
Day off	Day off	T2	E1b	
		20 min.		4:15
		2:00	0:45	
Day off or	S3 (optional)	E4	E2a	
strength train	4-8	~15-20 min. z4/5a		6:30-7:00
(see text)	0:30-1:00	2:30	1:30	
Day off or	S3 (optional)	E4	E2a	
strength train	4-8	~20-30 min. z4/5a		6:30-7:00
(see text)	0:30-1:00	2:30	1:30	
Day off	Day off	A1d	E1b	
				4:15
		2:00	0:45	
Day off or	S3 (optional)	A1c	E2a	
strength train	4-8			7:30-8:00
(see text)	0:30-1:00	3:00	2:00	
Day off or	S3 (optional)	A1c	E2a	
strength train	4-8			7:30-8:00
(see text)	0:30-1:00	3:00	2:00	
Day off	Day off	T2	E1b	
		20 min.		4:15
		2:00	0:45	

CONTINUED

TABLE 11.1 LEVEL II THREE-DAY TOUR, 40–50 MILES PER DAY CONTINUED

WEEK	MONDAY	TUESDAY	WEDNESDAY
10	P2 5–7 × 10 sec. (4 min. 50 sec. RI) 1:00	Day off or strength train (see text)	M7 4 × 90 sec. (3 min. RI) 0:45
11	P4 0:45	Day off or strength train (see text)	M6 (z1/5a) 0:45
12	Day off	M7 4 × 90 sec. (3 min. RI) 0:45	Day off

Weeks 4 and 5

This block begins on Monday, with power-building sprints. Note that the work time has increased to 20 seconds. The threshold workouts on Wednesdays continue, but the intensity has increased into zones 4 to 5a. The Saturday rides increase in intensity and length (to 2:30). The Sunday rides remain in zones 1 to 2 and hold at 1:30.

Week 6

Week 6 is a reduced-volume week for rest, with the weekday rides holding at 45 minutes. Do not be tempted to increase the ride length. The Saturday ride is a group ride that allows you to ride how you feel. If you do not ride with a group, ride at a how-you-feel level on your own, pushing the hills and randomly pushing the pace.

Weeks 7 and 8

The Monday workouts in this block move to all-out sprints that are 10 seconds long. The Wednesday intervals increase in length to eight minutes in Week 8.

The Saturday rides include fast group riding. Push yourself on hills and on some of the flat sections. Be very aware of your fueling and hydration during these rides, as it is easy to get distracted during group rides and neglect good nutrition practices. The Sunday aerobic sessions increase to two hours in this block.

THURSDAY	FRIDAY	SATURDAY	SUNDAY	WEEKLY TOTAL
Day off or	S3 (optional)	E4	E2a	
strength train	4-8			6:15-6:45
(see text)	0:30-1:00	2:30	1:30	
Day off	S3 (optional)	A1c	E1b	
	4-6			5:00
	0:30	2:00	1:00	
S7	Ride	Ride	Ride	
	40-50 mi.	40-50 mi.	40-50 mi.	7:30-10:15
0:30	2:15-3:10	2:15-3:10	2:15-3:10	

Week 9

This week is a repeat of Week 3, including the TT. Did you improve your speed?

You have some spare time this week because of reduced training, so take care of any tasks you may have been putting off. If you need new clothing or equipment before the tour, now is the time to find it. Get your bike scheduled for a pre-tour tune-up as well.

Weeks 10 and 11

Training volume begins to decrease during these weeks, though you are keeping some intensity in the program. Do not be tempted to increase volume right up to the tour. You want your legs to feel rested and strong for the event.

Week 12

Be sure to keep your training volume low this week. If you have been strength training, eliminate it completely. On the tour itself, try to hold back some on the first day. Pay close attention to your fueling and hydration. Keep alert to car traffic and to other riders who may get distracted and ride erratically.

Plan to ride very strong and fast on the second day of the tour. On the third and final day, end the tour on a high note. This might mean riding more slowly than usual and enjoying the day with good friends. Or it might mean riding very fast and enjoying the challenge of riding with old or newfound friends. Enjoy!

One-Week Tour
60–80 MILES PER DAY
Level I

I can still remember how I felt during my first weeklong bike tour. Although I was an experienced cyclist and I raced multisport events, I had never ridden my bicycle on seven consecutive days. Additionally, the tour was a hard route with lots of climbing. I worried that I wouldn't be able to complete the ride.

Not only did I complete the tour, but I also got hooked on weeklong bike tours and have done one every year since then. As I write this book, I'm heading into my tenth year of bicycle touring.

A weeklong bike tour is a great way to escape your normal routine. You spend a fabulous week thinking about nothing other than riding your bike from point A to point B, deciding what fuels to consume, and resting.

For some cyclists, the bike tour is the end of the training journey. For others, the tour is a nice boost of "crash training," or completing a period of riding volume and intensity that is much greater than normal. When properly planned and executed, crash training boosts your fitness significantly. The trick is to rest properly before and after the tour, as well as to take care of yourself with recovery fueling and plenty of rest during the tour.

If you are looking for a plan to help you prepare for a great week of cycling, read on.

PROFILE

This plan is designed for a cyclist who is at Level I in terms of weeklong touring. You are currently riding two weekdays for an hour each, whether outdoors or in an indoor spinning class. The rides may or may not include intensity. On weekends, your long ride is an hour long. Sometimes, though rarely, you get out for a second, short ride with friends or family. But most weeks, you ride three days per week total, for about an hour per ride.

For the duration of this 12-week training plan, you can commit to riding five days per week most of the time. Your longest rides on the weekends build gradually to three and four hours on Saturday and Sunday in Week 9, with options to extend those rides if you have more time and fitness. The longest ride is five hours on Sunday in Week 11.

Some of the strategies utilized in this plan include blocking long-ride days together, building the length of long rides, and building the volume of intensity at the same time you are building volume. This process must be managed with care.

Due to the volume of training in this program, you need to focus on recovery as much as on the training, especially the further you progress into the plan. Daily recovery is critical during your tour. This means getting adequate rest and eating nutrient-dense foods (see Chapter 3).

GOAL

Your goal is to ride six or seven days of a weeklong tour. Distances average between 60 and 80 miles per day, though some days the distance might be longer or shorter. You want to complete the tour, riding the distance each day. You estimate that you can average 12 to 15 mph for the entire tour.

THE PLAN OVERVIEW

Take a look at the plan in Table 12.1. The pattern is two or three weeks of building volume and intensity, followed by a week of rest. Rest weeks reduce training volume while maintaining some intensity throughout the plan. If you manage the plan correctly, you can build volume and intensity simultaneously.

Monday is an optional strength training day. If you currently have a strength training program, you can continue that program on your day off from cycling. You may find that you have to modify the routine, reducing sets, repetitions, or weight so that strength training doesn't negatively impact your cycling.

If you are not strength training but would like to incorporate a weight-room routine in your workout plan, I suggest beginning with the anatomical adaptation phase of strength training described in Chapter 22. Keep the weight relatively light for the first two weeks. As your body adapts to the routine, you can slightly increase the weight and reduce the number of repetitions to 12 to 15 (from the 15 to 20 suggested in Chapter 22).

Tuesday workouts are primarily form work. Wednesday workouts begin as form work and move to threshold intervals as the plan progresses. Thursdays are shown as days off.

Friday workouts begin as on-the-bike strength training and become aerobic workouts when they reach 90 minutes in length. Saturday and Sunday rides build in length. Additionally, one of the weekend rides builds in intensity.

PLAN DETAILS

Explanations of the workout codes used throughout this plan can be found in Chapter 21. Here, let's break down the plan by week.

Weeks 1 through 4

On Mondays, the plan notes "day off or strength train." As mentioned earlier, you can keep a current strength training routine or begin one; strength training, however, is not mandatory.

In this first training block, Tuesday and Wednesday workouts are intended to improve your form and build your aerobic endurance. Thursdays are days off. The Friday workouts are on-the-bike strength sessions; begin conservatively with these. Saturday and Sunday rides are aerobic and work on building your long-ride endurance. The Saturday ride in Week 4 includes a small volume of zone 3 intensity, or the beginning of lactate threshold training.

Week 4 is also your first rest week. Training volume totals 4:00 for this week, the same as during Week 1. Although a reduction from 6:30 to 4:00 of training may not seem like much, it is enough to give your body a break before Week 5 training, which totals 8:00.

Weeks 5 through 7

In this training block, you begin to work on lactate threshold in earnest. While Tuesday workouts remain form work, the Wednesday workouts move to low-end threshold intervals. Fridays remain on-the-bike strength days, and Saturdays remain aerobic endurance days.

On Sunday, the rides build in length and you add some zone 3 work, but don't get carried away with the zone 3 volume. If your bike tour includes a good deal of hill climbing, be sure your weekend rides include hills. Again, don't overload on force and intensity by attempting routes similar to the Alpe d'Huez. Save those off-the-chart rides for when you progress in your riding ability.

Weeks 8 through 10

This block caps off your training, wrapping up your lactate threshold training and building the length of your longest ride. At the end of Week 9, your ride time over three consecutive days should total about 8:30 to 9:30 for a weekly total of 12:00 to 13:00, not including strength training. This weekly total is approximately 50 percent of the ride time during your tour. If 50 percent seems low, rest assured it is plenty to achieve your goals.

TABLE 12.1 LEVEL I ONE-WEEK TOUR, 60–80 MILES PER DAY

WEEK	MONDAY	TUESDAY	WEDNESDAY	THURSDAY
1	Day off or	S1	S2	Day off
	strength train			
	(see text)	1:00	1:00	
2	Day off or	S1	S2	Day off
	strength train			
	(see text)	1:00	1:00	
3	Day off or	S1a	S3	Day off
	strength train	6–8 × 30 sec. (90 sec. RI)	6–8	
	(see text)	1:00	1:30	
4	Day off or	E1a	S4	Day off
	strength train			
	(see text)	0:45	0:45	
5	Day off or	S3	M2 (z3)	Day off
	strength train	6–8	5–7 × 3 min. (60 sec. RI)	
	(see text)	1:00	1:30	
6	Day off or	S3	M2 (z3)	Day off
	strength train	6–8	4–6 × 4 min. (60 sec. RI)	
	(see text)	1:00	1:30	
7	Day off or	E1a	S4	Day off
	strength train			
	(see text)	0:45	0:45	
8	Day off or	E2c	M2 (z4/5a)	Day off
	strength train		5–7 × 3 min. (60 sec. RI)	
	(see text)	1:00	2:00	
9	Day off or	E2a	M2 (z4/5a)	Day off
	strength train		4–6 × 4 min. (60 sec. RI)	
	(see text)	1:30	2:00	

FRIDAY	SATURDAY	SUNDAY	WEEKLY TOTAL
F1	E2c	E2a	4:00
0:30	0:30	1:00	
F1	E2c	E2a	5:00
0:30	1:00	1:30	
F1	E2c	E2a	6:30
0:30	1:30	2:00	
E2b	E3	Day off	4:00
	~10–15 min. z3		
0:30	2:00		
F1	E2a	E3	8:00
		~30 min. z3	
1:00	2:00	2:30	
F1	E2a	E3	9:00
		~20–30 min. z3	
1:00	2:30	3:00	
E2b	E4	Day off	4:00
	~15–20 min. z4/5a		
0:30	2:00		
E2b	E4	E2a	11:00
	~20–30 min. z4/5a		
1:30	3:00	3:30	
E2b	E4	E2a	12:00–13:00
	~30 min. z4/5a		
1:30	3:00	4:00–5:00	

CONTINUED

Tours

TABLE 12.1 LEVEL I ONE-WEEK TOUR, 60–80 MILES PER DAY CONTINUED

WEEK	MONDAY	TUESDAY	WEDNESDAY	THURSDAY
10	Day off or	A7	S4	Day off
	strength train	4 × 90 sec. (3 min. RI)		
	(see text)	1:00	1:30	
11	Day off	A7	S1a	Day off
		4 × 90 sec. (3 min. RI)	4-6 × 30 sec. (90 sec. RI)	
		1:00	0:45	
12	Ride	Ride	Day off	Ride
	(E3)	(A1d)		(E3)
	5:00	5:00		5:00

In Week 8, zone 4 to 5a intensity is added to the Wednesday intervals as well as to the Saturday ride. Note that the intensity has moved from the Sunday rides to the Saturday rides, as Sunday rides become primarily aerobic. For the Sunday ride at the end of Week 9, you can ride between four and five hours. If you're feeling great, aim for five.

You can see that the total volume in Week 10 isn't as low as in your other rest weeks. This is because your low-volume week begins with the Sunday at the end of Week 10 and goes through the Saturday of Week 11. The total training volume for that time period is 4:15.

Weeks 11 and 12

Week 11, then, is your rest week prior to the bike tour. This plan assumes the tour begins on the Sunday of Week 11 and goes through the Saturday of Week 12.

The ride times shown during the tour week serve multiple purposes. First, if you are not joining an organized tour but are planning your own, the ride times can be converted to mileage to help you plan your trip.

Another reason for showing ride times and intensities is to help you plan your riding so you can finish strong. All too often, cyclists begin the first day of a bike tour with too much intensity, too little fueling, and too little hydration. This combination can lead to time in the sag wagon or some miserable days on the bike.

FRIDAY	SATURDAY	SUNDAY	WEEKLY TOTAL
E2b	E4	A1d	
	-15-20 min. z4/5a		7:30
1:00	2:00	2:00	
Day off	S7	Ride	
		(E2a)	7:15
	0:30	5:00	
Ride	Ride	Day off	
(E2a)	(A1d)		25:00+/-
5:00	5:00		

Even though you are rested and feel fantastic, ride easy the first day. If a ride day is designated as E3, don't feel you have to spend any time in zone 3. If you are feeling extended, scale back the intensity.

Enjoy riding your bike, seeing the country (or the world), and building fitness that rewards you for a long time after the tour is over!

One-Week Tour
60–80 MILES PER DAY
Level II

You are a serious recreational athlete. You are already riding consistently at least five days per week and have done so for several months, perhaps years. You may or may not be an experienced bicycle-tour rider. In either case, you want to ride aggressively in an upcoming tour. That means fast—as if it were a stage race for you. And, in a way, it's a stage race with yourself. You want the best results possible.

Before beginning this training plan, you should either complete Chapter 20 training or have the fitness to slip easily into the routine of Week 1. The training volume and intensity of Week 1 are not more, or much more, than you are currently training.

Whether you are using this weeklong tour as a week of training to set you up for other events, or using it as your key event of the year, you want performance.

PROFILE

The plan in this chapter is designed for a Level II cyclist in terms of weeklong touring. You plan to average 16 to 18 mph for the entire tour, and you are currently riding three or four weekdays for an hour each, whether outdoors or in an indoor spinning class. The rides include some intensity. On weekends, your long ride is about three hours long and may or may not be a group ride. You typically do a second ride near the two-hour mark.

For the duration of this 12-week training plan, you can commit to riding five or six days per week most of the time. Your longest rides on the weekends build to approximately four and a half hours, sandwiched by Friday rides of two hours and Sunday rides of three and a half hours. Your longest training weeks are sixteen hours total.

The plan is written with top performance in mind. It also includes a good deal of volume. This schedule may or may not work for you. If you find you cannot fit in all of the rides, eliminate the Thursday rides. The second workouts to eliminate are the Monday strength training sessions. If you can do the frequency of days and the intensity but cannot do the volume of training during the week, cut down those days.

As the training plan progresses, intensity increases. Some athletes perform well on three days of intense riding, while others are better off with only two. You may find you need to take the intensity out of some of the rides or aim for the lowest number of repeats shown. In the optimal case, you are doing the number of workouts and the training volume and intensity that best improve *your* fitness.

Some of the strategies utilized in this training plan include blocking long-ride days together, building the length of long rides, and building intensity at the same time you are building volume. This process must be managed with care.

Due to the volume of training in this plan, you need to focus on recovery as much as on the training, especially since daily recovery is also critical during your tour. This means getting adequate rest and eating nutrient-dense foods (see Chapter 3).

GOAL

Your goal is to ride six or seven days of a weeklong tour. Distances average between 60 and 80 miles per day, though some days the distance might be longer or shorter. You want to complete the tour, riding the distance each day. You estimate that you can average 16 to 18 mph for the entire tour, including on flats, rolling terrain, and hills.

THE PLAN OVERVIEW

Take a look at the plan in Table 13.1. The pattern is two or three weeks of building volume and intensity, followed by a week of rest. Rest weeks reduce training volume while maintaining some intensity, to help you absorb the training and take your fitness to a new level. If you manage the plan correctly, you can build volume and intensity simultaneously.

Monday is an optional strength training day, noted on the plan as a strength maintenance (SM) workout (see Chapter 22). If you are not strength training and do not want to begin a routine, you can make Monday a day off. If you currently have a strength training program, you can continue that program on your day off from cycling. You may find that you have to modify the routine, reducing sets, repetitions, or weight so that strength training doesn't negatively impact your cycling.

If you are not strength training but would like to incorporate a weight-room routine in your workout plan, I suggest beginning with the anatomical adaptation phase of strength training described in Chapter 22. Keep the weight relatively light for the first two weeks. As your body adapts to the routine, you can slightly increase the weight and reduce the number of repetitions to 12 to 15 (from the 15 to 20 suggested in Chapter 22).

Tuesday workouts are primarily easy spins or aerobic maintenance days. Wednesday workouts are some of the key workouts for each week and include interval sessions. Thursdays are days off or easy recovery spins. Friday workouts are most often power workouts. Saturday and Sunday rides build in duration and help you improve your endurance. Additionally, the Saturday workouts include intensity throughout the plan.

PLAN DETAILS

Explanations of the workout codes used throughout this plan can be found in Chapter 21. Here, let's break down the plan by week.

Weeks 1 through 4

Monday strength training workouts are shown but, again, are optional. You can use your own routine. If you followed the Chapter 20 foundation fitness plan, move to the SM phase of strength training on Monday in Week 1 of this plan.

As mentioned previously, Tuesday is always an easy ride. In this first training block, Wednesday rides include lactate threshold training. Thursdays are days off or recovery rides.

The Friday workouts are power workouts. For Weeks 2 and 3, structure the workouts this way:

Friday of Week 2 (P3b): After a warm-up, do one set of descending intervals as follows. 45 sec. (4 min. 15 sec. RI), 30 sec. (4 min. 30 sec. RI), 20 sec. (4 min. 40 sec. RI), 10 sec. (4 min. 50 sec. RI). Repeat.

Friday of Week 3 (P3): After a warm-up, do 3 × 45 sec. (4 min. 15 sec. RI), 3 × 30 sec. (4 min. 30 sec. RI), 3 × 20 sec. (4 min. 40 sec. RI), 3 × 10 sec. (4 min. 50 sec. RI). Cool down.

Your Saturday rides are either hilly rides in which you push the pace or aggressive group rides. "Aggressive" means you try to ride fast. For this training block, ride hard during some portions of the Saturday rides and recover during other portions. The Sunday rides are mostly aerobic rides that build in duration.

Week 4 is a recovery week with reduced volume. Do not be tempted to do more; it may be to your benefit to do less. On your Saturday ride, keep the volume of intensity in zones 4 and 5 to less than 20 minutes.

TABLE 13.1 LEVEL II ONE-WEEK TOUR, 60–80 MILES PER DAY

WEEK	MONDAY	TUESDAY	WEDNESDAY	THURSDAY
1	SM	E2b	M2 (z4/5a)	E1b or day off
			3–4 x 8 min. (2 min. RI)	
	1:00	1:00	1:15	1:00
2	SM	E2b	M2 (z4/5a)	E1b or day off
			2–3 × 10 min. (3 min. 30 sec. RI)	
	1:00	1:00	1:15	1:00
3	SM	E1b	M4	E1b or day off
			20 min.	
	1:00	1:00	1:30	1:00
4	SM	Day off	P2	E1b or day off
			5 × 20 sec. (4 min. 40 sec. RI)	
	0:45		1:00	1:00
5	SM	E2b	A2	E1b or day off
			4–5 × 3 min. (3 min. RI)	
	1:00	1:15	1:30	1:00
6	SM	E2b	M2 (z3)	E1b or day off
			7–8 × 3 min. (60 sec. RI)	
	1:00	1:30	2:00	1:00
7	SM	Day off	P2	E1b or day off
			5 × 20 sec. (4 min. 40 sec. RI)	
	0:45		1:00	1:00
8	SM	E2b	A2	E1b or day off
			4–5 × 3 min. (3 min. RI)	
	1:00	2:00	2:00	1:00
9	SM	E2b	M2 (z3)	E1b or day off
			5–7 × 4 min. (60 sec. RI)	
	1:00	2:00	2:00	1:00

FRIDAY	SATURDAY	SUNDAY	WEEKLY TOTAL
P3a	E4 or A1d	E2a	
5–7 × 45 sec. (4 min. 15 sec. RI)			10:15
1:00	3:00	2:00	
P3b	E4 or A1d	E2a	
(see text)			11:30
1:15	3:30	2:30	
P3	E4 or A1d	E2a	
(see text)			13:00
1:30	4:00	3:00	
S4	E4	E1b	
	<20 min. z4+		7:15
1:00	2:30	1:00	
P7	E4 or A1c	E2a	
4–5 × 1 min. (4 min. RI)	(fast avg.)		14:00
1:45	4:30	3:00	
P7	E4 or A1c	E2a	
6–7 × 1 min. (4 min. RI)	(fast avg.)		15:30
2:00	4:30	3:30	
S4	E4	E1b	
	<20 min. z4+		7:15
1:00	2:30	1:00	
A8	E4 or A1c	E2a	
4–5 × 2 min. (8 min. RI)	(fast avg.)		16:00
2:00	4:30	3:30	
P7	E4 or A1c	E2a	
4–7 × 1 min. (9 min. RI)	(fast avg.)		16:00
2:00	4:30	3:30	

CONTINUED

Tours

TABLE 13.1 LEVEL II ONE-WEEK TOUR, 60–80 MILES PER DAY CONTINUED

WEEK	MONDAY	TUESDAY	WEDNESDAY	THURSDAY
10	SM	E1b	M6 (z1/5a)	Day off or E1b
	0:45	1:00	1:00	1:00
11	Day off	M7	S4	Day off or E1b
		4 × 90 sec. (3 min. RI)		
		1:00	0:45	1:00
12	Ride	Ride	Day off	Ride
	(A1c)	(A1d)		(E2a)
	5:00	4:00		4:00

Weeks 5 through 7

Training volume continues to build in this block. The key changes in this block are the anaerobic intervals on Wednesday of Week 5, followed by longer threshold intervals on Wednesday of Week 6. Power intervals continue on Fridays.

For the Saturday ride in this block, ride at the highest average speed you can manage for the entire ride. Obviously you don't want to thrash yourself during the first hour and fade to a slow grind for the remaining hours. Learning how to ride fast requires learning how to ride smart.

If you are riding with a group for the Saturday rides, manage your energy so you can ride both at the front of the group and in the slipstream of other riders for other parts of the ride. Make smart decisions about when to chase and when to let others go. Remember your aim is to ride strong and fast overall.

Weeks 8 through 10

This training block is very similar to the last training block and allows you to continue to increase your fitness. The workouts have subtle changes, and all the details can be found in the training plan table or in the Chapter 21 workout details.

Note that the volume in Week 10 isn't as low as in your other rest weeks. This is because your low-volume week begins with the Sunday at the end of Week 10 and goes through the Saturday of Week 11. The total training volume for that time period is 5:15.

FRIDAY	SATURDAY	SUNDAY	WEEKLY TOTAL
S4	A1d	E2a	
			8:15
1:00	2:00	1:30	
Day off	S7	Ride	
		(E2a)	7:45
	1:00	4:00	
Ride	Ride	Day off	
(A1d)	(A1c)		21:00+/-
4:00	4:00		

Weeks 11 and 12

Week 11, then, is your rest week prior to the bike tour. This plan assumes the bike tour begins on the Sunday of Week 11 and goes through the Saturday of Week 12.

The ride times shown during the tour week serve multiple purposes. First, if you are not joining an organized tour but are planning your own, the ride times can be converted to mileage to help you plan your trip.

Another reason for showing ride times and intensities is to help you plan your riding so you can finish strong. All too often, cyclists begin the first day of a bike tour with too much intensity, too little fueling, and too little hydration. This combination can lead to time in the sag wagon or some miserable days on the bike.

Even though you are rested and feel fantastic, ride easy the first day. If a ride day is designated as E2a, don't feel you have to maximize time in zone 2. If you are feeling extended, scale back the intensity.

Ride strong and fast!

PART IV

MOUNTAIN BIKE
TRAINING PLANS

Weekend-Warrior Mountain Biking
Level I

You love to mountain bike. You don't have a lot of time to spend on the bike, but when you ride on trails, you want enough fitness to really enjoy yourself for a couple of hours. If this paragraph describes you, this plan is the right one to help you enjoy your mountain biking even more.

If you need to build some foundation fitness *before beginning this plan*, Chapter 19 is a great option. Depending on how much time you have to train before hitting the trails, you can use Weeks 1 through 8 or Weeks 1 through 12 of Chapter 19 to establish the fitness you need to start Week 1 of this plan. If you use Chapter 19, one option is to mountain bike the Sunday rides shown on the plan. If you do use the mountain bike for Chapter 19, try to follow the intensity guidelines and hike-a-bike, or push your bike uphill while you walk, if necessary.

In some locations, using a mountain bike for foundation fitness is not possible due to the condition of the trails (icy, muddy, etc.), so using a road bike or an indoor training option works as well.

Ready to get dirty?

PROFILE

The plan in this chapter is designed for a Level I rider. You are limited to training no more than about seven hours per week; you are pinched for time. Weekday workouts can't be longer than an hour each, due to other commitments. You may or may not be able to get to a trail during the week.

Before beginning this plan, you are riding three or four days per week. You've included some intensity in your rides. On weekends, you get one day at the trail and your ride is limited to two hours most of the time. Your second weekend ride is usually easy and taken with others who don't ride as fast as you—which, because this second ride is a recovery ride, is perfect. Either you have been doing foundation, or base, fitness training on your own or you have completed the training outlined in Chapter 19.

For the duration of this 12-week training plan, you can commit to training five days per week, most of the time.

GOAL

Your goal is to improve your strength and endurance on two-hour mountain bike rides. Your benchmark comes from either your past rides or performance comparisons with some of your riding buddies.

THE PLAN OVERVIEW

Take a look at the plan in Table 14.1. The pattern is three-week cycles. Volume does not build in this training plan, but intensity does. Weekly training time shown on the plan doesn't go beyond six hours. If you have the time and desire to do more, some options are given.

Mondays are either strength training or skills days, noted on the plan as strength maintenance (SM) workouts (see Chapter 22) or power skills workouts.

If you currently have a strength training program, you can continue that program on one of your days off from cycling. You may find that you have to modify the routine, reducing sets, repetitions, or weight so that strength training doesn't negatively impact your cycling. If you are not strength training but would like to incorporate a weight-room routine in your workout plan, I suggest beginning with the anatomical adaptation phase of strength training described in Chapter 22. Keep the weight relatively light for the first two weeks. As your body adapts to the routine, you can slightly increase the weight and reduce the number of repetitions to 12 to 15 (from the 15 to 20 suggested in Chapter 22).

Tuesdays and Fridays are days off. If it works better for you to have different days off, you can move them accordingly. Wednesday workouts are some of the key workouts for the week and include interval sessions. You need to be rested before these sessions in order to get the most out of them. These workouts can be done on a mountain bike or a road bike.

Thursday workouts are either easy skills days on the mountain bike or easy road rides, your choice. Saturday rides are on the mountain bike (specified in the plan as MTB) and Sunday rides are easy recovery rides. The Sunday rides can be one to two hours in length, though one hour is displayed on the plan. You can switch the Saturday and Sunday rides if it works better for your schedule.

Every third week is a rest week. Volume is reduced while some intensity is maintained to help you absorb the training, keep your legs fresh, and take your fitness to a new level.

PLAN DETAILS

Explanations of the workout codes and exercises used throughout this plan can be found in Chapter 21. Here, let's break down the plan by week.

Weeks 1 through 3

Monday strength training workouts are shown but, again, are optional. You can use SM strength training (see Chapter 22) or your own routine, or you can make Monday an on-the-bike power workout day. If you followed the Chapter 19 foundation fitness plan, you can continue with the SM phase of strength training on Mondays. The other option for your Monday workouts is to work on your mountain bike skills on a short course with obstacles. (See Chapter 21 for more details on P8 workouts.)

As mentioned previously, Tuesday is a day off. In this first training block, the Wednesday rides are threshold workouts. These sessions can be done on a road bike, on a mountain bike, or on the trainer. The Thursday workouts are easy days to help you recover from Wednesdays.

Each week, after taking Friday off, head to the trails for some off-road fun. On Saturday of Week 1, accumulate about 20 minutes of zone 3 intensity. In Week 2, accumulate 20 to 30 minutes in zone 3.

The Saturday workout in Week 3 is a time trial, which can be completed either on the road or off-road. Just select a course you can use to repeat the time trial when you get to Week 9. Instead of aiming for a particular mileage goal, ride a course that takes you about 20 minutes to complete. Note the conditions, your starting and ending points, how you felt, and any other particulars you think are important.

Weeks 4 through 6

This training block follows the same format as the last block. In this block, the Wednesday threshold intervals are on an uphill course. If you are forced inside, try to simulate a hill. The Saturday rides allow more intensity; aim to accumulate about 20 minutes in zones 4 to 5a in Week 4 and 20 to 30 minutes in zones 4 to 5a in Week 5. During your rest week, be sure you reduce training volume.

TABLE 14.1 LEVEL I WEEKEND-WARRIOR MOUNTAIN BIKING

WEEK	MONDAY	TUESDAY	WEDNESDAY	THURSDAY
1	SM or P8	Day off	M2 (z4/5a)	E2b or S8
			5–6 × 3 min. (60 sec. RI)	
	1:00		1:00	1:00
2	SM or P8	Day off	M2 (z4/5a)	E2b or S8
			6–7 × 3 min. (60 sec. RI)	
	1:00		1:00	1:00
3	SM or P8	Day off	E2a	E1b or S8
	0:45		0:45	0:30
4	SM or P8	Day off	M3 (z4/5a)	E2b or S8
			4–5 × 5 min. (2 min. RI)	
	1:00		1:00	1:00
5	SM or P8	Day off	M3 (z4/5a)	E2b or S8
			3–4 × 6 min. (2 min. RI)	
	1:00		1:00	1:00
6	SM or P8	Day off	E2a	E1b or S8
	0:45		0:45	0:30
7	SM or P8	Day off	A2	E2b or S8
			4–5 × 3 min. (3 min. RI)	
	1:00		1:00	1:00
8	SM or P8	Day off	A2	E2b or S8
			4–5 × 3 min. (3 min. RI)	
	1:00		1:00	1:00
9	SM or P8	Day off	E2a	E1b or S8
	0:45		0:45	0:30

Mountain Bike

FRIDAY	SATURDAY	SUNDAY	WEEKLY TOTAL
Day off	MTB E3	E2a	
	~20 min. z3		6:00
	2:00	1:00	
Day off	MTB E3	E2a	
	~20–30 min. z3		6:00
	2:00	1:00	
Day off	MTB T2	E1a	
	20 min.		4:00
	1:00	1:00	
Day off	E4	E2a	
	~20 min. z4/5a		6:00
	2:00	1:00	
Day off	E4	E2a	
	~20–30 min. z4/5a		6:00
	2:00	1:00	
Day off	MTB A1d	E1a	
			4:00
	1:00	1:00	
Day off	MTB A1c	E2a	
			6:00
	2:00	1:00	
Day off	MTB A1c	E2a	
			6:00
	2:00	1:00	
Day off	MTB T2	E1a	
	20 min.		4:00
	1:00	1:00	

CONTINUED

Mountain Bike

TABLE 14.1 **LEVEL I WEEKEND-WARRIOR MOUNTAIN BIKING** CONTINUED

WEEK	MONDAY	TUESDAY	WEDNESDAY	THURSDAY
10	SM or P8	Day off	M3 (z4/5a) or	E2b or S8
			A8 or A2	
	1:00		1:00	1:00
11	SM or P8	Day off	M3 (z4/5a) or	E2b or S8
			A8 or A2	
	1:00		1:00	1:00
12	SM or P8	Day off	A7	S4
			3–5 × 90 sec. (3 min. RI)	
	0:45		0:45	0:30

Weeks 7 through 9

The Wednesday workouts in this block are at an even higher intensity, zone 5b. Try to do these workouts outside, on either a road bike or a mountain bike. This level of intensity is usually tough to achieve on an indoor trainer unless you are overheating. And while training in a hot room drives up your heart rate, it doesn't do much to improve power production.

The Saturday mountain bike rides include all intensities. Enjoy your fitness and ride strong.

The rest week includes a retest of your 20-minute time trial. Try to make the conditions of this test similar to those in the first test. If it isn't possible to make them similar, note the major differences between the two.

Weeks 10 and 11

In this training block, the Wednesday rides can be any of the following:

M3 (z4/5a): Do some combination of intervals so that the accumulated work time is 20 to 30 minutes. If you're on a road bike, make the interval length 4 to 10 minutes long with a recovery interval ratio of 3:1 or 4:1. If you're on a mountain bike, the recovery interval is the easy descent.

A8: 4–5 × 2 min. (4 min. RI)

A2: 4–5 × 3 min. (3 min. RI)

FRIDAY	SATURDAY	SUNDAY	WEEKLY TOTAL
Day off	MTB A1c	E2a	
			6:00
	2:00	1:00	
Day off	MTB A1c	E2a	
			6:00
	2:00	1:00	
Day off	MTB A1c	E1b	
			4:30
	2:00	0:30	

The Saturday rides are the same intensity as in the last training block; however, you should be seeing some fitness gains.

Week 12

The Wednesday workout in Week 12 includes just enough intensity to keep you feeling fast, but not so much to leave your legs feeling tired.

You can keep repeating Weeks 10 through 12 until your season ends. After your season is over, take a break, and then begin your foundation fitness plan for next season.

Mountain Bike Racing
Level II

You love to mountain bike and you are competitive. Being "competitive" may mean that you race and want to get faster, or it may mean that you do group rides and treat them as races. I have personally coached many cyclists who had no desire to enter fee-requiring races but had a real desire to put the hurt on their buddies—in a competitive but friendly way, of course!

One of the first ways to get faster is to be more consistent, which means riding year-round, whether indoors or outdoors. If you have not been consistent before beginning this plan, consider starting with the preparation plan in Chapter 20. I'm often asked, "What is the best way to get faster? More intervals? Longer rides?" My answer is always that consistency trumps all; first establish a consistent routine of fitness.

Ready to go faster and dust your competition? Read on.

PROFILE

This plan is designed for a Level II rider. You are a serious cyclist, and you maintain fitness all year. While you take breaks from cycling to recover or do other activities, you are not a fair-weather cyclist who begins a fitness program in the spring.

Before beginning Week 1 in this plan, you have either completed Weeks 1 through 12 of the Chapter 20 foundation fitness training plan or your training has been very similar to what is shown in that chapter. You are currently riding five or six days per week. Weekday rides range from one to two hours each, and you have access to a hilly course, either on a road or off-road. On weekends, your long ride—whether a group ride or a ride on your own—is three hours long and includes some intensity. Your second weekend ride is two hours long. You have already completed some lactate threshold training.

GOAL

Your goal is to improve your strength and endurance on three-hour mountain bike races or rides. Your benchmark comes from either your past races or performance comparisons with some of your riding buddies.

THE PLAN OVERVIEW

Take a look at the plan in Table 15.1. The pattern is three-week cycles, and training volume does not build much in this plan. You can follow the plan as written—Weeks 1 through 12, in order—or you can mix and match the three-week blocks to suit your own training needs. Each three-week block has a specific pattern of workouts. Remember that your body needs time to absorb the effects of a block of training and to show improvement. It may take as little as a couple of weeks or as long as eight or more weeks. Be patient.

For the first nine weeks, the week begins with a strength training day, noted on the plan as strength maintenance (SM) workout (see Chapter 22). If you currently have a strength training program, you can continue that program. You may find that you have to modify the routine, reducing sets, repetitions, or weight so that strength training doesn't negatively impact your cycling.

Some blocks have the key workouts scheduled on Tuesdays, Thursdays, and Saturdays. Other blocks have a different format, which will be discussed later in this chapter.

Every third week is a rest week. Volume is reduced while some intensity is maintained to help you absorb the training, keep your legs fresh, and take your fitness to a new level. Don't skimp on rest.

PLAN DETAILS

Explanations of the workout codes used throughout this plan can be found in Chapter 21. Here, let's break down the plan by week.

Weeks 1 through 3

If you followed the Chapter 20 foundation fitness plan, you can continue with the SM phase of strength training on Mondays. Or, as discussed in the plan overview, you can modify your own strength training program.

This training block contains three key workouts, scheduled on Tuesdays, Thursdays, and Saturdays. These are tough workouts, intended to take your fitness to a new level. The Tuesday rides are designed to work on lactate threshold while climbing. These rides can be on a mountain bike or a road bike. The Thursday workouts are designed to work on anaerobic power and can be on a road bike or a mountain bike. The Saturday rides are group rides, training races, or races within a series. These rides are obviously best done on a mountain bike (specified in the plan as MTB.) If you are racing on the weekend, you may find that you need to cut down the intensity in the Thursday workout. If the race is on Sunday rather than Saturday, simply swap these workouts.

The Wednesday, Friday, and Sunday rides are for recovery, to work on form or to maintain aerobic endurance.

Week 3 is a rest week. If you have an important race midway through the plan, Week 3 is one example of how to rest before the race.

Weeks 4 through 6

In this training block, the Tuesday rides work on lactate threshold, but the work does not need to be done on hills to be effective. Some mountain bike races have long sections of flats or gently rolling terrain where it is to your advantage to be strong. The Thursday workouts are aimed at working on anaerobic power again, this time in the two-minute range. The remaining workouts in this block are similar to those in Weeks 1 through 3.

Weeks 7 through 9

This training block moves the key workouts to Wednesdays, Saturdays, and Sundays. If you are racing two-day events, this format is good. Even if you are not racing two-day races, you may find that a training block with this format boosts your fitness.

The Tuesday rides in this block are easy skills rides on a mountain bike or easy road rides. The Wednesday rides are mountain bike rides including all intensity zones, and they are intended to work on technical skills as well. These rides help you decide when it is more effective to dismount and push your bike (i.e., hike-a-bike) or to build the skills to ride certain difficult trail sections. The Saturday rides work on lactate threshold power and the Sunday rides are multipurpose rides or races. You can switch the Saturday and Sunday rides if it better meets your needs.

Weeks 10 through 12

Many cyclists don't do a good job of resting before the final big race of the season. This training block shows you how to taper volume while maintaining some intensity to prepare for the final event. You may find that you do better by using a two-week taper of volume, in which case you may prefer using Weeks 10 and 12, Weeks 11 and 12, or Weeks 10 and 11.

TABLE 15.1 LEVEL II MOUNTAIN BIKE RACING

WEEK	MONDAY	TUESDAY	WEDNESDAY	THURSDAY
1	SM	M3 (z4/5a)	E2a	A2
		5–7 × 3 min. (60 sec. RI)		4–5 × 3 min. (3 min. RI)
	1:00	1:15	1:30	1:15
2	SM	M3 (z4/5a)	E2a	A2
		4–6 × 4 min. (60 sec. RI)		4–5 × 3 min. (3 min. RI)
	1:00	1:15	1:30	1:15
3	Day off	SM	S4	Day off
		0:45	1:00	
4	SM	M5	E2a	A8
		20–30 min.		4–5 × 2 min. (4 min. RI)
	1:00	1:15	1:30	1:15
5	SM	M4	E2a	A8
		20 min.		5–6 × 2 min. (4 min. RI)
	1:00	1:15	1:30	1:15
6	Day off	SM	S4	Day off
		0:45	1:00	
7	SM	E2b or S8	E4	E2a
			MTB + skills	
	1:00	1:15	2:00	1:15
8	SM	E2b or S8	E4	E2a
			MTB + skills	
	1:00	1:15	2:00	1:15
9	Day off	SM	S4	Day off
		0:45	1:00	

Mountain Bike

FRIDAY	SATURDAY	SUNDAY	WEEKLY TOTAL
E1b or day off	MTB A1c or race	E2b	
			11:00
1:00	3:00	2:00	
E1b or day off	MTB A1c or race	E2a	
			11:00
1:00	3:00	2:00	
S8	MTB A1c or race	E1b or day off	
			5:45
1:00	2:00	1:00	
E1b or day off	MTB A1c or race	E2b	
			11:00
1:00	3:00	2:00	
E1b or day off	MTB A1c or race	E2a	
			11:00
1:00	3:00	2:00	
S7	MTB A1c or race	E1b or day off	
			5:45
1:00	2:00	1:00	
S4 or day off	M5	MTB A1c or race	
	20–30 min.		11:30
1:00	2:00	3:00	
S4 or day off	M4	MTB A1c or race	
	20–30 min.		11:30
1:00	2:00	3:00	
S8	MTB A1c or race	E1b	
			5:45
1:00	2:00	1:00	

CONTINUED

Mountain Bike

TABLE 15.1 LEVEL II MOUNTAIN BIKE RACING CONTINUED

WEEK	MONDAY	TUESDAY	WEDNESDAY	THURSDAY
10	E1a	E2b or S8	MTB E4	E2a
			<20 min. z3	
	1:00	1:15	1:30	1:00
11	E1a	M5	A7	S4
		15 min.	4 × 90 sec. (3 min. RI)	
	1:00	1:00	1:00	1:00
12	E1a or day off	A7	A7 or day off	Day off
		3–5 × 90 sec. (3 min. RI)	3 × 90 sec. (3 min. RI)	
	0:45	1:00	1:00	

RECOVERY

After ending your last event of the season, be sure to take some time off the bike to recover. Weather may force you to do this naturally or you may have to force yourself to take a break. As well, if you find your riding is getting stale, take some time off. See Chapter 2 for recovery guidelines.

FRIDAY	SATURDAY	SUNDAY	WEEKLY TOTAL
S7 or day off	M2 (z4/5a)	MTB A1c or race	
	5 × 3 min. (60 sec. RI)		10:15
1:00	1:30	3:00	
Day off	MTB A1c or race	E2a	
			8:30
	3:00	1:30	
S7	MTB A1c or race	E1b	
			7:30
0:45	3:00	1:00	

100-Mile Mountain Bike Race
Level I

A 100-mile mountain bike race is not an easy task, no matter how you look at it. Depending on the course, only the best riders can expect to be under the 10-hour mark. On some courses, it takes a very strong rider to be under the 12-hour mark.

You are aiming for the 100-mile distance and you need to accomplish the mission with a minimal amount of weekly training time. Because your training time is limited, you need structure. You need a plan of attack.

PROFILE

Before beginning this plan, you are riding consistently and training five to six hours each week. Your long ride is about two hours long and includes some intensity as well as hill work. At least one other ride during the week contains some intensity, whether the ride is outdoors or in an indoor spinning class.

If your current fitness level does not meet the description above, use the training plan in Chapter 19 to build foundation fitness. After the last week of the Chapter 19 plan, begin with Week 1 of this chapter.

During the week, you are limited to an hour of training on three days. You need two days off for other activities. Additionally, you do not have time to commute to a mountain course, so the training needs to be on an indoor trainer, in a spin class, or on a road bike.

GOAL

Your goal is to comfortably complete a 100-mile mountain bike race. While you want to ride as fast as possible, you are restricted for training time. You want to achieve the best race time given your limited training time.

THE PLAN OVERVIEW

Take a look at the plan in Table 16.1 to get an overview of the training volume. The plan begins with two four-week cycles, each including three weeks of building volume and then a week of rest. As training volume increases, you move to two three-week cycles in order to help improve recovery. The final three weeks decrease in volume so you can be fully prepared for race day.

TABLE 16.1 OVERALL PLAN

WEEK	1	2	3	4	5	6	7	8	9	10	11	12	13	14	15	16
HOURS	6:00	7:00	7:30	5:15	8:30	9:00	10:00	5:15	11:00	11:30	5:15	12:30	13:30	5:15	6:00	2:15 + race
PERIOD	Pre-competitive Preparation 1				Pre-competitive Preparation 2				Pre-competitive Preparation 3			Pre-competitive Preparation 4			Competitive	

Now look at Table 16.2, Week 1, to see the overall pattern for the training plan. Monday workouts are either easy rides, skills rides, or form workouts. If you are currently doing a strength training program and want to keep strength training as part of your training, continue that program on Mondays rather than riding. You may find you need to reduce the weights, sets, repetitions, or some combination of all so that strength training doesn't negatively affect your cycling. If you are not strength training but want to add a routine, see Chapter 22 for a description of the strength maintenance (SM) phase of training. Plan to begin with very light weights and work your way into slightly heavier weights as the program progresses. There is no need to lift very heavy weights during this plan.

Tuesdays and Thursdays are days off. You may have to adjust the days off to better suit your personal needs. Wednesday workouts are typically interval sessions, and you need to be rested for these workouts to get the most out of them.

Friday workouts change some throughout the program, but they stay within the one-hour limit that you require. Saturday workouts are for honing mountain bike skills and building endurance. The Saturday rides combine with long rides on Sundays to pack a punch to build your overall race endurance. Also, the combination of the Friday, Saturday, Sunday, and Monday workouts gives you four solid days of riding each week.

On the long weekend rides, be certain you are working on your nutritional strategy for race day. Iron out any equipment choices prior to Week 12, so you have time to do final testing before race day.

PLAN DETAILS

Explanations of the workout codes used throughout this plan can be found in Chapter 21. Here, let's break down the plan by week.

Weeks 1 through 4

For this block of training, Mondays are easy ride days or can be strength training days. Wednesday sessions work on lactate threshold speed. Friday workouts are for aerobic endurance and Saturday workouts are on-the-bike strength training. The Saturday sessions can be on a mountain bike or on a road bike. The Sunday sessions work on threshold, climbing power, and endurance. Week 4 is a rest week to help you absorb training from the previous three weeks.

Weeks 5 through 8

Monday workouts in this block are intended to work on your mountain bike skills, but you have the option to do strength work. While skill workouts may not seem "hard" enough to contribute to your fitness, having solid skills can keep you from wasting precious energy due to inefficiency. Not all workouts that produce race-day results have to be hard.

The Wednesday workouts continue to work on lactate threshold speed and power. On-the-bike strength training moves to Fridays, and Saturdays become mountain bike days. The Saturday workouts include the higher-intensity work for the weekend, as well. The Sunday workouts continue to build your race-day endurance.

Weeks 9 through 11

The Monday workouts are form work or strength training. The Wednesday workouts continue to work on threshold, though they intentionally return to zone 3 training. While you may get into zones 4 and above during the race, you will need to limit your time in the upper zones. The main purpose of lactate threshold work is to increase the size of your aerobic engine.

The Wednesday workout in Week 10 is a special one, not covered by a particular code. After a good warm-up, ride for 10 minutes at a steady zone 3 intensity. Take 3 minutes of easy recovery spinning, then immediately begin two intervals of 5 minutes steady at zone 3 intensity. Recover for 2 minutes between the 5-minute efforts. Leave enough time to cool down at the end.

TABLE 16.2 LEVEL I 100-MILE MOUNTAIN BIKE RACE

WEEK	MONDAY	TUESDAY	WEDNESDAY	THURSDAY
1	E1b or SM	Day off	M2 (z3)	Day off
			3–4 × 6 min. (2 min. RI)	
	1:00		1:00	
2	E1b or SM	Day off	M2 (z3)	Day off
			3–4 × 8 min. (2 min. RI)	
	1:00		1:00	
3	E1b or SM	Day off	M1	Day off
			20 min.	
	1:00		1:00	
4	E1a or SM	Day off	M7	Day off
			3–4 × 90 sec. (3 min. RI)	
	0:45		0:45	
5	S8 or SM	Day off	M2 (z4/5a)	Day off
			5–7 × 3 min. (60 sec. RI)	
	1:00		1:00	
6	S8 or SM	Day off	M3 (z4/5a)	Day off
			5–7 × 3 min. (60 sec. RI)	
	1:00		1:00	
7	S8 or SM	Day off	M5	Day off
			20 min.	
	1:00		1:00	
8	E1a or SM	Day off	M7	Day off
			3–4 × 90 sec. (3 min. RI)	
	0:45		0:45	
9	S4 or SM	Day off	M2 (z3)	Day off
			4–5 × 5 min. (2 min. RI)	
	1:00		1:00	

FRIDAY	SATURDAY	SUNDAY	WEEKLY TOTAL
E2b	F1	E3	
	MTB or road		6:00
1:00	1:00	2:00	
E2b	F1	E3	
	MTB or road		7:00
1:00	1:30	2:30	
E2b	F1	E3	
	MTB		7:30
1:00	1:30	3:00	
S4	E3	E2a	
	MTB		5:15
0:45	2:00	1:00	
F1 or P1	E3	E2a	
5–7 × 10 sec. (4 min. 50 sec. RI)	MTB		8:30
1:00	2:00	3:30	
F1 or P1	E3	E2a	
5–7 × 10 sec. (4 min. 50 sec. RI)	MTB		9:00
1:00	2:00	4:00	
F1 or P1	E3	E2a	
5–7 × 10 sec. (4 min. 50 sec. RI)	MTB		10:00
1:00	2:30	4:30	
S4	E3	E2a	
	MTB		5:15
0:45	2:00	1:00	
E2a or S8	E4	E3	
	MTB (fast avg.)		11:00
1:00	3:00	5:00	

CONTINUED

Mountain Bike

TABLE 16.2   LEVEL I 100-MILE MOUNTAIN BIKE RACE CONTINUED

WEEK	MONDAY	TUESDAY	WEDNESDAY	THURSDAY
10	S4 or SM	Day off	See text	Day off
	1:00		1:00	
11	E1a or SM	Day off	M7	Day off
			3–4 × 90 sec. (3 min. RI)	
	0:45		0:45	
12	P1 or SM	Day off	E2b or S8	Day off
	5–7 × 10 sec. (4 min. 50 sec. RI)			
	1:00		1:00	
13	P1 or SM	Day off	E2b or S8	Day off
	5–7 × 10 sec. (4 min. 50 sec. RI)			
	1:00		1:00	
14	E1a or SM	Day off	M7	Day off
			3–4 × 90 sec. (3 min. RI)	
	0:45		0:45	
15	S8	Day off	E2b	Day off
	1:00		0:45	
16	S7	Day off	M7	Day off
			3 × 90 sec. (3 min. RI)	
	1:00		0:45	

FRIDAY	SATURDAY	SUNDAY	WEEKLY TOTAL
E2a or S8	E4	E3	
	MTB (fast avg.)		11:30
1:00	3:00	5:30	
S4	E3	E2a	
	MTB		5:15
0:45	2:00	1:00	
M4	E4	E3	
20 min.	MTB (fast avg.)	(limit z3)	12:30
1:00	3:30	6:00	
M4	E4	E3	
20 min.	MTB (fast avg.)	(limit z3)	13:30
1:00	4:00	6:30	
S4	E3	E2a	
	MTB		5:15
0:45	2:00	1:00	
S4	E4	F1	
	MTB <20 min. z4+		6:00
0:45	2:00	1:30	
Course preview	Race	Day off	
(see text)			2:15 + race
0:30			

The Friday workouts in this block can be aerobic workouts or skills workouts, your choice.

For the Saturday mountain bike rides, ride as fast as you can average for the entire three hours. Keep moving at a steady pace and minimize stopping time. Paired with the Sunday rides, these rides will help you continue to build endurance. The Sunday rides can include some zone 3, but keep it to a minimum. On race day, you will spend the majority of the event in zones 1 and 2. One goal of this plan is for you to develop the fitness necessary to ride as fast as possible at an aerobic intensity. The weekend workouts help you do that.

Week 11 is for recovery. Do not underestimate the need for rest in order to develop your fitness.

Weeks 12 through 14

This is the last big training block. The Monday sessions are to work on the "short power" necessary to climb over obstacles. The Wednesday sessions are aerobic or form workouts. The Friday, Saturday, and Sunday combinations are the final buildup of work toward your race fitness.

The Friday sessions are steady-state efforts. Keep the intensity in zones 2 and 3. Similar to the last training block, this block includes Saturday mountain bike rides at speeds as fast as you can average for the times shown on the plan. For the Sunday rides, limit the zone 3 intensity.

Week 14 is a well-deserved rest week. If you have been strength training, this is your last week of pushing iron in the gym.

Weeks 15 and 16

The training hours in Week 15 are bumped up slightly above Week 14's rest-week volume. Some intensity is included to keep your legs feeling fresh. If you have been strength training on Mondays, switch to riding your bike for the workout shown in the plan. If you find yourself still feeling tired by the Saturday workout, cut down that workout time. In any case, keep the zone 4 (and above) intensity of your ride to less than 20 minutes. Sunday is an aerobic force ride.

In the week heading into the race, expect to feel a little anxious but don't let this anxiety push you to do extra training. If anything, *reduce* your training. On the day before the race, ride the final few miles of the event. Knowing the final miles of the course can help you stay strong mentally during the race.

On race day, plan to ride a negative-split effort. Be careful not to get caught up in the starting frenzy, and ride at your own pace. If you wear your heart rate monitor, expect an elevated heart rate compared to your rate on a normal training day. Try to settle into an aerobic pace, *your* pace, as soon as you can. Using a mostly aerobic pace and the nutritional pace you practiced in training will propel you to a strong finish.

100-Mile Mountain Bike Race
Level II

Mountain bike racing at the 100-mile distance is increasingly popular. Some courses are near sea level, and others begin at elevations above 10,000 feet and go up from there. One course might be very technical, while another has minimal technical sections. Some courses have checkpoints and generous time cuts (points that you must pass through within a certain time; if you do not make the time cut, you are removed from the racecourse), others do not.

No matter what the course specifics are, you are competitive and want a fast race finish. This training plan is written for a cyclist who is currently fit and is looking for a solid performance in a 100-mile mountain bike race.

PROFILE

Before beginning this plan, you are training approximately nine hours per week, including two long rides. One ride is around two hours long and the second is roughly three hours. You are riding two or three other weekday rides that are an hour each. You may or may not be strength training.

This plan is designed to follow the Level II foundation fitness training plan found in Chapter 20. After completing 18 weeks of that plan, you can move directly into the plan in this chapter. This combination provides you with 32 weeks of training.

If you are not using the Chapter 20 training plan, review the workouts in that plan's last few weeks. You should be capable of completing those workouts (or similar ones), both in time and intensity, before beginning the plan in this chapter.

Due to the volume of training in this plan, you need to focus on recovery as much as on the training. Improved performance is accompanied by adequate rest and recovery techniques as well as by high-density nutrition (see Chapter 3).

GOAL

Your goal is to ride a 100-mile mountain bike race at a personal-best time. You want more than just to complete the event; you want to compete at the event. The competition may be for a spot on the podium or simply to beat that past personal record.

THE PLAN OVERVIEW

Take a look at Table 17.1 for an overview of the plan's training volume. The plan begins with a four-week block: three weeks of building volume, then a week of rest.

The first block of training is followed by a three-week block, which continues to build the overall training volume. After a rest week in Week 7, the training volume in Week 8 jumps off the page. This plan uses a "crash-training" week, during which volume and intensity are increased far beyond normal training. Crash training is effective only if the cyclist is rested going into the high-volume week and recovers the week following the training.

A crash-training week can significantly boost your fitness. Organized bicycle tours can make this week another highlight in your seaason or you can just ride the hours on your own. If you are unable to do all of the hours shown on the plan, I will give you tips on how to modify the training.

TABLE 17.1 OVERALL PLAN

WEEK	1	2	3	4	5	6	7	8	9	10	11	12	13	14
HOURS	9:00	10:00	11:00	5:45	12:30	13:30	4:45	22:00	6:45	13:30	12:30	10:45	7:00	3:30 + race
PERIOD	Pre-competitive Preparation 1				Pre-competitive Preparation 2			Pre-competitive Preparation 3			Pre-competitive Preparation 4			Competitive

Now look at Table 17.2 to see the overall training plan. Monday workouts are shown as strength training. If you are not strength training and do not want to begin a routine or you simply need a day of no training to recover, you can make Monday a day off. If you are currently doing a strength training program, you can continue that program. You may find you need to reduce the weights, sets, repetitions, or some combination of all so that strength training doesn't negatively affect your cycling. If you are not strength training but want to begin a routine, see Chapter 22 for a description of the strength maintenance (SM) phase of training. Plan to begin with very light weights and work your way into slightly heavier weights as the program progresses. There is no need to lift very heavy weights in this plan.

Tuesday workouts are typically form workouts or aerobic rides. The Wednesday workouts can be done on either a road bike or a mountain bike. If it's difficult for you to get to a trail—perhaps you live in a location where you must drive a long distance to reach one—a road bike works fine for these sessions.

Thursdays are rest days. Friday workouts are similar to those on Wednesdays, in that if it's not easy for you to get to a mountain bike trail, the ride can be done on a road bike.

The Saturday ride is your key mountain bike ride (specified as MTB in the plan) each week. Early in the plan, Saturday rides can be taken on a variety of trails. The closer you get to race day, the more you need to simulate course climbs and grades. Ride the actual racecourse if possible.

The Sunday rides are aerobic rides that are best done on a road bike or a mountain bike course that is not too technically demanding. The main goal for Sundays is to take a steady aerobic ride. The two weekend rides paired together build your overall race-day endurance while keeping your average power or speed as high as possible.

PLAN DETAILS

Before diving into details, I want to share some of the philosophy behind the plan. First, I am assuming you have worked on your foundation fitness and are coming into this plan fit. Your fitness has included some early work on lactate threshold.

At the beginning of this plan, you will find lactate threshold and anaerobic intervals. The purpose of this work for an experienced cyclist is to raise lactate threshold heart rate and speed. If your lactate threshold moves from 80 percent of your maximum heart rate to 90 percent of your maximum heart rate, you've increased the capacity of your aerobic engine. For example, if your maximum heart rate is 185 and you can move your lactate threshold from a heart rate of 148 to 167, you've got a larger aerobic engine. This increase can pay big dividends in an event that lasts 7 to 10 hours.

As the plan progresses and training volume builds, intervals are intended to simulate mountain bike terrain so they have less structure. Explanations of the workout codes used throughout this plan can be found in Chapter 21. Let's get started.

TABLE 17.2   LEVEL II 100-MILE MOUNTAIN BIKE RACE

WEEK	MONDAY	TUESDAY	WEDNESDAY	THURSDAY
1	SM	S8	A2	Day off
		MTB	4–5 × 3 min. (3 min. RI)	
	1:00	1:00	1:00	
2	SM	S8	M3 (z4/5a)	Day off
		MTB	4–5 × 4 min. (60 sec. RI)	
	1:00	1:00	1:30	
3	SM	S8	M4	Day off
		MTB	20 min.	
	1:00	1:00	2:00	
4	Day off	SM	S4	Day off
		0:45	1:00	
5	SM	S8	M3 (z4/5a)	Day off
		MTB	5–6 × 5 min. (2 min. RI)	
	1:00	1:00	2:00	
6	SM	S8	A2	Day off
		MTB	4–5 × 3 min. (3 min. RI)	
	1:00	1:00	2:00	
7	SM	E1a	M7	Day off
			4 × 90 sec. (3 min. RI)	
	0:45	1:00	1:00	
8	E4	E2b	M4	Day off
			20–30 min.	
	3:00	3:00	3:00	
9	Day off	SM	E1a	Day off
		0:45	1:00	

FRIDAY	SATURDAY	SUNDAY	WEEKLY TOTAL
F1	E4	E2a	
	MTB		9:00
1:00	2:00	3:00	
F1	E4	E2a	
	MTB		10:00
1:00	2:00	3:30	
F1	E4	E2a	
	MTB		11:00
1:00	2:30	3:30	
E1a	E4	E2a	
	MTB		5:45
1:00	2:00	1:00	
F1	E4	E2a	
	MTB		12:30
1:30	3:00	4:00	
F1	E4	E2a	
	MTB		13:30
1:30	3:00	5:00	
Day off	S4	S4	
	(see text)		4:45
	1:00	1:00	
E2a	E3	E2a	
	MTB (fast avg.)		22:00
3:00	6:00	4:00	
A7	E4	E2a	
4 × 90 sec. (3 min. RI)	MTB (fast avg.)		6:45
1:00	2:00	2:00	

CONTINUED

Mountain Bike

TABLE 17.2 LEVEL II 100-MILE MOUNTAIN BIKE RACE CONTINUED

WEEK	MONDAY	TUESDAY	WEDNESDAY	THURSDAY
10	SM	E2b	A1d	Day off
			MTB	
	1:00	1:00	2:00	
11	SM	E2b	A1d	Day off
			MTB	
	1:00	1:00	2:00	
12	SM	E2b	A1d	Day off
			MTB	
	0:45	1:00	2:00	
13	Day off	M7	A1d	Day off
		4 × 90 sec. (3 min. RI)	MTB	
		1:00	1:30	
14	E1a	S7	S8	Day off
	1:00	0:45	0:45	

Weeks 1 through 4

For this block of training, Mondays are strength training workouts or days off. Tuesdays are skills days. Wednesdays are interval workouts that can be done on the road or mountain bike. Thursdays are days off.

Friday workouts are intended to work on strength while you are on the bike. Saturday rides are your mountain bike days, and Sundays are aerobic endurance rides. During these weekend workouts, begin working on your race-day fueling strategies.

Weeks 5 through 7

Weeks 5 and 6 continue with the same basic structure of Weeks 1 through 4. If you are going to use Week 8 as a crash-training week, Week 7 needs to be a period of "aggressive" resting. To aid in recovery, feel free to eliminate or reduce any training session this week.

FRIDAY	SATURDAY	SUNDAY	WEEKLY TOTAL
S3	E4	E2a	
6–8	MTB (fast avg.)		13:30
1:30	5:00	3:00	
P1	E4	E2a	
5–7 × 10 sec. (4 min. 50 sec. RI)	MTB (fast avg.)		12:30
1:30	4:00	3:00	
F1	E4	E2a	
	MTB (fast avg.)		10:45
1:30	3:00	2:30	
F1	E4	S3	
	MTB (fast avg.)	5–7	7:00
1:00	2:00	1:30	
Course preview	Race	Day off	
(see text)			3:30 + race
1:00	3:30 + race		

If you are participating in an organized bike tour for your week of crash training, your event might begin on Sunday that ends Week 7. If this is the case, ride the first day of the tour at an aerobic pace. You may find it hard to keep the cap on your pace this first day, but doing so pays dividends later.

It is sometimes difficult to match the plan to the demands of the bike tour, so you may have to switch some days around. Just don't neglect your easy aerobic days and, if necessary, take a day off the bike.

If you are doing your own version of crash training in Week 8, keep Week 7's Sunday ride easy. One option is to keep the ride at an hour, as shown in Table 17.2. Another option is to add a longer day of aerobic riding, keeping the ride between two and three hours. The second option would be comparable to riding in a bike tour that begins on a Sunday and ends on a Sunday, which we'll consider more carefully now.

Week 8

If you are riding in an organized tour, the tour hours probably won't match those shown in the plan. It's more important that you try to match the intensities of the workouts shown in the plan, even if it requires that you reshuffle your plan to match the high-intensity workouts with the more demanding days of the tour.

For the Monday workout, push your pace on the climbs. On Tuesday, keep the intensity mostly aerobic. On Wednesday, include one segment during the ride that is crisscrossing threshold. If Thursday is not a day off, try to keep all the intensity in zone 1.

The Friday ride is mostly in zones 1 and 2. For the Saturday workout, ride at the fastest average pace you can for the entire six hours. Of course, you don't want to push the pace for the first two hours only to limp along for the last four. Ride smart.

For the Sunday workout, ride with whatever energy you have left. If you are feeling tired, take it easy. If you have the energy to ride faster, go for it.

If you are completing the Week 8 hours on your own or on a self-designed tour, here are some options:

- You can slide all rides forward one day, beginning your tour on Saturday. If you do this, eliminate the S4 ride and take the last Sunday off or put the S4 ride on that day.
- If your weekday schedule only allows two hours of riding each day, that works as well. Two hours is still more training than you would normally do, so you will get a fitness boost.
- If you do most of the crash training on your own but participate in an organized century ride on Sunday, just switch the Saturday and Sunday workouts. Keep the Saturday ride easy, in zones 1 to 2.

Week 9

You had a big week last week, so now you must recover. Your only goal this week is to feel recovered by Sunday. Cut down or eliminate rides, if you have to, to achieve this goal.

Weeks 10 through 13

This block tapers training volume into race day. The key workouts are on Wednesdays, Saturdays, and Sundays. Ride all intensities on the Wednesday rides, and ride on a mountain bike if possible. For Saturday mountain bike rides, aim for the fastest average speed you can manage for the time shown in the plan. Sunday rides should be kept mostly aerobic, and cycling on a road bike is fine.

Any bike maintenance should be done in Week 11 or 12 so you can take a few rides using any new parts. Also in Week 12, strength training should be lighter than normal. If you like, you can eliminate strength training beginning in this week.

In Week 13, do not be tempted to increase training volume. If anything, *decrease* the volume so you can be rested and ready for race day. Keep some intensity in some of the rides to keep your legs from feeling flat, but don't get carried away. Depending on your particular needs, the Saturday and Sunday rides in Week 13 can be cut down by 30 to 60 minutes.

Week 14

Please do not be tempted to do more than shown in the plan. If you have not had a chance to ride any of the course and you arrive in time on Friday, do a short ride on the course—but keep it controlled. Save your best for race day.

Plan to ride the race in a negative-split effort, riding the second half of the event stronger than the first half. With your fitness and fueling plan nailed, you are sure to have a great ride.

24-Hour Mountain Bike Racing on a Team
Crash-Training Program

Riding a mountain bike race as a team is great fun. Hanging with your buddies, tackling logistics, depriving yourself of sleep—what could be better?

This chapter gives you basic information about racing a 24-hour mountain bike race as a team. Let's assume that you, as an individual on that team, will be expected to ride four to six hours total, over the course of 24 hours. For beginners and cyclists pressed for training time, a six-week crash-training plan is included in this chapter. If you have more time, you can use the training plan from either Chapter 14 or Chapter 15 for a deeper level of fitness.

PROFILE

Before beginning this plan, you are riding at least three days per week for 45 to 60 minutes per ride, whether indoors or outdoors. If you have a greater level of fitness, take a look at the plans in Chapters 14 and 15.

GOAL

Your goal is to be ready to ride a 24-hour mountain bike race in six weeks. You are a member of a team, and your team expects you to ride about four to six hours total over the course of 24 hours.

TABLE 18.1 CRASH-TRAINING FOR A 24-HOUR MOUNTAIN BIKE RACE

WEEK	MONDAY	TUESDAY	WEDNESDAY	THURSDAY
1	Day off	E2a	Day off	S1a
				4–6 × 20 sec. (100 sec. RI)
		0:45		0:45
2	Day off	E2a	Day off	S1a
				4–6 × 30 sec. (90 sec. RI)
		1:00		1:00
3	Day off	E2b	Day off	S1
		1:00		1:00
4	Day off	E2b	Day off	S1
		1:00		1:00
5	Day off	E1b	Day off	S1a
				4–6 × 20 sec. (100 sec. RI)
		0:45		0:45
6	Day off	M7	Day off	S7
	4 × 90 sec. (3 min. RI)			
		0:45		0:30

THE PLAN

Take a look at the plan in Table 18.1. You ride four days per week. Your first week of riding totals three hours, and the weekly totals build to six hours two weeks before the event. The Tuesday rides are endurance rides. The Thursday rides include form work to improve your leg speed and neuromuscular coordination. The weekend rides help you build endurance. The Saturday rides include more intensity and are longer than Sunday rides.

All of the workout codes and terms are explained in Chapter 21. Also, be sure to look at the nutrition chapter (Chapter 3) for fuel, hydration, and recovery strategies that will be critical for you to follow between laps.

Mountain Bike

FRIDAY	SATURDAY	SUNDAY	WEEKLY TOTAL
Day off	MTB E3	E1b	
	-10 min. z3		3:00
	1:00	0:30	
Day off	MTB E3	E1a	
	-15 min. z3		4:30
	1:30	1:00	
Day off	MTB T2	E2a	
	-15-20 min. z3		5:30
	2:00	1:30	
Day off	E4	E2a	
	-20-30 min. z3		6:00
	2:00	2:00	
Day off	E4	Day off	
	-30-40 min. z3		4:00
	2:30		
Day off	24-hour race	Day off	
			1:15 + race

LOGISTICS

Some mountain bike races are located at the base of a ski area, with comfortable lodging just steps away. Other races are out in the boondocks, where lodging is a tent, a camper, or the back of a vehicle.

If you like a comfy situation, I suggest selecting a race that starts and ends the laps at the base of a ski area, close to a comfortable hotel or condominium. Having cushy sleeping quarters and a hot shower gives your team an advantage over the teams that are camping. Hearty campers might turn up their noses at the solid-wall dwellers—

until the weather turns cold and rain or snow begins to fall. (Or they might still turn up their noses, but then the noses are red-tipped and runny!)

If you are a hard-core outdoor enthusiast looking for more adventure than just riding over the course of 24 hours, then camping is the way to go. You will experience the full buffet of temperatures, weather, noises, and smells associated with the race.

No matter where you decide to sleep—or, rather, close your eyes for a brief period of time—I recommend you make a couple of lists to keep yourself organized. One should be a packing list for the actual race (similar to the one shown in Appendix B), and the other should keep track of all the items you will need for camping, eating, and sleeping.

If your camping quarters are outdoors or in a tight situation, earplugs and eye covers can help you get some rest. Also, when you are waiting for your teammates to roll into the exchange area at 1:00 a.m., temperatures can be pretty chilly. Be sure to bring enough clothes for the wait.

The final organizational item I suggest is a chart that lists the rider order, lap times, and expected clock arrival times. At first this will seem like overkill but as the hours wear on and sleep deprivation affects your thinking, a chart like this can keep you from making mistakes. You don't want to leave a teammate standing around and looking for you in the handoff area after busting his or her fanny riding the course.

Have fun and laugh a lot!

PART V

BUILDING
FOUNDATION FITNESS

Foundation Fitness Training Plan
Level I

This training plan is for a cyclist who is looking to build foundation fitness but is pinched for time. The plan can be used on its own or to help increase fitness preceding one of the other plans in the book.

Sometimes maintaining foundation fitness is challenging, so this plan also provides you with the framework and workouts to keep yourself fit. The plan can be used in the off-season or anytime you are looking to get or stay on track.

PROFILE

This plan is designed for a Level I rider. Before beginning the plan, you are riding two or three times per week, whether indoors or outdoors. Your workouts may not be consistent, but it is not a problem for you to ride for an hour. You are looking to build strength and endurance and to increase your riding speed. You'd like to start a weight training program, but you don't know where to begin.

One big issue you have is time: You don't have much of it to devote to staying fit. If you could find a plan that would whip you into shape based on three to six hours of training per week, you'd jump up and down.

Get ready to jump.

GOAL

Your goal is to work out consistently for 12 weeks to build foundation fitness. You want to complete 80 to 90 percent of the training hours in this plan. Although you know that simply riding will improve your fitness, you want to improve your riding speed as well. In addition, you want a long ride of about two hours to be comfortable and easy for you to complete.

THE PLAN OVERVIEW

Take a look at the plan overview in Table 19.1. If you begin this training plan the first week of January, you will be ready to ride comfortably for two hours by the time April arrives. Of course, you can begin the plan in any month.

TABLE 19.1 OVERALL PLAN

WEEK	1	2	3	4	5	6	7	8	9	10	11	12
HOURS	4:45	4:45	4:45	3:00	5:30	5:45	6:00	3:00	5:30	5:45	6:00	3:30
PERIOD	Specific Preparation 1				Specific Preparation 2				Specific Preparation 3			

The plan is structured in four-week cycles: Each block includes three weeks of training to build volume and intensity, followed by one week of recovery. In Table 19.1, you can see that your weekly training hours are manageable, six hours per week or less.

Now take a look at Table 19.2, which gives you the details of your training journey. Mondays and Wednesdays are strength training days. Tuesdays and Fridays are days off. Thursdays are form workouts, Saturdays are form or interval workouts, and Sundays are your long rides. If it works better for you to strength train on different days, move the workouts accordingly. Try to keep at least 48 hours between strength training sessions.

PLAN DETAILS

Explanations of the workout codes used throughout this plan can be found in Chapter 21. Strength training details in Chapter 22 can guide you through the AA, MS, and PE (Anatomical Adaptation, Maximum Strength, and Power Endurance) codes used for Monday and Wednesday sessions. Here, let's break down the plan by week.

Weeks 1 through 4

In this first block of training, weekly hours do not increase. This schedule is intentional, to allow you to adapt to the training load. One workout of note in Week 1 is the aerobic time trial on Saturday. This time trial repeats in Week 12. The purpose of the time trial is to give you an idea of the level of improvement you've made to your fitness over the course of the 12 weeks. The goal is to ride faster, for a given heart rate, after 12 weeks of training.

Weeks 5 through 8

In the second block of training, the strength training phase changes to MS (maximum strength; see Chapter 22). The Thursday workouts remain form workouts. On Saturdays, you begin to improve your lactate threshold speed and power. On Sundays, the length of your long ride increases. You can add up to 15 minutes to the length of each of these Sunday rides if you have the time and desire to do so. Be sure to fuel and hydrate appropriately for all rides over an hour long.

Weeks 9 through 12

In the third block of training, strength training changes again. The Thursday rides remain form rides. The Saturday rides in this block are aerobic, while the Sunday rides include a combination of endurance building and lactate threshold work.

In the last week of the training plan, you repeat the initial aerobic time trial to mark your fitness improvements. Make the conditions for both trials as close to identical as you can. When you look at your time improvement, consider weather conditions, as wind and heat can significantly affect your results.

After you've completed this foundation fitness plan, you are ready to move on to another training plan.

TABLE 19.2 LEVEL I FOUNDATION FITNESS

WEEK	MONDAY	TUESDAY	WEDNESDAY	THURSDAY
1	AA	Day off	AA	S2
				3–5 min./leg
	1:00		1:00	0:45
2	AA	Day off	AA	S2
				5–7 min./leg
	1:00		1:00	0:45
3	AA	Day off	AA	S2
				7–9 min./leg
	1:00		1:00	0:45
4	AA	Day off	AA	E1a
	0:45		0:45	0:30
5	MS	Day off	MS	S1
	1:15		1:15	0:45
6	MS	Day off	MS	S4
	1:15		1:15	0:45
7	MS	Day off	MS	S2
				7–9 min./leg
	1:15		1:15	0:45
8	MS	Day off	MS	E1a
	0:45		0:45	0:30
9	PE	Day off	PE	P1
				4–5 × 10 sec. (4 min. 50 sec. RI)
	1:00		1:00	0:45

Foundation Fitness

FRIDAY	SATURDAY	SUNDAY	WEEKLY TOTAL
Day off	T1	E1a	
	5 mi.		4:45
	1:00	1:00	
Day off	S4	E2a	
			4:45
	1:00	1:00	
Day off	S1a	E2c	
	4–6 × 20 sec. (100 sec. RI)		4:45
	1:00	1:00	
Day off	Day off	E2a	
			3:00
		1:00	
Day off	M2 (z3)	E2a	
	4–6 × 3 min. (60 sec. RI)		5:30
	1:00	1:15	
Day off	M2 (z3)	E2b	
	4–5 × 4 min. (60 sec. RI)		5:45
	1:00	1:30	
Day off	M2 (z3)	E2a	
	4–5 × 5 min. (2 min. RI)		6:00
	1:00	1:45	
Day off	Day off	E2b	
			3:00
		1:00	
Day off	E2a	E3	
		-20 min. z3	5:30
	1:00	1:45	

CONTINUED

TABLE 19.2 LEVEL I FOUNDATION FITNESS CONTINUED

WEEK	MONDAY	TUESDAY	WEDNESDAY	THURSDAY
10	PE	Day off	PE	P1a
				1–2
	1:00		1:00	0:45
11	PE	Day off	PE	P1
				4–5 × 10 sec. (4 min. 50 sec. RI)
	1:00		1:00	0:45
12	PE	Day off	PE	Day off
	0:45		0:45	

Foundation Fitness

FRIDAY	SATURDAY	SUNDAY	WEEKLY TOTAL
Day off	E2b	E3	
		~20–30 min. z3	5:45
	1:00	2:00	
Day off	E2a	E3	
		~30–40 min. z3	6:00
	1:00	2:15	
Day off	T1	E1a	
	5 mi.		3:30
	1:00	1:00	

Foundation Fitness Training Plan
Level II

This training plan is for an experienced cyclist who just had a great summer season of riding and wants to maintain strong off-season fitness, in order to enjoy improved performance next season. This plan can be used by cyclists who intend to race or who want to improve their speed for group rides. While the plan is written as an off-season training guide, it can be used to build foundation fitness at any time of the year.

PROFILE

This plan is designed for a Level II cyclist who is already riding three or four times per week. You are capable of comfortably completing a ride of 2 hours, 30 minutes, and your current long ride is mostly aerobic but may include a small amount of intensity. Also, you are looking to build strength and endurance and to increase your riding speed for next season. You want to start a weight training program that will deliver this on-the-bike speed later. Your schedule allows you to train six or seven days per week.

GOAL

Your goal is to have an off-season training plan that gives you a jump on your summer fitness. You want to complete 80 to 90 percent of the training hours and workouts in this plan.

Two measures of progress include improved speed for an aerobic time trial and improved speed for an all-out time trial. A third measure is better performance during regular group rides, which could mean the ability to ride with a faster group or to ride with less effort than in the past. Less effort can be measured by average heart rate values for a given distance or average heart rate for a given power output.

THE PLAN OVERVIEW

Take a look at the plan overview in Table 20.1. If you begin this training plan the first week of January, you will be ready to start racing or to go to higher-intensity training in mid-April. If you are preparing for early season racing, you may need to begin this plan in October or November.

TABLE 20.1   OVERALL PLAN

WEEK	1	2	3	4	5	6	7	8	9	10	11	12	13	14	15	16	17	18
HOURS	7:45	7:45	5:45	8:30	8:30	5:45	8:45	9:00	5:45	9:30	9:30	4:45	9:00	9:00	5:30	9:00	9:00	4:15
PERIOD	Specific Preparation 1			Specific Preparation 2			Specific Preparation 3			Specific Preparation 4			Pre-competitive Preparation 1			Pre-competitive Preparation 2		

The plan is structured in three-week cycles: Each block includes two weeks of training to build volume and intensity, followed by one week of recovery. Although some cyclists can do well on a four-week cycle, I have found that a three-week cycle keeps the quality of workouts high while helping riders avoid deep fatigue. This is even more the case as the relative volume or intensity of training increases.

Now look at Table 20.2, which gives the details of the plan. Mondays and Wednesdays are strength training days. Fridays are shown as days off; however, depending on your personal needs, Fridays can be optional strength training days or optional easy rides.

If you decide to strength train on Fridays, keep the AA (anatomical adaptation; see Chapter 22) phase of training on this day throughout the entire plan. If you decide to ride for an hour on Fridays, keep the intensity of the ride mostly in zones 1 to 2. You can use this day to work on cycling skills as well. See form or speed workouts in Chapter 21.

Tuesday and Thursday workouts vary throughout the plan, but the time stays around an hour on each day. If you have the time and energy, you can increase these workouts by up to 30 minutes each. Remember that adding more volume won't necessarily make you a faster rider. More volume or intensity is only good if your body can use it for positive adaptations. Choose wisely.

Saturday rides on the plan are the longer and more intense rides of the weekend. These can be group rides; try to follow the intentions of the workouts shown on the plan within your group rides. If your group rides are on Sundays rather than Saturdays, just exchange the two workouts.

Sundays are aerobic rides. If you are tired from Saturday, don't feel you have to push zone 2 at all. Fitness improvements are achieved by stress followed by recovery, in the form of total rest or active recovery.

PLAN DETAILS

Explanations of the workout codes used throughout this plan can be found in Chapter 21. Strength training details are in Chapter 22. Here, let's break down the plan by week.

Weeks 1 through 6

Week 1 begins with strength training on Monday and your first aerobic time trial on Tuesday. In order to get a good test for this time trial, make the first weight workout very, very light. Because you are adapting to the weight training, these workouts will be stressful. The other stressful workouts are the zone 3 intervals on Tuesdays and the zone 3 intensity portions included in the Saturday rides. Note that the volume of zone 3 builds throughout the block. The length of the Saturday rides does not build during this block.

Weeks 7 through 12

Decrease the weight you lift on Monday of Week 7 so you can produce your best results during the Tuesday aerobic time trial. Use the results in conjunction with the results from other workouts to determine if your fitness is improving.

This training block moves to the more difficult MS (maximum strength; see Chapter 22) phase of strength training. The MS phase tends to leave your legs feeling flat and tired. However, you should not feel sore after every workout. If you have lingering soreness, reduce the amount of weight you are lifting.

Because of the MS weight training, only one ride with intensity on the bike is included per week, on Saturdays. Some cyclists find they are unable to achieve intensity above zone 3. If you are one of them, don't worry about it. Use zone 3 efforts and limited zone 4 (and above) for your threshold improvement.

At the end of this training block—and the end of your rest week in Week 12—is an all-out time trial. Be sure you lighten the weights or reduce the sets you do on strength training days in both rest weeks, Weeks 9 and 12, to facilitate recovery. An additional option is to strength train only one day during a recovery week.

TABLE 20.2 LEVEL II FOUNDATION FITNESS

WEEK	MONDAY	TUESDAY	WEDNESDAY
1	AA	T1	AA
	(see text)	5 mi.	
	1:15	1:00	1:15
2	AA	M2 (z3)	AA
		4–6 × 3 min. (60 sec. RI)	
	1:15	1:00	1:15
3	AA	Day off	AA
	1:00		1:00
4	AA	M2 (z3)	AA
		4–6 × 4 min. (60 sec. RI)	
	1:15	1:00	1:15
5	AA	M2 (z3)	AA
		4–5 × 5 min. (2 min. RI)	
	1:15	1:00	1:15
6	AA	Day off	AA
	1:00		1:00
7	AA	T1	MS
	(see text)	5 mi.	
	1:15	1:00	1:30
8	MS	P1a	MS
		2–3	
	1:30	1:00	1:30
9	MS	Day off	MS
	(see text)		(see text)
	1:00		1:00

THURSDAY	FRIDAY	SATURDAY	SUNDAY	WEEKLY TOTAL
S2	Day off	E3	E2b	
3-5 min./leg		<20 min. z3		7:45
0:45		2:30	1:00	
S2	Day off	E3	E1a	
5-7 min./leg		<30 min. z3		7:45
0:45		2:30	1:00	
S4	Day off	E2c	E1b	
				5:45
0:45		2:00	1:00	
S1	Day off	E3	E2a	
		~30-40 min. z3		8:30
1:00		2:30	1:30	
S1	Day off	E3	E2b	
		~30-40 min. z3		8:30
1:00		2:30	1:30	
S4	Day off	E2c	E1a	
				5:45
0:45		2:00	1:00	
S2	Day off	E4	E2b	
7-9 min./leg		<20 min. z4/5a		8:45
1:00		2:30	1:30	
E1b	Day off	E4	E2b	
		<30 min. z4/5a		9:00
1:00		2:30	1:30	
S4	Day off	E2c	E1a	
				5:45
0:45		2:00	1:00	

CONTINUED

Foundation Fitness

TABLE 20.2 LEVEL II FOUNDATION FITNESS CONTINUED

WEEK	MONDAY	TUESDAY	WEDNESDAY
10	MS	P1	MS
	5–7 × 10 sec. (4 min. 50 sec. RI)		
	1:30	1:00	1:30
11	MS	P1a	MS
		3–4	
	1:30	1:00	1:30
12	MS	Day off	MS
	(see text)		(see text)
	1:00		1:00
13	PE	E2b	P1
			5–7 × 10 sec. (4 min. 50 sec. RI)
	1:00	1:00	1:00
14	PE	E2b	P2
			5–7 × 10 sec. (4 min. 50 sec. RI)
	1:00	1:00	1:00
15	PE	Day off	P2
			5 × 20 sec. (4 min. 40 sec. RI)
	0:45		1:00
16	PE	E1b	P3a
			5–7 × 30 sec. (4 min. 30 sec. RI)
	1:00	1:00	1:00
17	PE	E1b	P3b
			2–3
	1:00	1:00	1:00
18	PE	Day off	P1
			5 × 10 sec. (4 min. 50 sec. RI)
	0:45		0:45

Foundation Fitness

THURSDAY	FRIDAY	SATURDAY	SUNDAY	WEEKLY TOTAL
S2	Day off	E4	E2a	
8–10 min./leg		~30–40 min. z4/5a		9:30
1:00		3:00	1:30	
E1b	Day off	E4	E2a	
		~30–40 min. z4/5a		9:30
1:00		3:00	1:30	
S4	Day off	E2b	T2	
			5 mi.	4:45
0:45		1:00	1:00	
M2 (z4/5a)	Day off	A1c	E2a	
5–6 × 3 min. (60 sec. RI)				9:00
1:00		3:00	2:00	
M2 (z4/5a)	Day off	A1c	E2a	
5–6 × 4 min. (60 sec. RI)				9:00
1:00		3:00	2:00	
S4	Day off	A1a	E1b	
				5:30
0:45		2:00	1:00	
M2 (z4/5a)	Day off	A1c	E2a	
4–5 × 5 min. (2 min. RI)				9:00
1:00		3:00	2:00	
M2 (z4/5a)	Day off	A1c	E2a	
4–5 × 6 min. (2 min. RI)				9:00
1:00		3:00	2:00	
S4	Day off	E2b	T2	
			5 mi.	4:15
0:45		1:00	1:00	

Weeks 13 through 18

In this Pre-competitive block, strength training is reduced to one day per week and moves to the PE (power endurance; see Chapter 22) phase. Some cyclists find they benefit from two days in the weight room during this block of training. If you would like to keep two strength training days, you can substitute a day of PE training in place of each Wednesday workout shown in this block.

If you were unable to achieve intensity above zone 4 in the last block of Saturday rides, use the guidelines for Weeks 7 through 12 to replace the guidelines for Weeks 13 through 18. At the end of this training plan is another all-out time trial to check your progress.

After completing this plan, you are ready to head into a training plan designed for your specific event goal—whether it's road racing, aggressive group riding, or mountain bike racing.

PART VI

SUPPORTING INFORMATION

Workout Codes

All the workout codes that appear in the training plans are detailed here. Workout codes followed by an asterisk (*) are not included in any of the training plans, but as you refine your training more you might enjoy substituting them for similar workouts. The specific workouts are based on the training zones you determined for yourself by doing one of the tests in Chapter 2.

The workout times listed in any plan include warm-up and cool-down time. A warm-up is typically between 10 and 30 minutes, depending on the particular workout and how much time is assigned. If the ride is mostly in zone 1 to zone 2, begin and end the ride in zone 1. Before beginning intervals, tempo rides, or races, be certain to include a good warm-up. If the workout is a high-intensity session, begin the ride in zone 1 and slowly increase speed, so that your heart rate is close to being in the zone in which you will be doing the work intervals. If you are unable to get your heart rate into the specified zone by the third interval, admit that it's simply not your day, spin easy, and head home.

After all workouts and races, take an easy spin to cool down. By the end of the cool-down, heart rate should be in zone 1 or lower. Stretch muscles shortly after your cool-down (see Chapter 23 for stretching exercises).

Some of the workouts specify a rolling course or a hilly course. "Hilly" is relative to where you live. In general, a rolling course has grades up to about 4 percent and a hilly course has steeper grades. If you live in Flat City, simulate pedaling up hills by shifting up a gear or two.

Strength training codes (AA, MS, PE, SM) can be found in Chapter 21.

WORKOUT CODES

Endurance Workouts

E1a—Recovery, 90 rpm Ride in the small chainring at 90 revolutions per minute (rpm) on a flat course, keeping your heart rate in zone 1. If you are unable to maintain 90 rpm, coast and rest until you can resume 90 rpm.

E1b—Easy Ride Ride at rate of perceived exertion (RPE) zone 1 or below. This should be very easy, a "noodle ride."

E2a—Endurance, Rolling This level is used for aerobic maintenance and endurance training. Heart rate should stay primarily in zones 1 to 2. How much time is spent in each zone depends on how you feel that day. The goal of an E2 ride is not to see how much time you can spend in zone 2. Ride on a rolling course, if possible, with grades up to 4 percent. For reference, most highway off-ramps are 4 percent grade. Riding in a slightly larger gear can simulate a gentle hill if there are no hills where you live. Remain in the saddle on the hills. If you ride with a group, inner discipline is necessary to let the group go if it wants to hammer.

E2b—Endurance, 90 rpm Ride in zones 1 to 2 on a flat to gently rolling course at 90+ rpm. If you're unable to spin at 90+ rpm, coast and recover until you can.

E2c—Endurance, Negative-Split Begin the first half of the workout in zone 1. Control your intensity; it should feel too easy. When you reach the halfway mark, increase intensity a bit to zone 2. The second half of the workout is mostly zone 2 but can include some zone 1. If you ride an out-and-back course, you should return in less time than it took you to go out.

E3—Endurance This workout is used for endurance training and the beginning of lactate threshold training. Ride a rolling course in zones 1 to 3. Stay seated on the hills to build or maintain hip power. Ride a course and use gearing that allows work intensity into zone 3, but don't get into zones 4 and 5. Some plans suggest an amount of time to accumulate in zone 3. For example, the designation "~15–20 min. z3" means you should accumulate 15 to 20 minutes in zone 3. If the progression is not detailed in a plan, accumulated time is up to you—begin conservatively.

E4—Endurance This ride is a multifaceted workout for building endurance, speed, and strength. The first time you do an E4 workout, keep your heart rate in zones 1 to 4.

As training progresses, and depending on the specifics of the plan you're following, you can spend some time in zone 5. As your fitness improves, you should find you can spend progressively larger amounts of time in zones 4 and 5. Some plans suggest an amount of time to accumulate in zones 4 to 5a. For example, the designation "~20 min. z4/5a" means you should accumulate about 20 minutes in zones 4 to 5a. If the progression is not detailed in the plan, accumulated time is up to you—begin conservatively.

Form or Speed Workouts

S1—Spin Step-ups   This workout is intended to work on pedaling form and neuromuscular coordination. On an indoor trainer: Warm up with low resistance and at a pedaling cadence of 90 rpm. After warming up for 15 to 20 minutes, increase cadence to 100 rpm for 3 minutes, 110 rpm for 2 minutes, and 120+ rpm for 1 minute. If time allows, spin easy for 5 minutes to recover, and repeat. If you are just beginning to increase your pedaling speed, you may want to cut all of the times in half in order to maintain the recommended speeds. Using low resistance is important so that you focus on the speed of the feet and not on the force on the pedals. This workout can be done on the road if the road is flat or slightly downhill.

S1a—Spin-ups   This workout is intended to work on pedaling form and neuromuscular coordination. After a good warm-up, include the designated number of 20- to 30-second repeats, building your pedaling speed throughout. Spin at a high rpm while keeping your torso quiet—no swinging shoulders or bouncing butt. This is relaxed speed. Take a 90- to 100-second easy rest interval between spin-ups.

S2—Isolated Leg   This workout helps work the dead spots out of pedal strokes. On an indoor trainer: After a warm-up with light resistance, do 100 percent of the work with one leg while the other leg is resting on a stool. The bottom of the stroke is similar to the motion of scraping mud off the bottom of your shoe. The top of the stroke can be improved by driving toes forward. In all positions, keep the toes relaxed. Do not allow them to curl up and clench the bottom of your shoe.

This workout can be done outdoors by relaxing one leg while the other leg does 90 percent of the work. Change legs when fatigue sets in, or set a specific time interval to prevent excess fatigue. Work your way up to a work interval of 30 to 60 seconds per leg. After doing a work segment with each leg, spin easy with both legs for a minute and then go back to single-leg work.

Stop pedaling with one leg when form becomes sloppy. Do not worry about achieving any particular heart rate; smooth pedaling form is most important. Begin with a cumulative time of 3 to 5 minutes on each leg (or as specified in your plan) and build time as you become stronger.

S3—Accelerations   This workout is intended to work on leg speed and neuromuscular pathways. Warm up well, then complete the specified number of 30-second accelerations, spinning easy for 2 minutes and 30 seconds between accelerations. The end of the 30-second acceleration should be faster than the beginning. If only S3 appears in the plan, the total number of repeats is left to your discretion.

S4—Fartlek (Speed Play)   Ride mostly in zones 1 to 2 with a few 10- to 20-second accelerations placed throughout the workout—your choice. Spin for a generous amount of time between each of the accelerations so your legs recover before beginning another acceleration.

S5—Cadence   Ride in zones 1 to 2 on a flat to gently rolling course at 90+ rpm. If you're unable to spin at 90+ rpm, coast and recover until you can. Focus on smooth leg speed and don't worry about reaching a set amount of time in zone 2. Endurance training is not the focus of this workout.

S7—Pre-event Check   Ride mostly in zones 1 to 2 with a few 10- to 20-second accelerations placed throughout the workout—your choice. Run through all the gears at some point during the ride to ensure smooth shifting.

S8—Mountain Bike Skills   After a warm-up, practice skills in a grassy park or in a mountain bike skills park. The focus is on balancing (track stands) and negotiating turns equally well in both directions. Begin with large-radius turns and work your way to smaller and tighter corners. Practice on both flat and sloped terrain. This workout should be performed entirely at an intensity lower than zone 2.

Force Workout

F1—Hills, Low Cadence   Ride a hilly course using a gear or two larger than you would normally use on the uphill sections. This strategy will require you to use more force on the pedals and to ride at a lower cadence. Aim for a cadence of about 60 rpm when you are going uphill. Ride at your normal cadence on flat sections of the course, and increase cadence to 90+ rpm on the downhill sections. Most of the ride is in zones 1 to 2. *This workout can be used in place of strength training.*

Muscular Endurance Workouts

M1—Tempo   This workout is the beginning of lactate threshold speed work and is used for a good portion of training for events lasting more than three hours. After a warm-up on a mostly flat course, ride in zone 3 for the time indicated in the plan.

M2 (z3)—Cruise Intervals   These intervals also begin work on lactate threshold speed and power. On a mostly flat course or indoor trainer, complete the number of intervals given in the plan, allowing your heart rate to rise into zone 3 over the course of the interval. For example, "4–5 × 4 min. (60 sec. RI)" means after the warm-up, ride 4-minute intervals 4 or 5 times, allowing your heart rate to rise into zone 3 and no higher. After heart rate is in zone 3, try to hold it there until the end of the interval. Begin timing the interval as soon as you begin an increased effort; do not wait to begin the clock until your heart rate reaches zone 3. All work intervals begin when effort is increased and end when effort is decreased. Spin easy and recover for 60 seconds between efforts.

M2 (z4/5a)—Cruise Intervals*   These intervals work on lactate threshold speed as the season and your fitness progress. On a mostly flat course or indoor trainer, complete the number of intervals shown in the plan, allowing heart rate to rise into zones 4 to 5a over the course of the interval. For example, "4–5 × 4 min. (60 sec. RI)" means after your warm-up, ride 4 or 5 times for 4 minutes each, allowing your heart rate to rise into zones 4 to 5a and no higher. After heart rate is in zones 4 to 5a, try to hold it there until the end of the interval. Take 60 seconds of easy spinning between work intervals to recover.

M3 (z3)—Hill Cruise Intervals*   Same as M2 (z3), except on a long hill with a 2 to 4 percent grade.

M3 (z4/5a)—Hill Threshold Cruise Intervals   Same as M2 (z4/5a), except on a long hill with a 2 to 4 percent grade.

M4—Crisscross Threshold   On a mostly flat or rolling course, begin with a warm-up and slowly increase effort to the lower range of the zones specified. For example, if the plan says "M4 20 min. z4/5a," once you reach the bottom of zone 4, you will begin timing. Gradually build speed until you achieve the top of zone 5a. Then gradually reduce speed until you are back in the lower range of zone 4. To ride the zones from low to high to low again (i.e., crisscross) should take about 2 minutes. Continue this pattern for the time stated in the plan—in this example, you would crisscross for 20 minutes.

M5—Tempo   This workout improves lactate threshold speed. After a warm-up on a mostly flat course, ride steady in zones 4 to 5a for the time indicated in the plan.

M6 (z1/3)—Negative-Split   Begin the first half of the workout in zones 1 to 2. Control your intensity; it should feel too easy. When you reach the halfway mark, increase intensity a bit to zone 3. The second half of the workout is mostly in zones 2 to 3 but can include some zone 1. If you ride an out-and-back course, you should return in less time than it took you to go out.

M6 (z1/5a)—Negative-Split, Threshold   Begin the first half of the workout in zones 1 to 2. Control your intensity; it should feel too easy. When you reach the halfway mark, gently increase intensity to zone 4. Include steady time in zones 4 to 5a in the second half of the workout for the time indicated. Avoid zone 3. If you ride an out-and-back course, you should return in less time than it took you to go out.

M7—Taper Intervals   After a good warm-up, complete the designated number of 90-second accelerations, getting your heart rate into zone 3. Take 3 full minutes to recover and get your heart rate back into zone 1 before starting the next interval. These intervals help keep legs feeling fresh and speedy while volume is tapering prior to a race or important ride.

Speed Endurance (Anaerobic) and Taper Workouts

A1a—Easy Group Ride   This particular workout is not anaerobic but is part of a series of group rides. Ride with a group and stay mostly in zones 1 to 3.

A1b—Faster-Paced Group Ride*   Ride with a group and stay mostly in zones 1 to 4. Some time can be spent in zone 5, but keep it minimal.

A1c—Fast, Aggressive Group Ride   Ride with a group, and ride in all zones. Be aggressive and power up the hills, chase riders who might have been faster than you in the past, and have fun.

A1d—Ride as You Feel   If you are feeling great, ride aggressively with some time in all zones. If tired, take it easy.

A2—Speed-Endurance Intervals   After a good warm-up on a mostly flat course, do the specified number of intervals, allowing heart rate to climb into zone 5b. The intervals may be done on a flat or slightly uphill course. In the plans, the designation "4–5 × 3 min. (3 min. RI)" means ride 4 or 5 3-minute intervals, getting your heart rate into zone 5b and keeping it there until the end of the interval. Timing begins when effort increases and ends when effort ends. Take 3 minutes between intervals.

A6—90-Second Hill Reps*   After a good warm-up, ride a 6 to 8 percent grade hill and complete the specified number of 90-second hill repetitions. Stay seated for the first 60 seconds as you build to zone 5b, then shift to a higher gear, stand, and drive the bike to the top, allowing heart rate to climb into zone 5c. Recover completely for 3 to 4 minutes between repetitions.

A7—Taper Intervals   After a good warm-up, complete the specified number of 90-second accelerations, getting heart rate into zones 4 to 5a. Take 3 full minutes to recover and get heart rate back into zone 1 before starting the next interval. In the plans, the intervals may be noted as something like "4–5 × 90 sec. (3 min. RI)." If the number of repeats is not specified in the plan, do 3 to 5. Remember that doing more is not necessarily better. These intervals help keep legs feeling fresh and speedy while volume is tapering prior to a race or an important ride.

A8—High Power Average   Warm up for 15 to 20 minutes. After the warm-up, complete the designated number of 2-minute intervals indicated in the plan. Put as much power into each work interval as possible; don't worry if power fades during the workout. Recover for 4 minutes. For example, "4–5 × 2 min. (4 min. RI)" means complete 4 or 5 intervals of 2 minutes each, producing the highest average power possible on each one. Recover for 4 minutes between work bouts. These intervals can be on a flat or slightly uphill road. Cool down at the end.

Power Workouts

P1—Sprints, Getting Started   Warm up for 15 to 20 minutes. After the warm-up, complete the designated number of sprints and then spin very easy with a low load and a high cadence for the amount of time in parentheses. For example, "5–7 × 10 sec. (4 min. 50 sec. RI)" means complete 5 to 7 sprints of 10 seconds each, building power throughout. Recover for 4 minutes and 50 seconds between sprints. During each of these sprints, begin with moderate force and end with high power output. The power output at the end of each sprint should be very similar. Leave 10 to 20 minutes to cool down.

P1a—Sprints, Form   After a good warm-up, ride mostly at zone 1 to 2 intensity and include 1 to 4 repeats of this sprint routine, per your training plan:

30 sec. each leg (isolated leg)
2 min. at 90+ rpm
30 sec. acceleration
2 min. at 90+ rpm
10 sec. all-out sprint
1 min. 50 sec. easy spinning recovery

Cool down and stretch.

P2—Sprints, All-Out   Warm up for 15 to 20 minutes. After the warm-up, complete the designated number of sprints for the time indicated in the plan. Sprint as forcefully as you can—don't worry if power fades; just put as much power as possible into each sprint. Recover for the time indicated in the plan. For example, "5–7 × 10 sec. (4 min. 40 sec. RI)" means complete 5 to 7 all-out sprints of 10 seconds each. Recover for 4 minutes and 40 seconds between sprints. Cool down at the end.

P3—Power Combination, Short Descending   Warm up for 15 to 20 minutes. After the warm-up, begin the high-power-output interval. Complete the following set in its entirety before repeating according to the number of sets designated in your plan.

$$3 \times 45 \text{ sec. (4 min. 15 sec. RI)}$$
$$3 \times 30 \text{ sec. (4 min. 30 sec. RI)}$$
$$3 \times 20 \text{ sec. (4 min. 40 sec. RI)}$$
$$3 \times 10 \text{ sec. (4 min. 50 sec. RI).}$$

Leave time for cooling down at the end.

P3a—Short, High Power Average Warm up for 15 to 20 minutes. After the warm-up, complete the designated number of high-power intervals for the time indicated in the plan. Work interval time is less than 60 seconds. Put as much power into each work bout as possible; don't worry if power fades during the workout. Recover for the time indicated on the plan. For example, "5–7 × 45 sec. (4 min. 15 sec. RI)" means complete 5 to 7 sprints of 45 seconds each—producing the highest average power possible on each one—and recover for 4 minutes and 15 seconds between sprints. Cool down at the end.

P3b—Power Combination, Short Warm up for 15 to 20 minutes. After the warm-up, complete the designated number of sets of this combination of high-power-output intervals and rest intervals:

$$45 \text{ sec. (4 min. 15 sec. RI)}$$
$$30 \text{ sec. (4 min. 30 sec. RI)}$$
$$20 \text{ sec. (4 min. 40 sec. RI)}$$
$$10 \text{ sec. (4 min. 50 sec. RI)}$$

Repeat the cycle as indicated in the plan. Leave time for cooling down at the end.

P4—Sprints, Seated, as You Please Ride mostly in zones 1 to 2 on a flat or rolling course. On hills, stay seated. Include several powerful 10-pedal-stroke sprints as the mood strikes you. Take at least 3 minutes between sprints to recover.

P5—Sprints, out of the Saddle* After you warm up, do the designated number of sprints and get out of the saddle during each one. Sprint as forcefully as you can—don't worry if power fades; just put as much power as possible into each sprint. Recover for the time indicated in the plan. For example, "5–7 × 8–12 sec. (3 min. RI)" means complete 5 to 7 all-out sprints of 8 to 12 seconds each. Recover for 3 minutes between sprints. Cool down at the end.

P6—Sprints, in and out of the Saddle* After you warm up, do the designated number of sprints, riding the first half of the time in the saddle and the last half out of the saddle. Sprint as forcefully as you can—don't worry if power fades; just put as much power as possible into each sprint. Recover for the time indicated in the plan. For example, "5–7 × 8–12 sec. (3 min. RI)" means complete 5 to 7 sprints of 8 to 12 seconds each, in which you begin seated for 4 to 6 seconds and finish with 4 to 6 seconds out of the saddle. Recover for 3 minutes between sprints. Cool down at the end.

P7—Long, High Power Average   Warm up for 15 to 20 minutes. After the warm-up, complete the designated number of 1-minute intervals indicated in the plan. Put as much power into each work bout as possible. Don't worry if power fades during the workout; just aim for the highest average power you can. Recover for the time indicated in the plan. For example, "4–5 × 60 sec. (4 min. RI)" means complete 4 to 5 high-power-average intervals of 60 seconds each, producing the highest average power possible on each one. Recover for 4 minutes between work bouts. Cool down at the end.

P8—Mountain Bike Power and Technical Skills   Select a course that is rolling and includes short climbs with obstacles. Avoid courses with long, sustained climbs. Warm up for at least 20 minutes at mostly zone 1 to 2 intensity. Then work on powering over obstacles. You can do repeats on a select number of obstacles or just ride a course with multiple small obstacles. Recover fully after each obstacle so you can give each one your best effort. Spin down easy at the end.

Test Workouts

T1—Aerobic Time Trial (ATT)   This time trial is best done on an indoor trainer with a power meter or on a trainer with a rear-wheel computer pickup. In either case, you need a heart rate monitor as well. It can also be done on a flat section of road, but weather conditions will affect the results. After a warm-up, ride 5 miles with your heart rate 9 to 11 beats below lactate threshold heart rate. Use a single gear and do not shift during the test. In your training journal, record the gear used, time, power output, your current weight, and how you felt. Each time you repeat the test, try to make the testing conditions the same. As your aerobic fitness improves, your time should decrease. If you're using a power meter, your power-to-weight ratio (average power produced in watts divided by your weight in pounds or kilograms) should increase.

T2—As-Fast-as-You-Can-Go Time Trial (TT)   After a 15- to 30-minute warm-up, complete a 5- to 8-mile time trial as fast as you can possibly ride. If you are a novice, ride 5 miles. You may need to use a distance somewhere between 5 and 8 miles, because the available course dictates the exact length. Your course needs to be free of stop signs and heavy traffic. You can use a course with a turnaround point. Use any gear you wish, and shift at any time. In your training journal, record weather conditions, gears used, average heart rate, time, power output, your current weight, and how you felt. Each time you repeat the test, try to make the testing conditions (wind, temperature, subjective feelings, and outside stressors) as similar as possible. As your lactate threshold fitness improves, your time should decrease. If you're using a power meter, your power-to-weight ratio (average power produced in watts divided by your weight in pounds or kilograms) should increase.

Crosstraining

XT* It can be a good idea to crosstrain with other sports, such as hiking, aerobics, running, cross-country skiing, and in-line skating. Keep in mind that your crosstraining sport heart rates will not match your cycling heart rate. Use RPE (see Chapter 2) to estimate correct training zones. These workouts should be mostly easy. Be cautious with running. Even if you are cycling for several hours at a time, begin running for short times. For example, you may want to alternate running 1 minute and walking 4 minutes for a total of 30 minutes. You can build your running endurance from there.

CHAPTER 22

Strength Training

A strength workout is included in the designs of most, but not all, of the training plans. In some plans, strength training is optional. Each plan provides information to help you decide whether or not to include strength training. The first priority for getting you through a long-distance cycling event is always to build your endurance for the event, which primarily means spending time on your bike. Strength training can be a great way to augment your training, but it's not always essential.

If you already have a strength training routine, you can continue to use your current program in place of the workouts suggested in a plan. If a plan has no strength training day designated, you can add one if you have the time and energy for the additional workout. Try to strength train on a day shown as a "day off" or on a day that has a less strenuous workout. If you decide to strength train more than one day a week, separate your lifting days by at least 48 hours. If you find that strength training makes you sore or leaves your legs or arms feeling "dead" for endurance workouts, you may want to reduce the weight you are lifting, the number of sets, the number of repetitions, or some combination of the three.

Prior to any strength training session, warm up with 10 to 30 minutes of aerobic work. A good choice is easy spinning on the bike. You can also run, if you are a runner. Some plans have an aerobic session of cycling scheduled prior to strength training; in these plans, use this workout as your warm-up. After each strength session, include about 10 minutes of easy cycling to cool down. Running is not suggested after a strength training session because running on fatigued legs may put you at a higher risk for injury.

The strength training program suggested in this chapter prioritizes exercises that use multiple joints and muscles in a single exercise. These exercises are intended to improve the strength of the primary muscles utilized in cycling. As you develop a strength training and endurance routine, you can modify this program to meet your personal goals. For example, eliminating the upper-body exercises will have less impact on a road cyclist than on a mountain bike rider. Off-road riders need more upper-body strength than roadies.

STARTING A STRENGTH TRAINING PROGRAM

If you do not have experience weight training, it is worth your time to ask a qualified trainer at a gym to help with setting up weight training machines and establishing proper lifting form. It's also a good idea to ask someone you trust to recommend a trainer and to ask the trainer for his or her credentials.

When strength training, maintain good postural alignment whenever possible. This means that when you're standing in a normal, relaxed position, your head is supported by your neck, which is part of the spine and has a normal curvature. The spine too has a curvature that is normal for you. For example, when you're doing squats, your neck should be in a position that allows the curvature of your spine to be in a normal position—that is, your head is not craned toward the ceiling, nor is your chin tucked in toward your chest.

In any strength exercise, always maintain control of the weight on the concentric and the eccentric contractions. This means using muscles, not momentum, to lift and lower the weight. On a concentric contraction, the working muscles are shortening to overcome the force of the weight. This motion is often called the lift phase. On an eccentric contraction, the working muscles are lengthening to resist the force of the weight. The eccentric contraction means lowering the weight while using muscles to control the speed. Do not allow gravity to do all the work! Avoid using your muscles only at the end of the motion to stop the weight; they should be engaged throughout the lowering motion.

STRENGTH TRAINING PHASES

The training plans in this book include one or more of four strength training phases. The phases are summarized in Table 22.1. You can make a copy of this page and take it to the gym with you to use as a handy reference.

TABLE 22.1 STRENGTH TRAINING PHASES

PHASE	AA	MS*	PE*	SM*
Total sessions per phase	8+	8–12	6–12	4+
Days per week	2–3	2	1–2	1–2
Exercises, minimum (in order of completion)	1 2 3 4 5 (circuit)	[1 2][3 4] 5	[1 2][3 4] 5	[1 2][3 4] 5
Exercises, recommended additional (optional)	1 2 3 6 7 8 9 4 5 10 11 12 13	[1 2][3 6] [8 9] [4 5] [7 10] [11 12] 13	[1 2][3 6] [8 9] [4 5] [7 10] [11 12] 13	1 2 3 4 5 + additional exercises as time allows
Load — Rough percentage of 1-Rep Max and how it should feel	40–60 (feels light)	80–95 (feels challenging)	65–85 (feels moderate)	Sets 1–2 at 60 Set 3 at 80 (Sets 1–2 feel moderate; set 3 feels slightly challenging.)
Sets per session	3–5	3–6	3–5	2–6
Repetitions (reps) per set	15–20	3–6	8–15	Sets 1–2 at 12; sets 3–6 at 6–8
Speed of movement	Slow	Slow–moderate	Moderately fast or explosive**	Slow–moderate
Minutes of recovery (between sets)	1–1.5	2–4	3–5	1–2

Minimum exercises in order of completion:
1. Hip extension (squat, step-up, or leg press)
2. Supine dumbbell chest press or push-up
3. Seated row
4. Abdominal curl
5. Floor back extension (single arm and single leg)

Recommended additional exercises (optional):
6. Hip extension (select a different exercise than #1 above to include two hip-extension exercises in your routine)
7. Standing bent-arm latissimus (lat) pull-down or seated cable lat pull-down
8. Knee flexion (also called hamstring curl)
9. Knee extension
10. Heel raise
11. Standing machine hip adduction
12. Standing machine hip abduction
13. Additional core body work to strengthen the trunk

Notes for exercises:
1. Do not continue any exercise that causes pain or causes joints to "pop" or "crack," including any exercise that results in sharp pain during the exercise or pain that lasts for days after the strength training session.
2. Before and after each strength training session, warm up and cool down with 10 to 20 minutes of aerobic activity. Easy spinning on the bike is a good choice. Running is a warm-up option. Do not use running to cool down.
3. Exercises in brackets [ ] can be done in a superset manner, alternating between the two exercises.

* **Boldfaced** exercises follow the guidelines for each particular phase for mountain bike riders. Road riders can follow the same plan as mountain bike riders or keep upper-body exercises at AA sets, weight, and reps. Exercises not in bold are to be completed at AA sets, weight, and reps for all phases of weight training.
** Explosive movements are done only if equipment described in the chapter is available; otherwise, movements are done at moderately fast speeds.

The list of "minimum exercises" in Table 22.1 is for busy athletes looking for efficiency. If you are very busy and want to do the least amount of strength training that will help you reach your goals, utilize the minimum exercise list. If you typically utilize additional exercises but find yourself pinched for time, do the minimum exercises first. The "recommended additional exercises" list is for cyclists who have more time to train or who have physical weaknesses that limit race performance.

If you happen to know your 1-Rep Max weight (the maximum weight you can lift one time), you can use the chart to guide the amount you lift in each phase. If you do not know your 1-Rep Max, just use the rate of exertion descriptions (see "how it should feel" under "load" in Table 22.1) to estimate the weight to lift in each phase.

During the recovery time between exercises, you can stretch. Stretching exercises are outlined in Chapter 23.

Anatomical Adaptation (AA)

Anatomical adaptation (AA) is the initial phase of strength training, designed for the beginning of a racing season or when an athlete is just starting a strength training program. Its purpose is to prepare tendons and muscles for greater loads in a subsequent strength training phase. As part of an endurance sport program, strength training also helps prepare muscles and tendons for greater sport loads, such as moving between flat terrain and rolling or hilly terrain when riding a bicycle. Some training plans use the AA phase for an optional third day of strength training. It is typically an "easy" day of lifting in the maximum strength phase (see "Maximum Strength").

Routine
Complete 2 to 3 sets of 15 to 20 repetitions (reps) of exercises 1 through 5 in Table 22.1. Exercises 6 through 13 are optional. The weight, or load, you lift should feel light, as if you could lift more weight. The exercises can be done in a circuit fashion, doing one set of each exercise before progressing to the second set. Or complete one set of one exercise and rest 1 to 2 minutes before completing the second set of the same exercise. Rest 1 to 2 minutes before completing the third set. Move to the next exercise after completing all sets of one exercise.

In this strength training phase, as well as the others, have alternative exercises in mind in case the weight room is very busy. Additionally, if you are pressed for time, you can rearrange the order of the exercises.

Maximum Strength (MS)

In the MS phase, your form should be to slowly exert force on the weight to move it. Do not use explosive force (e.g., like a rocket booster on the leg press machine). Using explosive force to raise a heavy weight can lead to knee or back problems. Lifting more slowly may mean you struggle a bit to raise the weight the first time, which is fine.

Many athletes find this phase fun because strength gains come quickly as loads increase. Be cautious not to extend this phase beyond the recommended number of sessions. Continuing this phase for too long may result in muscle imbalances, particularly in the upper leg, which could lead to hip or knee injuries.

Routine

The maximum strength (MS) phase is used to teach the central nervous system to recruit high numbers of muscle fibers. For exercises designated MS in Table 22.1, do a warm-up set with a light weight—something you are able to lift 15 or 20 times. When you add more weight, begin the first set conservatively. Use a weight you are certain you can lift 6 to 8 times.

After resting and stretching, add 5 to 10 pounds and lift again. Continue these sequences until up to 6 sets are complete. At some point, you may find it impossible to add more weight and you'll have to lift the final 2 or 3 sets at the same weight. If you find your last set easy, at the next strength training session you can begin the entire sequence 5 to 10 pounds heavier.

Exercises to do while lifting heavier weight include hip extensions, chest presses, seated rows, and latissimus (lat) pull-downs. For all other exercises, do 2 or 3 sets of 15 to 20 reps each. You can "superset" the exercises in brackets, which means alternate between the two exercises. It is important to recover fully between the heavier sets.

Power Endurance (PE)

The PE strength training phase is intended to combine strength with velocity. Making fast movements with weights, however, is controversial. At least one study has shown that when lifters were asked to move a weight as quickly as possible while maintaining contact with the weight bar, power decreased. On a separate occasion, the same group was asked to move the weight as quickly as possible but to release the weight. The lifters' power and speed of movement increased in the second scenario. In theory, the body tries to protect itself in the first scenario, attempting to keep joints from being injured. The body appears to use opposing muscles to slow the weight down, decreasing power. So when you begin the PE phase, ask yourself if the particular piece of equipment or exercise you are using will increase or decrease your power.

One of the best options for a hip-extension exercise with fast movements is a leg press machine that allows you to explosively jump off the platform with a load and return to the starting position at a moderate speed. In other words, the machine does not allow the entire load to come slamming down on your shoulders. The type of equipment I am most familiar with positions the athlete on an incline bench, and the travel of the platform is parallel to the ground. If your gym does not have this type of leg press machine, moderate your speed to reduce the risk of injury and to be certain you are not losing power.

The jumping exercise just described is a form of plyometrics. Plyometrics are exercises aimed at linking strength with speed of movement to produce power. The conventional wisdom used to be that plyometrics was only for sprinters and football players until one study showed that 5K running performance was improved in well-trained endurance athletes using plyometrics.

An example of a plyometric exercise for the upper body—in place of lat pull-downs—is an exercise using a medicine ball. While standing, hold the medicine ball above your head and, as fast and forcefully as possible, slam the ball into the ground. Rowing is difficult to mimic as a plyometric exercise. One option is to lie facedown on a bench, hanging one side of the body off the bench. Quickly lift a medicine ball off the ground and release it at maximum height. Another upper-body option includes quickly tossing a medicine ball between two people, keeping your elbows high, similar to a chest-press position.

This book doesn't have the space to discuss detailed plyometric programs, but you can find more information in Donald A. Chu's *Jumping into Plyometrics*, published by Leisure Press. If you don't have access to machines that allow you to safely perform plyometric movements or you feel uncomfortable experimenting with plyometrics, don't try to use explosive movements. Just do the sets and repetitions designated for this phase and make the movements at moderate, controlled speeds.

Routine

For each exercise, complete 3 to 5 sets of 8 to 15 reps. Follow the same routine of sequence and supersets that you did in the MS phase. You may have to reduce the number of exercises you do in this phase to streamline your training. Eliminate the optional exercises first, unless you have a particular weakness you need to address.

Strength Maintenance (SM)

The SM phase of strength training is often used by experienced athletes to maintain gains made in the MS and PE phases. For beginners, this phase is sometimes included to make small gains in strength without compromising endurance performance.

Routine

Keep the same exercises you used in the AA phase or, if you have less time, use only exercises numbered 1 through 5. For hip extensions, chest presses, seated rows, and lat pull-downs, begin each with a set of 15 to 20 reps at a light weight. Increase the weight slightly and complete 1 or 2 sets of 12 to 15 reps. The load should feel moderate. "Moderate" means challenging, but not so challenging that you must struggle to move the load. Increase the load a small amount on the designated exercises only and complete 1 to 2 sets of 6 to 10 reps. For all other exercises, do 2 to 3 sets of 12 to 15 reps.

RECOVERY WEEKS

As part of your periodization plan, some weeks reduce the volume of training to allow rest and recovery. You can apply this strategy to strength training by reducing the number of strength training days during a rest week, decreasing the time spent in each strength session by reducing the number of sets within a workout, slightly reducing the weight lifted on each exercise, or a combination of any of these three adjustments.

STRENGTH EXERCISES

The strength exercises illustrated in this chapter are not an exhaustive list but are some of the more common exercises. Unfortunately, performing the exercises incorrectly is also common. To help you learn and maintain correct form, each exercise description includes the start position, movement instructions, and the finish position as well as some common errors to avoid. Each exercise is also accompanied by illustrations showing the start and finish positions. If you don't have access to the exact kinds of equipment illustrated, try to find equipment that allows you to make a similar move. You can also ask a trainer for help. Finally, each exercise includes recommended stretches for the muscle(s) you are working. Detailed descriptions of all the stretches can be found in Chapter 23.

START   FINISH

Start Position
- Stand with your toes pointing forward and your feet about shoulder width apart.

Movement and Finish Position
- Keeping the normal curvature of your back and head forward, squat until your upper thighs are about halfway to being parallel to the floor, about the same angle as the knee bend at the top of the pedal stroke when riding a bicycle. The beginning of the squat movement is similar to the movement you make to sit in a chair.
- Keep knees and feet pointed forward the entire time.
- Keep knees over the feet; don't let them wander inward or outward.
- Return to the start position.

Common Errors
- Looking at the floor and bending at your waist, losing the normal curvature of your spine at the bottom of the lift
- Squatting too low
- Placing your feet about 20 inches apart and toes pointing out
- Rocking your knees inward or outward on the way up

Stretches
- Standing quadriceps stretch and standing hamstring stretch

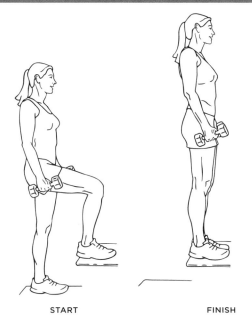

START   FINISH

Start Position
- Use dumbbells or a bar loaded with weight.
- Place your right foot on a sturdy platform about mid-shin high with toes pointing straight ahead.

Movement and Finish Position
- Step up using the muscles in your right leg and touch the platform with your left foot. Pause only a moment and return to the starting position.
- Keep knees and feet pointed forward the entire time.
- Return to the start position.
- Complete all repetitions working the right leg, then repeat with the left leg.

Common Errors
- Looking at the floor and bending at your waist
- Allowing your toes to point out
- Allowing your knees to sway inward or outward
- Toeing off your bottom leg—for example, in the movement description above, pushing off your left leg to make the step instead of using the muscles in your right leg to make the motion

Stretches
- Standing quadriceps stretch and standing hamstring stretch

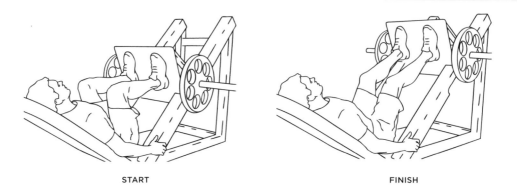

START   FINISH

Start Position

- If the seat is adjustable, angle the seat so you'll have about an arm's length between your torso and your knees when extended.
- Place your feet flat on the platform, about 8 inches apart with your toes pointing forward and your feet aligned with your knees.

Movement and Finish Position

- Press the platform away from you until your legs are straight, knees almost locked.
- Lower the platform until your upper and lower leg form an 80- to 90-degree angle.
- Point your knees and feet forward and keep them about shoulder width apart the entire time.
- Keep your knees aligned with your hips and toes during the entire motion up and down.
- Return to the start position.

Common Errors

- Placing your feet too high on the platform, such that your ankles are in front of your knee joints
- Placing your feet too low so that your heels hang off the platform
- Raising your heels off the platform during the lift phase
- Lowering the platform so that your knees touch your chest—which generally relaxes some of the muscles that should be working, lifts your butt off the seat pad, rocks your pelvis forward, and eliminates the normal curvature of the spine
- Not controlling the weight in both directions

Stretches

- Standing quadriceps stretch and standing hamstring stretch

SUPINE DUMBBELL CHEST PRESS

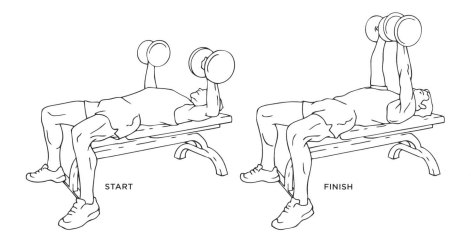

START   FINISH

Start Position

- Lie on your back on a bench with your back in a neutral position that allows the normal curvature of your spine.
- Position your feet so they touch the floor or are on the bench, whichever is most comfortable.
- Hold weights straight up above your chest, keeping your wrists aligned with your elbows and shoulder joints. (A barbell can be used when going to heavier weight.)

Movement and Finish Position

- Retract the shoulders—squeeze your shoulder blades together.
- Lower the weights by leading with your elbows until your elbows align with your shoulder blades.
- Keep your forearms perpendicular to the floor throughout the movement.
- Pause for a moment and return to the start position by keeping your hands directly above your elbows throughout the movement.

Common Errors

- Allowing the dumbbells to drift toward the centerline of your body or away from your body on the upward movement
- Arching your back when lifting heavier weights
- Not retracting your shoulders

Stretches

- Standing upper-torso stretch

Start Position
- Begin with hands placed slightly wider than the shoulders, fingers pointing forward or slightly in.
- The floor contact points will be your hands and either your knees or your toes.

Movement and Finish Position
- Keeping your body rigid and your abdominal muscles tight, push your chest away from the floor until your elbows are extended and nearly locked.
- Lower your body toward the floor in a controlled manner until the angle between your upper and lower arm is between 90 and 100 degrees.
- Pause for a moment before pushing back up again.
- Keep your head aligned with your body, as if you were in a standing position.
- Repeat the action until all repetitions are complete.

Common Errors
- Relaxing all muscles on the downward motion
- Allowing your body to sag in the middle, arching your back

Stretches
- Standing upper-torso stretch

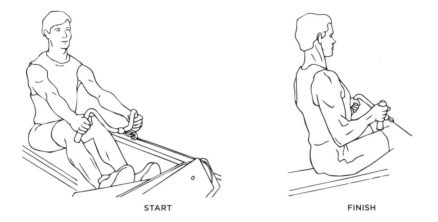

START   FINISH

Start Position

- Use a handle that puts your hands in a position similar to the one you use when holding the hoods of your bicycle handlebars. Your gym may have many handles to choose from; use the widest one. Or use one of the short bars available at most gyms and put your hands the same distance apart as if you were holding the handlebar tops.
- Seated, with your torso and thighs (or upper legs) forming close to a 90-degree angle, place your feet flat on the footplates.
- Keep your head and neck upright, eyes looking forward.
- Make sure your elbows are nearly straight when handles are held at arm's length and when there is tension in the cable.
- Start with your shoulder blades relaxed and separated (abducted) to help train the muscles of your upper back.

Movement and Finish Position

- Initiate the pull by retracting your shoulder blades, then pulling the handle or bar toward your chest, leading with your elbows.
- After a brief pause at your chest, return the handle or bar to the start position by moving first at your elbows, then at your shoulders.
- After your elbows are nearly straight, allow your shoulder blades to separate slightly, returning to the start position.
- Keep your back still throughout the entire exercise, flexing it only to return the bar to the floor when the exercise is complete.
- Keep your abdominal muscles contracted to stabilize your torso.

Common Errors
- Flexing or bending at your waist and using your back to initiate the movement
- Not beginning with your shoulder blades abducted

Stretches
- Standing upper-torso stretch

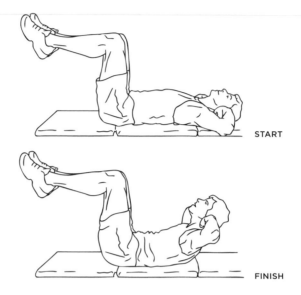

START

FINISH

Start Position

- Lying on your back, bend your knees so your feet rest comfortably on the floor, then lift your feet so your knees stack over your hips.
- Place your hands either behind your head for support (do not pull on the head) or crossed across your chest.

Movement and Finish Position

- Contract your abdominal muscles and lift your torso, bringing your bottom ribs toward your hip bones.
- Your shoulders, neck, and head will lift too; elbows stay wide, and chin stays lifted.
- Pause for a moment, keeping your shoulders lifted
- Lower slowly back to the start position until you are just before the point of losing the contraction of your abdominal muscles. In other words, don't relax on the floor before the next repetition.

Common Errors
- Pulling on your head with your hands
- Hunching your shoulders
- Using a rocking motion and momentum instead of controlling the movement

Stretches
- While lying on the floor on your back, reach your hands and feet in opposite directions.

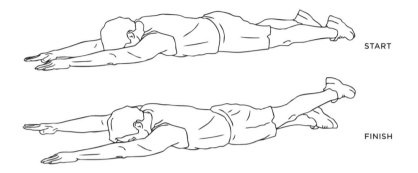

START

FINISH

Start Position
- Lying facedown on the floor, place your arms forward.

Movement and Finish Position
- Using your back muscles, raise one arm and the opposite leg off the ground, keeping your pelvic bones on the floor. (Note: A more advanced move is to raise both arms and both legs off the floor.)
- Keep your neck aligned with your spine, maintaining its normal curvature.
- Pause for a moment.
- Keeping your back muscles contracted, lower your arm and leg back to the starting position.
- Switch to the other arm and the other leg.

Common Errors
- Attempting to use your head and momentum to get your arm and leg off the floor
- Totally relaxing your back muscles when returning to the start position
- Hyperextending your neck, pushing your chin toward the ceiling

Stretches
- Seated back, hip, and gluteus stretch

START   FINISH

Start Position
- Grasp the bar with your arms extended, arms bent at the same angle as when riding a mountain bike.
- Step back enough to lift the weights off the stack while arms are extended in the start position.
- Keep your knees bent and your feet about shoulder width apart.

Movement and Finish Position
- Pull the bar toward your thighs by first depressing your shoulders away from your ears, then retracting your shoulder blades—pulling them together.
- Follow by pulling with your arms.
- Pause for a moment.
- Return the weight to the start position by moving your arms, then your shoulders.

Common Errors
- Jerking the weight to begin and using a lot of torso movement to get the weight started (using your body weight instead of back and arm muscles to move the weight)
- Relaxing your muscles when returning the weight to the start position and allowing the weight to jerk your arms instead of using back and arm muscles to control the weight on the return to the start

Stretches
- Standing upper-torso stretch

SEATED CABLE LAT PULL-DOWN

START   FINISH

Start Position
- Grasp the bar with your arms fully extended and hands about shoulder width apart, using an overhand grip.
- Sit on the bench with your feet flat on the ground and your knees bent at about a 90-degree angle.
- Adjust the thigh pads so they help keep you seated.

Movement and Finish Position
- Leaning slightly back, pull the bar toward your upper chest, by first depressing your shoulders away from your ears, followed by pulling with your arms.
- Pull down and in until the bar just touches or is very close to your breastbone.
- Pause for a moment.
- Return the weight by moving your arms, then your shoulders.

Common Errors
- Jerking the weight and using a lot of torso movement
- Leaning back to get the weight started (using your body weight instead of your muscles to move the weight)

Stretches
- Standing upper-torso stretch

KNEE FLEXION (HAMSTRING CURL)

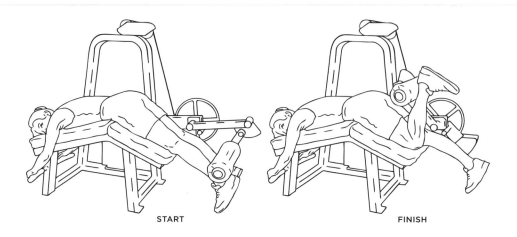

START   FINISH

Start Position
- Begin with the support pad a few inches above your heel.
- Align the center of your knee joint with the pivot point on the equipment.
- Relax your foot; don't try to flex it.

Movement and Finish Position
- Curl one leg up as far as possible.
- Pause for a moment.
- Return the rotating arm to the start position, keeping your hamstring muscles contracted.
- Complete all repetitions in a set with one leg before switching to your other leg.

Common Errors
- Stopping short by not curling your leg as far as possible
- Relaxing your hamstring muscles when lowering the weight
- Arching your back to complete the lift
- Using momentum to complete the lift

Stretches
- Standing hamstring stretch

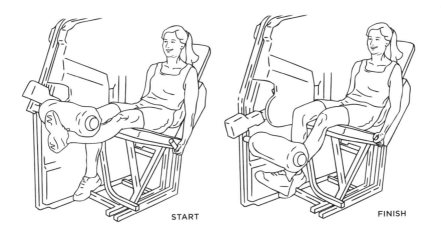

START   FINISH

Start Position

- Adjust the seat so you have back support and the center of your knee joint aligns with the pivotal joint on the exercise equipment.
- Begin with both legs fully extended, lifting a weight you can lift with a single leg.
- Keep your knees and hips aligned throughout the exercise.

Movement and Finish Position

- Use one leg to lower the weight about 8 inches, to just before the point where your quadriceps muscles lose contraction. (Do not go all the way down.)
- Return to the starting position and pause for a moment.
- Complete all repetitions in the set with one leg before switching to your other leg.

Common Errors

- Lowering the weight past the point of keeping your quadriceps muscles contracted (you can put your hand on your quadriceps and feel when they are contracted and tight and when they are relaxed)
- Using momentum to swing the weight up and down instead of using a controlled motion
- Arching your back in the lift phase
- Allowing your butt to lift off the seat pad
- Allowing your knees to rotate in or out

Stretches

- Standing quadriceps stretch

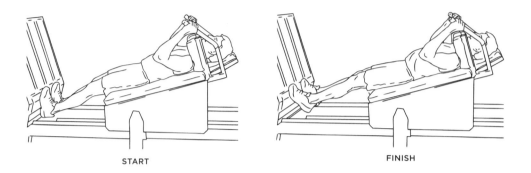

START   FINISH

Start Position

- Use a leg press machine, a standing calf raise machine, or a riser block.
- If using a leg press or a standing calf machine, you can work both legs at once or one at a time.
- Using a riser block, you can either use your body weight or hold a dumbbell.
- Doing single- or double-leg heel raises, point the foot of your working leg(s) forward.
- The ball of your foot is on the platform and your heel is as low as possible, allowing you to maintain an eccentric contraction in the calf muscle. (Calf muscle is not totally relaxed.)
- Your knee is straight but not locked.

Movement and Finish Position (from the heel-down position)

- Contract your calf (push up onto your tiptoes) until you are on the ball of your foot, as high as you can go.
- Pause for a moment at the top position.
- In a controlled manner, return to the start position.
- If you are doing single-leg exercises, complete all repetitions in a set with one leg, then switch legs.

Common Errors

- Not going as high as possible
- Going too low and losing tension on your calf muscle
- Relaxing your muscles on the down motion
- Not doing the exercise in a controlled manner

Stretches

- Standing lower-leg stretch

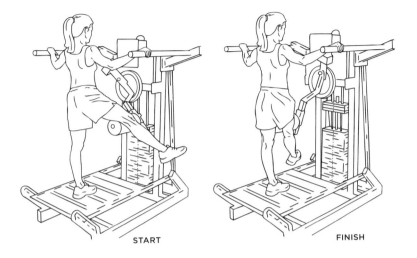

START   FINISH

Start Position

- Stand comfortably with your spine in neutral alignment. (Don't arch your back or lean forward.)
- Position yourself so the pad on the machine is just above your knee on the inside.
- The angle of the padded arm puts a very slight, but not excessive, stretch on your adductors (inner thigh).

Movement and Finish Position

- Move your leg toward the midline of your body.
- Move your leg across the midline of your body without twisting your torso.
- Pause for a moment and return to the start position by controlling the speed of the weight.

Common Errors

- Arching your back
- Swinging and twisting your torso, not keeping hips facing the machine
- Beginning with too much stretch on your adductors
- Moving the weight with an explosive start
- Relaxing muscles on the return to start and allowing the weight to slam down

Stretches

- Seated adductor stretch

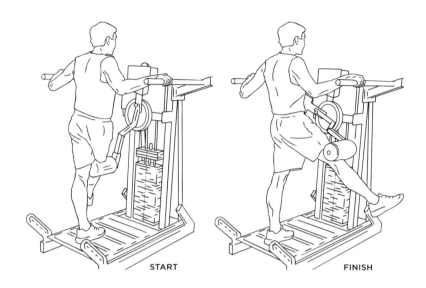

START   FINISH

Start Position

- Stand comfortably with your spine in neutral alignment. (Don't arch your back or lean forward.)
- Position yourself so the pad on the machine is just above your knee on the outside.
- The angle of the padded arm puts a very slight, but not excessive, stretch on your abductors (outer thigh).

Movement and Finish Position

- Keeping your trunk stable, move your working leg away from the midline of your body.
- Pause for a moment and return to the start position by controlling the speed of the weight.

Common Errors

- Arching your back
- Swinging and twisting your torso, not keeping hips facing the machine
- Moving the weight with an explosive start
- Relaxing muscles on the return to start and allowing the weight to slam down

Stretches

- Seated back, hip, and gluteus stretch

Stretching

Flexibility has been shown to improve neuromuscular coordination, physical efficiency, balance and muscular awareness, and performance. It increases blood supply and nutrients to joint structure and can even improve strength.

Two basic types of flexibility are *static* and *dynamic*. Static flexibility is the range of motion relative to a joint, with little emphasis on speed of movement. An example is the flexibility in the hamstring, lower back, and upper back that is necessary for cyclists to ride in a time trial position or endure a long ride. Dynamic flexibility is resistance to motion at the joint and involves speed during physical performance. For example, a cyclist needs dynamic flexibility in a short sprint to pass a competitor at the finish line. A good cyclist must have both types of flexibility.

In a study, swimmers, football players, and runners did contract-relax flexibility training for the knee extensors and flexors for eight weeks, three days per week. Contract-relax flexibility training involves a passive stretch of a muscle after an isometric contraction. The researchers found that flexibility training increased the range of motion of the knee joint by about 6 percent and that stretching improved knee joint torque. Eccentric knee extension torque increased 19 to 25 percent, depending on particular velocity of measurement. Eccentric knee flexion torque increased 16 to 18 percent, again depending on the velocity of measurement. Concentric knee flexion torque increased 8 to 10 percent, while knee flexion isometric torque increased 11 percent.

In short, the contract-relax flexibility training increased the strength of the knee flexors and extensors (hamstrings and quadriceps, respectively, to name some of the major muscles involved) during eccentric actions. The training also increased the strength of the knee flexors during concentric actions.

While this study showed a positive correlation between stretching and sport strength, not all studies support these findings. In fact, a review of the literature doesn't result in enough evidence either to endorse or to discourage a stretching routine. So stretching—whether it helps everyone or not and whether it should be done at all—remains somewhat controversial.

Literature aside, several athletes have found themselves faced with activity-limiting injuries. Many times, their rehabilitation and future prevention routines include a stretching regimen. Because the research literature is inconclusive and many recreational and elite athletes have benefited from a stretching protocol, I continue to recommend stretching as part of a fitness routine. If you are an athlete who has never stretched and you haven't experienced any problems due to your lack of flexibility, I don't see a reason to add stretching to your routine until it is needed.

HOW TO STRETCH

Good times to stretch are after your cool-down, following an aerobic session, and during rest periods between strength training sets. There are many stretching methods, but I recommend proprioceptive neuromuscular facilitation (PNF). This technique has many variations. Here is one easy-to-follow version:

1. Static stretch (stretch and hold) the muscle for about 8 seconds. Remember to breathe.
2. Contract, or flex, the same muscle for about 8 seconds. (Leave out the contraction step when stretching during the rest interval of strength training and just hold static stretches for about 15 seconds.)
3. Stretch and hold the stretch again for about 8 seconds. Breathe.
4. Continue alternating muscle contractions and stretches until you have completed 4 to 8 static stretches. End with a stretch and not a contraction.

Each time you repeat the stretch, you should find you are able to stretch further, or increase your range of motion.

STRETCHES FOR CYCLING AND WEIGHT ROOM

Some of the following exercises stretch multiple muscles, so they can save time for the hurried athlete. Do them in the order listed. Some of these stretches may not work for you. If you want further ideas for stretching exercises, a couple of good resources are *Sport Stretch* by Michael J. Alter and *Stretching* by Bob Anderson.

STANDING QUADRICEPS STRETCH

- While balancing against something with your left hand, use your right hand to grasp your right foot behind your butt.
- Static stretch by gently pulling your foot up and away from your butt.
- Stand erect and keep your hip, knee, and ankle in alignment.
- Contract by pushing against your hand with your foot. Begin with a gentle force.
- Repeat with your left leg.

Common Errors
- Pulling your foot against your butt and compressing your knee joint
- Bending over at your waist

STANDING HAMSTRING STRETCH

- Bend over at your waist, balancing yourself against something stable.
- Place one leg forward and the other leg about 12 inches behind it, toes pointing forward.
- With your weight mostly on your front leg, press your chest toward the front kneecap and relax your back muscles.
- You should feel the stretch in the hamstring muscles of your front leg.
- Contract your front leg by trying to pull it backward against the floor. (There is no movement.)
- Repeat with your other leg.

Common Errors
- Allowing your toes to point out
- Not relaxing your back muscles

STANDING UPPER-TORSO STRETCH

(stretches your latissimus dorsi, trapezius, pectoralis, and triceps muscles)

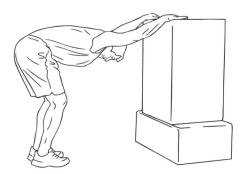

- Hold on to something stable for support, with hands placed slightly wider than shoulder width, feet about shoulder width apart, and knees slightly bent.
- Allow your head to relax between your arms.
- For the contraction phase, push against the support with your arms, contracting the muscles in your upper back.

> *Common Errors*
> - Not relaxing all the muscles in your arms, chest, and upper back

SEATED BACK, HIP, AND GLUTEUS STRETCH

(stretches your gluteus, tensor fasciae late, and latissimus muscles as well as your iliotibial tract)

- Sit on the ground with one leg extended in front of you and your opposite hand behind your back for support.
- Cross one foot (your left foot as shown) over the opposite (right) leg and slide your left heel toward your butt.
- Place your right elbow on the outside of your left knee.
- Look over your left shoulder while turning your torso. Gently pushing on your knee with your right elbow increases the stretch.
- Hold the stretch for 15 to 30 seconds.
- Contract by pushing your knee against your elbow, resisting the force with your elbow.
- Repeat with your other leg and arm.

> *Common Errors*
> - Keeping your shoulders, back, and butt muscles tense—take a deep breath and relax.

STANDING LOWER-LEG STRETCH

(stretches your gastrocnemius, soleus, and Achilles tendon)

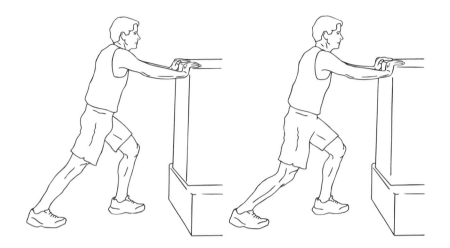

- Lean against an immovable support object, with one leg straight behind you and the other leg forward.
- Point your toes forward.
- Press the heel of your back leg into the ground and move your hips forward, keeping your back knee straight. The farther forward you press your hips, the more stretch you should feel in your back leg's lower muscles.
- Slightly bend your back knee to stretch different calf muscles.
- Contract your calf muscles by pushing against the support object as if you were pushing it away using your back leg.

Common Errors
- Pointing your toes in or out
- Not putting most of your weight on your back leg

SEATED ADDUCTOR STRETCH

(stretches your adductor magnus, adductor brevis, adductor longus, pectineus, and gracilis)

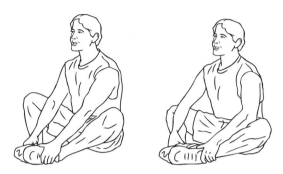

- Sit on the ground with your spine in a natural position, not leaning forward or backward. (You can also put your back against a wall.)
- Grasp your ankles and pull them toward you, enough to feel a light stretch. Your knees should be pointing out to the sides.
- Place elbows on your inner legs and gently push your legs toward the floor.
- Contract by pushing your legs upward against your elbows, resisting the push with your elbows.

> **Common Errors**
> - Rounding your back
> - Pushing too hard on your inner leg

HEALTH QUESTIONNAIRE

Questions 1 through 6 give you a health snapshot, including hereditary health issues.

1. What is my family history of health disorders?	
2. What is my personal health history? What problems have I had in past years?	
3. What health problems do I currently have?	
4. What is my diet currently like?	
5. Have I made recent changes to my diet?	
6. What does my most recent blood chemistry work say about my health?	

CONTINUED

If you answer yes to several of the following questions, your diet may not be serving your needs. Chapter 3 can help you modify your diet; alternatively, consider seeking the help of a registered dietitian specializing in sports nutrition.

7. Am I frequently awake throughout the night?	
8. Does my hair grow slowly? Is it dry or brittle?	
9. Do I have acne, or wounds that heal slowly?	
10. Are my nails weak and brittle?	
11. Am I frequently ill or injured?	
12. Do I often feel tired or have low energy?	
13. Do I often have to skip training or reduce workout intensity because I have no energy?	
14. (Women) Are my periods irregular, often skipping months?	

Event Checklist

If you are traveling to an event, a checklist is a handy way to stay organized. A sample list is shown in Table B.1. This list includes more items than you will likely need for a single event, though if you are traveling to several events—especially if they are different types or in different kinds of weather—then this list will cover many of your needs. But you should feel free to modify it or to create your own checklist.

Some of the items on this list might seem unusual:

- **Compression socks:** These are used for airline travel and long car trips to reduce or eliminate lower-leg swelling. At minimum, these socks can speed recovery from the post-travel, heavy-leg feeling. At the extreme, they can help prevent deep vein thrombosis (DVT). DVT is a condition in which blood clots form in the body's deep veins, particularly in the legs. Sometimes a clot can break off and travel elsewhere in the body, where it can cause major problems, such as obstructing a vessel in the lungs and causing pulmonary embolism. According to Airhealth.org, "About 85% of air travel thrombosis victims are athletic, usually endurance-type athletes like marathoners. People with slower resting blood flow are at greater risk of stasis, stagnant blood subject to clotting. Also, they are more likely to have bruises and sore muscles that can trigger clotting."

- **Pledge® wipes:** These can be used for a final wipe down and polish of your bike frame before the event.

- **Hydration system:** This item refers to a backpack-style hydration system, which is primarily used for mountain biking. Some cyclists use them for road riding as well.

- **Lighting system:** Generally you won't need a lighting system unless you plan to do a 24-hour race. Regardless, sometimes it's nice to have a small headlamp if you need to do any packing or repairs in the dark.

- **Post-event bag:** A small post-event bag of clean up items is nice to take into a small locker room or bathroom. Cleaning up immediately after a ride can help prevent saddle sores.

Make a copy of your own personalized checklist and check off the items after you place them into your travel bag. Take the list with you to your event and use "Last-Minute Checks" on the morning of the event.

TABLE B.1 EVENT CHECKLIST

BACKPACK	GENERAL	EQUIPMENT BAG(S)	POST-EVENT BAG
☐ House keys	☐ Toothbrush/paste	☐ Jerseys	☐ Towel
☐ Race instructions	☐ Contact supplies	☐ Shorts	☐ Shower items
☐ Driver's license	☐ Underwear	☐ Arm warmers	☐ Clothes for post race
☐ Cash, coins	☐ Extra clothes	☐ Leg warmers	☐ Sunscreen, lip balm
☐ Charge card	☐ Extra shoes	☐ Jacket	☐ Sandals
☐ Sunglasses	☐ Sweats	☐ Vest	☐ Towelettes
☐ Maps	☐ Tights	☐ Socks	☐ Hat
☐ Music	☐ T-shirts	☐ Helmet	☐ First-aid kit
☐ Travel food	☐ Jeans	☐ Bike shoes	☐ Deodorant
☐ Travel H_2O bottle	☐ Shorts	☐ Gloves	☐ _____
☐ Camera	☐ Hat	☐ Sunglasses	☐ _____
☐ Phone and charger	☐ Sleepwear	☐ Clear lenses	☐ _____
☐ Computer and plug-in	☐ Long-sleeved shirt	☐ Body Glide	☐ _____
		☐ Cool-weather gear	☐ _____
AIR TRAVEL	**REPAIRS AND SPARES**	☐ Ear band	☐ _____
☐ Airline tickets	☐ Spare tubes	☐ Helmet cover	
☐ Passport	☐ Spare tire	☐ Toe covers/booties	
☐ Medications	☐ CO_2 cartridges	☐ (_____) H_2O bottles	
☐ Vitamins	☐ Floor pump	☐ Flat-repair kit	
☐ Compression socks	☐ Chain lube	☐ _____	
☐ Clear bag for liquids	☐ Extra cleaning rags	☐ _____	
	☐ Pledge® wipes		
FUEL	☐ Frame cleaner	**MOUNTAIN BIKE**	
☐ Energy drink powder	☐ Chain cleaner	☐ Hydration system	
☐ Energy bars	☐ Bike tools	☐ Arm/leg guards	
☐ Electrolyte tablets	☐ Safety pins	☐ Lighting system	
☐ Gels	☐ Tape	☐ Charger for lighting	
☐ Food	☐ Black marker	☐ Shock pump	
☐ _____	☐ Scissors	☐ _____	
☐ _____	☐ Lock and cable	☐ _____	

LAST-MINUTE CHECKS	
☐ Water bottles full?	☐ Brakes centered, wheels spun?
☐ Energy drink in race bottle?	☐ Chain lubricated?
☐ Gears set for start of the bike?	☐ Bike number on?
☐ Computer zeroed?	☐ Bike stripped to the bare minimum?
☐ Tires inflated?	☐ Did you warm up?
	☐ Sunscreen on? Lip sunscreen?

You are physically prepared. You love challenges. You are mentally strong. You are a winner!

Illness and Injury

This appendix is a collection of information I've found useful over the years. *Please note that nothing here is intended to substitute for a physician's advice or treatment.* You need to determine when a trip to the doctor is in order: Be honest with yourself when deciding if the situation is discomfort (something you can handle yourself) or pain that needs professional treatment.

COMMON CYCLING INJURIES

Saddle Sores

Sores in the groin, upper leg, and butt areas can be a nuisance—or worse, force you to take time off the bike. The best approach is prevention. The most common types of sores include blocked or infected glands, which show up as lumps, pain in the pelvic bone area where your weight may be resting, and chafing problems.

Prevention

- Be sure your bike is set up correctly by referring to Chapter 4. Better yet, get a professional bike fit done by a knowledgeable expert. A saddle that is too high can cause you to reach for the pedals, resulting in either pressure or chafing. A saddle that is too low doesn't allow your legs to support your body and puts excess pressure on your crotch area.

- To help prevent chafing, slather your genital area and upper thighs with a good emollient. Several such emollients are made for cycling and other sports, and some combine lubrication and antifungal properties.
- Wear padded cycling shorts without underwear. Cycling shorts are designed to reduce friction from seams and give you some padding to help reduce pressure on sensitive areas.
- After the ride, get out of those dirty shorts. Good hygiene is essential. Wash your crotch and don't wear those shorts again until they have been cleaned.
- Don't suddenly increase weekly or daily mileage on the bike.
- If you shave your upper legs, a light application of antibiotic ointment after shaving may help prevent red spots and infected bumps.
- Be certain the bike seat isn't tilted too far up or down, causing pressure or making you constantly push yourself back in the saddle.
- If problems persist, a different saddle may help, especially one with a soft or cutout area near the nose.

Self-Treatment
- Soaking in comfortably hot bathwater one to three times per day will help boils surface and drain.
- Antibiotic ointments can aid healing.
- Moleskin with an area cut out around the sore may help keep pressure off the sore itself.

Road Rash

As an old saying goes, "There are two kinds of cyclists: those who have crashed and those who are going to crash." When your flesh meets earth in a sliding-type accident, most of the time you'll have some kind of skin damage. Softball players sometimes call it a "strawberry" due to the red and dotted appearance. Cyclists call it road rash.

This kind of skin injury occurs in degrees, similar to burns. Third-degree road rash, the worst condition, won't be covered here. This condition means skin has been entirely removed, with underlying layers of fat and other tissues exposed, and it requires a physician's attention—and perhaps skin grafting. First-degree road rash occurs when only the surface of the skin is reddened. It usually does not require active treatment, but keeping the wound clean is recommended. Second-degree road rash occurs when the surface layer of the skin is broken and a deep layer remains that will allow the skin to heal and repair itself.

Treatment
After damage assessment, the goal is to heal as quickly as possible while minimizing time off the bike. Past healing recommendations included keeping the wound covered with

bandages and plenty of antibiotic ointment. The treatment cycle included soaking in a hot bath to soften and scrub off any scabs that had formed under the bandage to minimize scarring.

This soaking-and-scrubbing method is no longer the preferred treatment. Diana Palmer, the head athletic trainer and sports medicine program director for Westmont College in Santa Barbara, recommends moist wound care. Her extensive experience patching up cyclists and other outdoor athletes gives her firsthand experience in administering wound care and teaching wound-care techniques.

The wound-care process includes a product named Tegaderm™, manufactured by 3M Corporation. It is a thin, clear dressing with adhesive on one side. It keeps water, dirt, and germs away from the wound, yet it lets skin breathe. This property keeps the wound healthy and does not allow deep, scarring scabs to form. Because the dressing is clear, you can constantly monitor the healing process, which is a real advantage. It is available over the counter at some drugstores and pharmacies.

If the crash caused you to hit your head, you may want to take a trip to the emergency room. Even if the hospital does a head scan that comes up negative, internal bleeding can develop 24 hours to 7 days post-trauma. Also, concussions can't show up on scans or in MRI (magnetic resonance imaging). If you've had a head injury, avoid holding your breath when lifting anything. Steer clear of pushing down hard and holding your breath, as when using the toilet. Avoid sharp changes in pulse rate or blood pressure, such as suddenly standing on the pedals of your bike to climb hard. Give your head a rest for a few days.

Healing Self-Care Wounds
If your wounds are the self-care type, the tips below can help you heal quickly:

- Clean the wound with clean water. If you are in the backcountry, do not use stagnant stream water. Sterile saline wound wash can be used in place of water and is often included in athletic trainer kits because it puts out a stream that helps flush wounds. Use a soft, child's toothbrush (or a sponge) and soap. Baby shampoo works well as soap because it is mild. The biggest issue is cleaning the wound thoroughly; many people don't clean their own wounds well enough because it is really painful. If you or someone you know cannot do a good job of cleansing the wound, go to an urgent care office. The last thing you want is a nasty infection.
- If the wound is an abrasion and not free-bleeding, use hydrogen peroxide for the first day only.
- Get a tetanus shot if you have not had one within the last 10 years.
- Put an antibiotic on the wound (e.g., bacitracin, Polysporin®, Neosporin®) and cover it with Tegaderm. Keep in mind that antibiotic ointments can be overused and cause skin reactions or allergic responses as well as set up a bacterial-resistance growth cycle.

Using Ointments for Minor Wounds

If you use an ointment on your minor wounds, follow these suggestions:

- Be sure your wound is well cleansed before applying any antibacterial ointment, to avoid "sealing in" bacteria.
- Apply a very thin layer of ointment to coat and protect the wound. Use a clean swab or sterile gauze to apply the ointment. Do not apply ointments directly from the tube to avoid contaminating the tube and any future wounds. You can apply ointments up to two times daily; however, always clean the wound before each new application of ointment.
- Remove the Tegaderm by peeling it from the top to the bottom. Unless there are signs of infection, you can stop using antibacterial ointments after 24 to 48 hours, but continue to cover the wound with Tegaderm.
- Watch the wound daily. Change the Tegaderm as needed, particularly if excessive exudite (wound pus) develops. Some fluid buildup under the Tegaderm is normal, but watch for dark yellow, green, or brown exudite; excessive redness; increasing pain; fever; or red streaks moving up the extremity. You can also change the dressing as necessary, but see your medical professional if any worrisome conditions develop.
- Keep the wound covered with Tegaderm until the redness, the wound, or both are gone.

Protect the newly healed wound from the sun by using sunscreen with a sun protection factor of 30 or higher. New skin is very sun sensitive.

OTHER HEALTH CONCERNS

While we would all like to be riding in ideal conditions at all times, sometimes the seasons or race conditions mean that you might be on your bike in extreme heat or cold, or dealing with the inconvenience of gastrointestinal problems, namely diarrhea. If you are adequately prepared and well informed you can ride more comfortably in adverse conditions and recognize warning signs before the situation becomes serious.

Heat Illness

Even if you are careful about proper hydration and conditioning, you may encounter times when either the weather suddenly becomes hot or you travel from a cool climate to a hot climate to ride in an event. (Heat acclimatization takes 10 to 14 days.) For these reasons, you should know how to prevent heat illness and how to recognize its stages.

Prevention

1. Adding a small amount of salt to food, if you do not have problems with sodium, and drinking extra water will help. With prolonged exercise in the heat, sweat loss may deplete the body of sodium.

2. Avoid alcohol and caffeine; they are diuretics.
3. Frequent rests may be necessary in hot weather.
4. Cold fluids are absorbed faster than warm fluids.
5. Drink diluted, 4 to 8 percent glucose solutions before, during, and after exercise in the heat. During prolonged exercise—60 to 90 minutes or longer—drink 4 to 8 ounces every 15 to 20 minutes. In other words, drink before becoming thirsty.
6. Wear loose-fitting, light-colored clothing or fabrics that wick moisture.
7. Some prescription drugs may increase heat sensitivity; be aware of the side effects of any medications you're taking.

Stages of Heat Illness

Stage 1: Heat cramps
- Muscle pain and involuntary spasm often occur.
- Body temperature is not necessarily elevated.

Stage 2: Heat exhaustion
Heat exhaustion is often reported during the first heat wave of summer. It is caused by ineffective circulatory adjustments compounded by a depletion of extracellular fluid, especially blood volume, due to excess sweating. Symptoms include:
- Weak, rapid pulse
- Low blood pressure in the upright position
- Headache, dizziness, and general weakness.

To aid the situation, stop physical work or exercise, move to a cooler environment, and administer fluids. In extreme cases, intravenous therapy may be needed.

Stage 3: Heatstroke
Heatstroke is the most serious and complex of heat-stress maladies. It requires *immediate* medical attention. It is the failure of heat-regulating mechanisms in the body, brought on by excessive body temperatures.
- Sweating usually ceases, skin becomes hot and dry, body temperature rises to 104°F or higher, and excessive strain is put on the circulatory system.
- Some individuals may continue sweating, but heat gain by the body outstrips the avenues for heat loss.

Untreated, heatstroke can result in circulatory collapse, central nervous system damage, and death. *Heatstroke is a medical emergency*.

Cold Stress and Hypothermia

I once attended a seminar by Papa Bear Whitmore, a noted authority on wilderness survival. As a cyclist, I was struck by some of his observations about cold-weather activities. He noted that when the weather is cold—say, 20°F to 30°F—people know it's cold and prepare accordingly. Problems can occur when the temperature is in the range of 40°F–50°F and people are unprepared for a sudden change in the weather. Or an accident keeps them out longer than expected. In addition, cyclists who travel to new places for events may simply be unaware of the dangers associated with cool- and cold-weather riding.

One possible scenario: Two cyclists set out for a two-hour ride with a beginning temperature of about 40°F. The cyclists expect the weather to warm up as they ride, and each takes one bottle of energy drink and one bottle of water. Halfway through the ride, one cyclist gets a flat, and the temperature is not warming up as the riders expected. It looks like it might rain. One of the cyclists realizes that only one of his fluid bottles is filled with water—the second one is empty. He was distracted and forgot to fill the bottle with energy drink.

The story has a couple of potential endings. In one, mechanical problems force the cyclists off the bikes again to make repairs. It begins raining and the wind starts to blow. The cyclists end up being out in weather they didn't expect for an hour longer than intended. They have only 150 calories of energy drink between them, after racing each other for the first hour. On the way home, both experience hypothermia.

In a second ending, one cyclist is carrying a cell phone and calls for a lift home. Lucky break.

Prevention

Cold is a relative term. An acceptable riding temperature for one person may be blue-lip weather for another. Regardless, dressing properly is the key to staying warm in cold-weather riding. Appropriate layers can keep your body from losing heat (see sidebar).

The layer worn next to the skin of your upper body should be a moisture-wicking material. Fibers such as cotton retain moisture, which keeps you feeling chilled. If your neck typically gets cold, use a moisture-wicking turtleneck as a base layer.

The second layer on your upper body can be a cycling jersey with arm warmers or a long-sleeved jersey made of fleece, depending on the temperature. If you will be peeling layers off, down to short sleeves, go for the cycling jersey with arm warmers. If temperatures don't allow bare-arm exposure, stick with a long-sleeved jersey.

Your outer layer should be a breathable, wind-and-moisture barrier made of a fabric such as Gore-Tex®. If the weather is extremely wet, go with a waterproof shell.

For your lower torso and legs, you can find cycling tights and pants made specifically for cold and wet weather. If the weather is cool and dry, cycling shorts and a pair of regular tights or leg warmers usually do the trick. For colder weather, a pair of propylene thermal underwear between your cycling shorts and your tights may help. Very wet cold-weather riding may require waterproof pants to cover your tights.

Head, ears, nose, fingers, and toes seem to be the areas that get cold first. Wind covers for helmets are available to protect the head. You can also find helmets that come with special inserts for cold weather. Some cyclists prefer to wear a cover made specifically for the head. Covering your head and wearing ear warmers will help keep the wind chill off these sensitive areas. You can wear a balaclava under your helmet and pull it over your

How Your Body Loses Heat

Body heat is lost primarily through four methods:

Radiation occurs when your exposed skin loses heat to the atmosphere via electromagnetic waves. For example, you lose radiated heat when you are standing in cool weather with no wind, waiting for a riding partner to arrive.

Convection heat loss is associated with air moving across your body. Your body warms air molecules that come in contact with your skin; then the air molecules move away, taking precious body heat with them. This process is the basis for the wind chill factor—why wind, such as the kind created when you're riding, can drive down skin (and eventually internal body) temperature to be lower than actual air temperature. The wind chill factor can make bearable air temperatures downright dangerous. For example, an ambient temperature of 40°F changes to 34°F on your skin with a wind of 10 mph. Add a cycling speed of 20 mph to that headwind and the wind chill takes the temperature to a subfreezing 28°F.

Conduction is like convection, except body heat is lost through a cold object instead of the air, such as when you're sitting on a cold surface or holding a cold bar. Heat is drawn from your body to warm the cold object.

Evaporation is heat loss that occurs when water changes to vapor. Wet skin (or skin underneath wet clothing) loses heat several times faster than dry skin. Also, many materials, such as cotton, lose their insulating properties when they become wet.

nose when necessary. If your ears get especially cold, ear warmers can be worn under the balaclava.

A wide variety of gloves is available, featuring varying thicknesses of insulation for warmth. Different outer coverings can protect against conditions ranging from simple chill to cold and wet weather. Layering can work for your hands as well. An inner liner of propylene next to your hands and fingers wicks moisture away, while a second glove layer insulates and protects from the elements.

For your feet, you can choose from several types of booties. Some are simply wind covers, while others insulate toes from cold and water. Be careful not to wear socks that are so thick they cramp your feet. Cramped feet don't have adequate circulation, resulting in cold toes. If your toes get cold even with booties, you can use chemical packs that are often used by skiers. These packs, which generate heat once opened, can be found at sporting goods stores and some cycling stores. Carry a spare package or two in your cycling jersey in case of a flat tire, because in addition to warming toes, they can be very helpful for warming cold fingers.

For overall body warmth, another trick is to fill a hydration pack (such as a CamelBak®) with a warm, apple-flavored sports drink. The warm bladder against your body will help you stay toasty, and the fluid is like hot apple cider.

Stages of Cold Stress and Hypothermia

Recognizing the early signs of cold stress will help you keep exposure to the cold from becoming dangerous. Cold stress on the body has four stages:

Stage 1: A two-degree drop in temperature

The body shivers to exercise muscles and produce heat as core temperature drops from about 98.6°F to 96°F. Women's body temperatures often run lower than men's, but in general, a two-degree drop from what is normal will most likely produce shivering.

Stage 2: 91°F to 95°F

When body temperature drops to 91°F to 95°F, shivering becomes violent, speech is difficult, thinking is slow, and amnesia may occur.

Stage 3: 86°F to 90°F

When body temperature drops to 86°F to 90°F, muscles may become rigid and skin will become blue and puffy. When shivering stops, it is a critical sign. The person may experience poor coordination, muddled thinking, and muscle spasms that appear as jerking. The person may still be able to sit or stand unassisted.

Stage 4: 78°F to 85°F

A body temperature of 78°F to 85°F will usually result in the person becoming unconscious with reflexes depressed.

Stage 5: Below 78°F

When body temperature dips below 78°F, the person usually experiences ventricular fibrillation and cardiac arrest.

Treatment

The first step in the treatment of hypothermia is to remove the affected person from the cold environment. If possible, get her out of any wet clothing and into dry gear. Heat can be added to the body with hot drinks high in carbohydrates and by electric heat or fire. Blankets or spare clothing can be used to trap air and heat next to the person's body.

In a case of extreme hypothermia, the person can be immersed in a tub of water heated to 105°F to 110°F. Submerge *only the torso,* leaving arms and legs out of the hot water, to allow warming of the body core and a gentle warming of the limbs. This gradual warming process helps prevent a condition called "after drop." If the entire body is submerged, the hot water stimulates the circulation of large volumes of cold blood from the extremities to the heart, which can cause cardiac arrest.

The chance that you will ever experience the latter stages of hypothermia on a bicycle is slim unless you are riding in extreme conditions. All stages of cold stress are included here for informational purposes. This knowledge can also be helpful if you participate in winter sports for crosstraining.

Diarrhea

I have worked with a number of cyclists, including elite racers, who put up with diarrhea and hope it will go away. Sometimes the diarrhea is caused by nerves, and in some of these cases, practicing visualization and relaxation techniques can help eliminate nervous diarrhea. Other cases require a combination of relaxation techniques and diet changes.

If you have one loose bowel movement, don't panic. But if diarrhea continues, do something about it. Continued loose stools contribute to dehydration and loss of valuable nutrients. You can't reach optimum performance if your body is depleted.

Treatment and Prevention

For a short-term remedy, nonprescription products are available from a pharmacy. After you have the condition under control, do some troubleshooting to see if your diarrhea is related to particular foods or drinks.

In general, high-fiber foods or foods that cause gas combined with lots of fluid can cause problems. Some foods that may cause or contribute to these problems include

- Fresh fruits (except bananas)
- Dried fruits such as prunes, apricots, and figs
- Vegetables
- Unprocessed wheat bran
- Whole-grain breakfast cereals
- Whole-grain breads
- Legumes (beans, lentils, chickpeas, etc.)

Before workouts and races, avoid foods that cause you problems. This process will likely require some experimentation. Recurring diarrhea that doesn't respond to over-the-counter remedies or changes in your diet needs the attention of a physician.

Resources

Airhealth.org. www.airhealth.org.

American Heart Association. www.americanheart.org.

Baker, A., MD. *Bicycling Medicine*. San Diego, CA: Argo, 1995.

Mayo Clinic. www.mayoclinic.com.

McArdle, William D., Frank I. Katch, and Victor L. Katch. *Exercise Physiology, Energy, Nutrition, and Human Performance,* 3rd ed. Malvern, PA: Lea & Febiger, 1991.

National Weather Service. "Windchill: Frequently Asked Questions, Terms, and Definitions." www.nws.noaa.gov/om/windchill/.

Palmer, D. Personal interview, July 2006.

Vickery, D. M., MD, and J. F. Fries, MD. *Take Care of Yourself*, 5th ed. Upper Saddle River, NJ: Addison-Wesley, 1994.

Whitmore, Papa Bear, and J. Bunstock. *The W.I.S.E. Guide to Wilderness Survival*. Lincoln, NE: Astonisher Press, 1992.

BIBLIOGRAPHY

Alter, M. J. *Sport Stretch*. Champaign, IL: Human Kinetics, 1998.

American Council on Exercise. *Research Matters*, no. 1 (May 1995).

Anderson, B. *Stretching*. Bolinas, CA: Shelter, 1980.

Anderson, J. C. "Stretching Before and After Exercise: Effect on Muscle Soreness and Injury Risk." *Journal of Athletic Trainers* 40, no. 3 (July 2005): 218–220.

Anderson, O. "Are Women Better Than Men in the Long Run?" *Running Research News* 10, no. 6 (November–December 1994).

————. "Dad, Mom, and You: Do Your Genes Determine Your Performances?" *Running Research News* 11, no. 8 (October 1995).

————. "Question and Answer Section." *Running Research News* 11, no. 4 (May 1995).

Armstrong, L. E. "Caffeine, Body Fluid–Electrolyte Balance, and Exercise Performance." *International Journal of Sport Nutrition and Exercise Metabolism* 12 (2002): 189–206.

————. *Performing in Extreme Environments*. Champaign, IL: Human Kinetics, 2000.

Balch, J. F., and P. A. Balch. *Prescription for Nutritional Healing*. Garden City Park, NY: Avery, 1997.

Barr, S. "Women, Nutrition, and Exercise: A Review of Athletes' Intakes and a Discussion of Energy Balance in Active Women." *Progress in Food and Nutrition Science* 11, nos. 3–4 (1987): 307–361.

Bean, A. "Runner's Guide to Pain." *Runner's World*, November 1997.

Bernhardt, G. *Bicycling for Women*. Boulder, CO: VeloPress, 2008.

————. *The Female Cyclist: Gearing up a Level*. Boulder, CO: VeloPress, 1999.

————. *Training Plans for Multisport Athletes*, 2nd ed. Boulder, CO: VeloPress, 2007.

————. *Triathlon Training Basics*. Boulder, CO: VeloPress, 2004.

Bishop, D., et al. "The Effects of Strength Training on Endurance Performance and Muscle Characteristics." *Medicine and Science in Sports and Exercise* 31 no. 6 (June 1999): 886–891.

Book, C. Interview by Gale Bernhardt, July 7, 1998, McKee Medical Center, Loveland, Colorado.

Burke, E. R., PhD. *Serious Cycling*. Champaign, IL: Human Kinetics, 1995.

Burke, L. *The Complete Guide to Food for Sports Performance*. New York: Allen & Unwin, 1995.

Callanan, T. *Playing to Win: Playbook and Study Guide*. Minneapolis: Pecos River Learning Centers, Inc., 1992.

Chu, D. A. *Jumping into Plyometrics*, 2nd ed. Champaign, IL: Human Kinetics, 1998.

Coggan, A. "Coggan Power Levels." Two Wheel Blogs. http://www.twowheelblogs.com/training-with-power/power-levels-0.

Coleman, E. *Eating for Endurance*. Palo Alto, CA: Bull, 1997.

Colgan, M. *Optimum Sports Nutrition*. Ronkonkoma, NY: Advanced Research Press, 1993.

Correll, D. "Young Girls Attempt to Mimic Model Bodies." *Loveland Reporter-Herald*, June 21, 1998 (Sunday ed.).

Cox, G. R., et al. "Effect of Different Protocols of Caffeine Intake on Metabolism and Endurance Performance." *Journal of Applied Physiology* 93, no. 3 (September 2002): 990–999.

Coyle, E. F. "Substrate Utilization during Exercise in Active People." *American Journal of Clinical Nutrition* supplement b1 (1995): 968S–979S.

Daniels, A. C. *Performance Management*. Tucker, GA: Performance Management Publications, 1989.

Davis, J. M., et al. "Central Nervous System Effects of Caffeine and Adenosine on Fatigue." *American Journal of Physiology* 284, no. 2 (February 2003): R399–R404.

Eades, M. R., and M. Eades. *Protein Power*. New York: Bantam, 1996.

Eastman Kodak Company. *Ergonomic Design for People at Work*, vol. 1. New York: Van Nostrand Reinhold, 1983.

———. *Ergonomic Design for People at Work*, vol. 2. New York: Van Nostrand Reinhold, 1986.

Edwards, S. *The Heart Rate Monitor Book*. Finland: Polar Electro Oy, 1992.

Frentsos, J. A., and J. T. Baer. "Increased Energy and Nutrient Intake during Training and Competition Improves Elite Triathletes' Endurance Performance." *International Journal of Sports Nutrition* 1 (March 1997): 61–71.

Friedlander, A. L., et al. "A Two-Year Program of Aerobics and Weight Training Enhances Bone Mineral Density of Young Women." *Journal of Bone and Mineral Research* 10 (1995): 574–585.

Friel, J. *The Cyclist's Training Bible*. Boulder, CO: VeloPress, 1996.

———. *The Triathlete's Training Bible*. Boulder, CO: VeloPress, 1998

Graham, T. E. "Caffeine and Exercise: Metabolism, Endurance, and Performance." *Sports Medicine* 31, no. 11 (2001): 785–807.

Gremion, G. "Is Stretching for Sports Performance Still Useful? A Review of the Literature." *Review of Medicine Suisse* 1, no. 28 (July 2005): 1830–1834.

Henry Dreyfuss Associates. *The Measure of Man and Woman: Human Factors in Design*, Rev. ed. New York: Wiley, 2002.

Hickson, R. C. "Potential for Strength and Endurance Training to Amplify Endurance Performance." *Journal of Applied Physiology* 65, no. 5 (November 1988): 2285–2290.

Ingraham, S. J. "The Role of Flexibility in Injury Prevention and Athletic Performance: Have We Stretched the Truth?" *Minnesota Medicine* 86, no. 5 (May 2003): 58–61.

Jackson, N. P., et al. "High Resistance/Low Repetition vs. Low Resistance/High Repetition Training: Effects on Performance of Trained Cyclists." *Journal of Strength and Conditioning* 21, no. 1 (February 2007): 289–295.

Janssen, G. M., et al. "Marathon Running: Functional Changes in Male and Female Subjects during Training and Contests." *International Journal of Sports Medicine* supplement (October 10, 1989): S118–S123.

Janssen, P. G. J. M. *Training Lactate Pulse-Rate*. Finland: Polar Electro Oy, 1987.

Kerr, D., et al. "Exercise Effects on Bone Mass in Postmenopausal Women Are Site-Specific and Load-Dependent." *Journal of Bone and Mineral Research* 11, no. 2 (February 1996): 218–225.

Klesges, R. C. "Changes in Bone Mineral Content in Male Athletes: Mechanisms of Action and Intervention Effects." *Journal of the American Medical Association* 276, no. 3 (July 1996): 226–230.

Kraemer, W. J., and S. J. Fleck. "Exercise Technique: Classic Lat Pull-Down." *Strength and Health Report* 1, no. 6 (June 1997).

———. "Exercise Technique: Machine Standing Calf Raise." *Strength and Health Report* 2, no. 1 (March 1998).

———. "Exercise Technique: Seated Cable Row." *Strength and Health Report* 1, no. 3 (June 1997).

Lampert, E. V., et al. "Enhanced Endurance in Trained Cyclists during Moderate Intensity Exercise Following 2 Weeks of Adaptation to a High Fat Diet." *European Journal of Applied Physiology* 69, no. 4 (1994): 287–293.

LaRoche, D. P., et al. "Effects of Stretching on Passive Muscle Tension and Response to Eccentric Exercise." *American Journal of Sports Medicine* 34, no. 6 (June 2006): 1000–1007.

Liebman, B. "3 Vitamins and a Mineral: What to Take." *Nutrition Action*, May 1998.

———. "Avoiding the Fracture Zone: Calcium—Why Get More?" *Nutrition Action*, April 1998.

Loehr, J. E., EdD. *Mental Toughness Training for Sports*. Harrisburg, VA: R. R. Donnelley & Sons, 1987.

Loehr, J. E., EdD., and P. J. McLaughlin. *Mentally Tough*. New York: M. Evans, 1986.

Lutter, J. M., and L. Jaffee. *The Bodywise Woman*, 2nd ed. Champaign, IL: Human Kinetics, 1996.

Marcinik, E. J., et al. "Effects of Strength Training on Lactate Threshold and Endurance Performance." *Medicine and Science in Sports and Exercise* 23, no. 6 (June 1991): 739–743.

Martin, D. E., PhD, and P. N. Coe. *Better Training for Distance Runners*, 2nd ed. Champaign, IL: Human Kinetics, 1997.

McArdle, W. D., et al. *Exercise Physiology, Energy, Nutrition, and Human Performance*, 3rd ed. Malvern, PA: Lea & Febiger, 1991.

———. *Exercise Physiology, Energy, Nutrition, and Human Performance*, 5th ed. Philadelphia: Lippincott Williams & Wilkins, 2001.

———. "The Big Jolt: Mountain Biking's Love Affair with Coffee." *Mountain Biker*, February 1998.

McCarthy, J. P., et al. "Compatibility of Adaptive Responses with Combining Strength and Endurance Training." *Medicine and Science in Sports and Exercise* 27, no. 3 (March 1995): 429–436.

Nelson, A. G. "Acute Muscle Stretching Inhibits Muscle Strength Endurance Performance." *Journal of Strength and Conditioning Research* 19, no. 2 (May 2005): 338–343.

Nelson, A. G., et al. "Chronic Stretching and Running Economy." *Scandinavian Journal of Medicine and Science in Sports* 11, no. 5 (October 2001): 260–265.

Newton, R. U., et al. "Kinematics, Kinetics, and Muscle Activation during Explosive Upper Body Movements: Implications for Power Development." *Journal of Applied Biomechanics* 12, no. 1 (1996): 31–43.

Noakes, Tim, MD. *The Lore of Running*. Southern Africa: Oxford University Press, 2003.

Norager, C. B., et al. "Caffeine Improves Endurance in 75-Year-Old Citizens: A Randomized, Double-Blind, Placebo-Controlled, Crossover Study," *Journal of Applied Physiology* 99, no. 6 (December 2005): 2302–2306.

O'Connor, D. M., et al. "Effects of Static Stretching on Leg Power during Cycling." *Journal of Sports Medicine and Physical Fitness* 46, no. 1 (March 2006): 52–56.

Paavolainen, L., et al. "Explosive-Strength Training Improves 5-Km Running Time by Improving Running Economy and Muscle Power." *Journal of Applied Physiology* 5, no. 86 (May 1999): 1527–1533.

Paluska, S.A. "Caffeine and Exercise." *Current Sports Medicine Reports* 2, no. 4 (August 2003): 213–219.

Pruitt, A., EdD. *Andy Pruitt's Complete Medical Guide for Cyclists.* Boulder, CO: VeloPress, 2006.

Roberts, A. T., et al. "The Effect of an Herbal Supplement Containing Black Tea and Caffeine on Metabolic Parameters in Humans." *Alternative Medicine Review* 10, no. 4 (December 2005): 321–325.

Ryan, M. "Less Is More: Taking the Sensible Approach to Shedding Weight." *Inside Triathlon*, July 1998.

———. *Sports Nutrition for Endurance Athletes.* Boulder, CO: VeloPress, 2002.

Sabo, D., et al. "Modification of Bone Quality by Extreme Physical Stress: Bone Density Measurements in High-Performance Athletes Using Dual-Energy X-Ray Absorptiometry." *Z Orthop Ihre Grenzgeb* 143, no. 1 (January–February 1996): 1–6.

Sears, B. *The Zone.* New York: HarperCollins, 1995.

Seiler, S. "Gender Differences in Endurance Performance Training." MAPP, March 1998. http://home.hia.no/~stephens/gender.htm.

Sharkey, B. J. *Fitness and Health.* Champaign, IL: Human Kinetics, 1997.

Shrier, I. "Does Stretching Improve Performance? A Systematic and Critical Review of the Literature." *Clinical Journal of Sports Medicine* 14, no. 5 (September 2004): 267–273.

Shulman, D., Exercise physiologist. Interviews by Gale Bernhardt, July 1998.

Tanaka, H., and T. Swensen. "Impact of Resistance Training on Endurance Performance. A New Form of Cross-training?" *Sports Medicine* 25, no. 3 (March 1998): 191–200.

Thacker, S. B. "The Impact of Stretching on Sports Injury Risk: A Systematic Review of the Literature." *Medicine and Science in Sports and Exercise* 36, no. 3 (March 2004): 371–378.

Ulene, A. *The NutriBase Nutrition Facts Desk Reference.* Garden City Park, NY: Avery, 1995.

USA Cycling Elite Coaching Clinic Manual. Colorado Springs, CO: USA Cycling, February 17–19, 1997.

Yeo, S. E., et al. "Caffeine Increases Exogenous Carbohydrate Oxidation during Exercise." *Journal of Applied Physiology* 99, no. 3 (September 2005): 844–850.

Witvrouw, E., et al. "Stretching and Injury Prevention: An Obscure Relationship." *Sports Medicine* 34, no. 7 (2004): 443–449.

Zinn, L. Personal communication, January 2–5, 2004.

Zinn, L. *Zinn's Cycling Primer.* Boulder, CO: VeloPress, 2004.

INDEX

ABOUT THE AUTHOR

Gale Bernhardt has been an athlete and coach for more than thirty-four years. With a Level I coaching certification from USA Cycling and a Level III coaching certification from USA Triathlon, Gale is among the nation's premier endurance coaches. She coached the 2004 USA men's and women's triathlon teams at the Olympics in Athens, Greece, and the triathlon teams at the 2003 Pan American Games; she also serves as a World Cup Coach for the International Triathlon Union (ITU) Sport Development squad. Her athletes are Olympic and professional cyclists; top national-level masters road cyclists; ultra-endurance cyclists; and runners, triathletes, and multisport athletes with podium finishes at Olympic trials, national championships, and world championship events. Tens of thousands of amateur athletes have used a training plan from Gale Bernhardt to prepare for a big race or event, whether they find it in a book, magazine, or Web site.

Gale is the author of several VeloPress books, including *Bicycling for Women*, *Training Plans for Multisport Athletes*, and *Triathlon Training Basics*, and series editor of the popular Workouts in a Binder® series: *Swim Workouts for Triathletes* (coauthor); *Workouts for Swimmers, Triathletes, and Coaches*; *Indoor Cycling*; and *Run Workouts for Runners and Triathletes*. She lives and trains in Loveland, Colorado.